People called Methodists

A collection of anecdotes

compiled and edited by

John A. Vickers

ISBN: 978-1-5272-5993-5

Cover painting of 'The Fire at Epworth Rectory, South Yorkshire' by Henry Perlee Parker
Copyright © Oxford Brookes University; reproduction courtesy of
The Oxford Centre for Methodism and Church History

Printed and bound by HSDC, Waterlooville, PO7 8AA

Acknowledgements

I would like to thank my son Stephen and my friends Jane Gregory and James
Brown for their contributions to the making of this book.

JAV

Contents

Prologue

The collection of anecdotes that follow is a by-product of more than half a century's study of Methodist history. There was always the thought in the back of my mind that I might share them with others, but until now this has been elbowed out by more serious tasks. Now that I have reached my nineties, it is a case of 'now or never'. My hope is that I survive long enough to see them in print. The arrangement is chronological by year of birth.

In August 1709 a fire swept through the Epworth rectory that might well have caused the death of the five-year-old Jacky Wesley. His mother Susanna Wesley wrote an account of it, to which many years later her son added his own recollections.

Epworth, Aug. 24, 1709… On Wednesday night, February the ninth, between the hours of eleven and twelve, some sparks fell from the roof of our house, upon one of the children's feet. She immediately ran to our chamber and called us. Mr. Wesley, hearing a cry of fire in the street, started up… and opening his door, found the fire was in his own house. …Then he ran and burst open the Nursery door and called to the maid to bring out the children… She snatched up the youngest and bade the rest follow; which the three elder did. When we were got into the hall, and were surrounded with flames, Mr. Wesley found he had left the keys of the doors above stairs. He ran up and recovered them, a minute before the staircase took fire. When we opened the street door, the strong North East wind drove the flames in with such violence that none could stand against them. But some of our children got out through the windows, the rest through a little door into the garden.

When Mr. Wesley had seen the other children safe, he heard the child in the nursery cry. He attempted to go up the stairs, but they were all on fire, and would not bear his weight.

Many years later John Wesley took up the story.

I believe it was just at that time I waked: for I did not cry as they imagined, unless it was afterwards. I remember all the circumstances as distinctly, as though it were but yesterday. Seeing the room was very light, I called to the maid to take me up. But none answering, I put my head out of the curtains and saw streaks of fire on the top of the room. I got up and ran to the door, but could get no farther, all the floor beyond it being in a blaze. I then climbed upon a chest, which stood near the window; one in the yard below saw me and proposed running to fetch a ladder. Another answered, "There will be no time. But I have thought of another expedient. Here I will fix my feet against the wall: lift a light man, and set him on my shoulders." They did so, and he took me out at the window. Just then the whole roof fell in; but it fell inward, or we had all been crushed at once. When they brought me into the house where my father was, he cried out, "Come, neighbours,! Let us kneel down; let us give thanks to God! He has given me all my eight children: let the house go: I am rich enough!"

Coke and Moore, *Life of the Rev John Wesley*, A.M., pp. 38–41

Apart from the Epworth fire, there is only one place from which a collection of Methodist anecdotes can set out and that is John Wesley's often repeated account of his experience in Aldersgate Street, London on the evening of 24th May 1738. What is less widely known, however, is that his younger brother Charles had had a similar experience three days earlier. So we begin with their own accounts of what happened to each of them.

Charles Wesley, recovering from pleurisy, wrote on Pentecost Sunday, May 21ˢᵗ, 1738:

I waked in hope and expectation of His coming. At nine my brother and some friends came, and sang an hymn to the Holy Ghost. My comfort and hope were hereby increased. In about half-an-hour they went: I betook myself to prayer... I was composing myself to sleep, in quietness and peace, when I heard one come in (Mrs. Musgrave, I thought, by the voice) and say, "In the name of Jesus of Nazareth, arise, and believe, and thou shalt be healed of all thy infirmities." I wondered how it should enter into her head to speak in that manner. The words struck me to the heart. I sighed and said within myself, "O that Christ would but speak thus to me!" I lay musing and trembling.: then thought, "But what if it should be Him? I will send at least to see." I rang, and, Mrs. Turner coming up, I desired her to send up Mrs. Musgrove. She went down, and, returning, said, "Mrs. Musgrove had not been here." My heart sunk within me at the word, and I hoped it might be Christ indeed. However, I sent her down again to inquire, and felt in the meantime a strange palpitation of heart. I said, yet feared to say, "I believe, I believe!" She came up again and said, "It was I, a weak, sinful creature, spoke; but the words were Christ's; he commanded me to say them, and so constrained me that I could not forbear..."

I now found myself at peace with God, and rejoiced in hope of loving Christ. My temper for the rest of the day was, mistrust of my own great, but before unknown, weakness. I saw that by faith I stood; by the continual support of faith, which kept me from falling, though of myself I am ever sinking into sin. I went to bed still sensible of my own weakness, (I humbly hope to be more and more so), yet confident of Christ's protection.

John Wesley wrote:

Wednesday, May 24th... In the afternoon I was asked to go to St. Paul's. The anthem was, "Out of the deep have I called unto Thee, O Lord: Lord, hear my voice."...In the evening I went very unwillingly to a society in Aldersgate Street, where one was reading Luther's preface to the *Epistle to the Romans*. About a quarter before nine, while he was describing the change which God works in the heart through faith in Christ, I felt my heart strangely warmed. I felt I did trust in Christ, Christ alone for salvation; and an assurance was given me that He had taken away *my* sins, even *mine*, and saved *me* from the law of sin and death...

After my return home, I was much buffeted with temptations; but cried out, and they fled away. They returned again and again. I as often lifted up my eyes, and He "sent me help from His holy place". And herein I found the difference between this and my former state chiefly consisted. I was striving, yea, fighting with all my might under the laws, as well as under grace. But then I was sometimes, if not often, conquered; now, I was always conqueror.

John Wesley (1703–1791)

In January 1776, when preaching at All Hallows, Lombard Street, John Wesley recalled preaching there for the first time extempore over forty years earlier. It was a charity sermon in aid of St. Ethelburga's Children's Society. One of his hearers on that momentous occasion, Thomas Letts of Clapham, many year's later gave an account of it to William Myles.

Dec. 28, 1788. Two Sermons were preached at the Parish Church of Allhallows, Lombard-Street, London, for the benefit of forty-eight poor children belonging to St. Ethelburga Society; that in the morning by the Rev. George Patrick, LL.B.; and that in the afternoon, by the Rev. John Wesley, A.M., who thus notices it in his Journal: 'Sunday, 28: I preached at Allhallows Church, on these words in the service: "His commandments are not grievous." The congregation was exceedingly large, and seemed to taste the good word.' Mr. Letts, by virtue of his office as a Steward of the Charity, was appointed to attend on Mr. Wesley, who, while he was putting on his gown in the vestry, said to him, 'It is above fifty years, Sir, since I first preached in this Church; I remember it from a particular circumstance that occurred at that time. I came without a Sermon; and, going up the pulpit stairs, I hesitated, and returned to the vestry, under much mental confusion and agitation. A woman, who stood by, noticed my concern and said, 'Pray, Sir, what is the matter with you?' I replied, I have not brought a Sermon with me. She said, putting her hand on my shoulder, 'Is that all? Cannot you trust God for a Sermon?' This question had such an effect upon me, that I ascended the pulpit, preached extempore, with great freedom to myself, and acceptance to the people; and I have never since taken a written Sermon into the pulpit.

Wesleyan Methodist Magazine, 1825, pp. 105–6

It is important to remember that we have only Wesley's version of the following well-known encounter with Beau Nash, the leading figure in Bath society.

Tue. 5 [June, 1739]. There was great expectation at Bath of what a noted man was to do to me there, and I was much entreated 'not to preach, because no one knew what might happen'. By this report also I gained a much larger audience, among whom were many of the rich and great. I told them plainly, the Scripture had concluded them all under sin, high and low, rich and poor, one with another. Many of them seemed not a little surprised and were sinking apace into seriousness, when their champion appeared and, coming close to me, asked by what authority I did these things. I replied, 'By the authority of Jesus Christ, conveyed to me by the (now) Archbishop of Canterbury, when he laid his hands upon me and said, "Take thou authority to preach the gospel."' He said, 'This is contrary to Act of Parliament. This is a conventicle.' I answered, 'Sir, the conventicles mentioned in that Act (as the Preamble shows) are *seditious* meetings. But this is not such. Here is no shadow of sedition. Therefore it is not contrary to that Act.' He replied, 'I say it is. And beside, your preaching frightens people out of their wits.' 'Sir, did you ever hear me preach?' 'No.' 'How then can you judge of what you never heard?' 'Sir, by common report. Common report is enough.' 'Give me leave, sir, to ask, Is not your name Nash?' 'My name is Nash.' 'Sir, I dare not judge of you by common report. I think it is not enough to judge by.' Here he paused awhile, and having recovered himself asked, 'I desire to know what this people comes here for.' On which one replied, 'Sir, leave him to me. Let an old woman answer him. You, Mr. Nash, take care of your body. We take care of our souls, and for the food of our souls we come here.' He replied not a word but walked away.

John Wesley, *Journal*

On the strength of the following well-known incident Wesley's convert Thomas Maxfield has been credited with being Methodism's first lay preacher, though the claim is not indisputable and a case can be made for John Cennick. Wesley had left Maxwell in charge of the London society while he was busy in Bristol. But there was a significant difference between leading the people in prayer as part of his pastoral care and preaching.

This young man, being fervent in spirit, and mighty in the Scriptures, greatly profited the people. They crowded to hear him; and, by the increase of their number, as well as by their earnest and deep attention, they insensibly led him to go further than he had, at first, designed. He began to *preach*, and the Lord so blessed the word that many were not only deeply awakened and brought to repentance, but were also made happy in a consciousness of pardon. The Scripture marks of true conversion – inward peace and power to walk in all holiness – evinced the work to be of God.

Some, however, were offended at this irregularity, as it was termed. A complaint was made in form to Mr. Wesley, and he hastened to London in order to put a stop to it. His mother then lived in his house, adjoining to the Foundery [Moorfields, London]. When he arrived, she perceived that his countenance was expressive of dissatisfaction and inquired the cause. 'Thomas Maxfield,' said he abruptly, 'has turned preacher, I find.' She looked attentively at him and replied, 'John, you know what my sentiments have been. You cannot suspect me of favouring readily anything of this kind. But take care what you do with respect to that young man, for he is as surely called of God to preach as you are. Examine what have been the fruits of his preaching and hear him also yourself.' He did so. His prejudice bowed before the force of truth and he could only say, 'It is the Lord: Let him do what seemeth him good.'

Henry Moore, *Life of the Rev. John Wesley*, 1824, vol. 1, pp. 505–6

In the early years of his itinerant ministry, opposition to Wesley's field-preaching took varied forms.

Friday 19 [March, 1742]. I rode once more to Pensford, at the earnest request of several serious people. The place where they desired me to preach was a little green spot near the town. But I had no sooner begun than a great company of rabble, hired (as we afterwards found) for that purpose, came furiously upon us, bringing a bull which they had been baiting, and now strove to drive in among the people. But the beast was wiser than his drivers, and continually ran, either to one side of us or the other, while we quietly sang praise to God and prayed for about an hour. The poor wretches, finding themselves disappointed, at length seized upon the bull, now weak and tired, after having been so long torn and beaten both by dogs and men, and by main strength partly dragged and partly thrust him in among the people. When they had forced their way to the little table on which I stood, they strove several times to throw it down, by thrusting the helpless beast against it, who of himself stirred no more than a log of wood. I once or twice put aside his head with my hand, that the blood might not drop upon my clothes, intending to go on as soon as the hurry should be a little over. But the table falling down, some of our friends caught me in their arms and carried me right away on their shoulders; while the rabble wreaked their vengeance on the table, which they tore bit from bit. We went a little way off, where I finished my discourse without any noise or interruption.

John Wesley, *Journal*

19 September 1769: I preached ... on White's Hill near Bradford [on Avon] in the evening. By this means, many had an opportunity of hearing who would not have come to the room. I had designed to preach there again the next evening, but a gentleman in the town desired me to preach at his door. The beasts of the people[1] were tolerably quiet till I had nearly finished my sermon. Then they lifted up their voice, especially one, *called a gentleman*, who had filled his pockets with rotten eggs. But a young man, coming unawares, clapped his hands on each side and mashed them all at once. In an instant, he was perfumed all over – though it was not so sweet as balsam!

John Wesley, *Journal*

Wednesday 9 [June, 1742]. I rode over [from Epworth] to a neighbouring town [Crowle] to wait upon a Justice of Peace, a man of candour and understanding; before whom (I was informed) their angry neighbours had carried a whole waggon-load of these new heretics. But when he asked what they had done, there was a deep silence, for that was a point their conductors had forgot. At length one said, 'Why, they pretend to be better than other people. And besides, they prayed from morning to night.' Mr. S[tovin] asked, 'But have they done nothing besides?' 'Yes, sir,' said an old man, 'an't please your worship, they have *converted* my wife. Till she went among them she had such a tongue! And now she is as quiet as a lamb.' 'Carry them back, carry them back,' replied the Justice, 'and let them convert all the scolds in the town.'

John Wesley, *Journal*

John Nelson, the Yorkshire stonemason, accompanied Wesley on his first visit to Cornwall in 1743. His account of that visit reveals something of the hardship of their itinerant life.

All that time Mr. Wesley and I lay on the floor: he had my greatcoat for his pillow, and I had *Burkitt's Notes on the New Testament* for mine. After being here near three weeks, one morning, about three o'clock, Mr. Wesley turned over, and finding me awake, clapped me on the side saying, 'Brother Nelson, let us be of good cheer: I have one whole side yet, for the skin is off but one side.' We usually preached on the commons, going from one common to another, and it was but seldom any one asked us to eat and drink.

One day we had been at St. Hilary Downs, and Mr. Wesley had preached from Ezekiel's vision of dry bones, and there was a shaking among the people as he preached. As we returned, Mr. Wesley stopped his horse to pick the blackberries, saying, 'Brother Nelson, we ought to be thankful that there are plenty of blackberries; for this is the best country I ever saw for getting a stomach, but the worst that ever I saw for getting food. Do people think that we can live by preaching?' I said, 'I know not what they may think; but one asked me to eat something as I came from St. Just, when I ate heartily of barley-bread and honey.' He said, 'You are well off: I

---

[1] One of Wesley's favourite expressions for the mobs he encountered.

had thought of begging a crust of bread of the woman where I met the people at Morva, but forgot it till I had got some distance from the house.'[2]

Lives of the Early Methodist Preachers, 1871, pp. 74–5

The following incident occurred while Wesley was hurrying to visit a dying friend at Donington Park.

The next afternoon [21st May, 1742] I stopped a little at Newport Pagnell, and then rode on till I overtook a serious man, with whom I immediately fell into conversation. He presently gave me to know what his opinions were; therefore I said nothing to contradict them. But that did not content him. He was quite uneasy to know whether I held the doctrine of the decrees as he did. But I told him over and over, 'We had better keep to practical things, lest we should be angry at one another.' And so we did for two miles, till he caught me unawares and dragged me into the dispute before I knew where I was. He then grew warmer and warmer, told me I was rotten at heart, and supposed I was one of John Wesley's followers. I told him, 'No, I am John Wesley himself.' Upon which... he would gladly have run away outright. But being the better mounted of the two I kept close to his side and endeavoured to show him his heart, till we came into the street of Northampton.

John Wesley, *Journal*

In his Journal for July 20th, 1766, Wesley records attending the church of St. Saviourgate in York and being invited to preach. An eye-witness account of this event was printed in the Wesleyan Methodist Magazine for 1827.

At that time, the Rev. Mr. Cordeux was incumbent of the living of St. Saviour's, and he warned his congregation against hearing 'that vagabond Wesley preach'. Mr. Wesley came to the city on a Saturday, preached in Peasholm-Green Chapel, and again on the Sunday morning; in the forenoon of that day he went to St. Saviour's Church, dressed in his canonicals. The clergyman in the course of reading prayers saw a stranger cleric and sent an official to invite him to take the pulpit. He accepted the invitation and took his text from the Gospel of the day, Matthew 7:21, 'Not everyone that saith unto me, Lord, Lord, shall enter the kingdom of heaven.' After the service the vicar asked the clerk if he knew who the stranger was. 'Sir,' said he, 'he is the vagabond Wesley of whom you warned us.' 'Aye, indeed,' was the reply, 'we are trapped; but never mind, we had a good sermon.' The Dean heard of the affair and threatened to lay a complaint before the Archbishop. Mr. Cordeux, afraid of the consequences, took an early opportunity, when some occasion brought him into the presence of his Grace, to tell him that he had allowed Mr. Wesley to occupy his pulpit. 'And you did right,' said the Prelate. The matter of the complaint was never more heard of, and Mr. Cordeux was so far from repenting of what

---

[2] William Clowes, the Primitive Methodist preacher, recalled this occasion when he was on a tour of Cornwall in 1825: 'I had expected that I should receive an invitation to dine at a certain house, but I was disappointed. I went to the top of Charn Bay Rock... I thought of what Mr. Wesley had said to John Nelson when they were in Cornwall, namely that it was an excellent country to get an appetite, but not so excellent to get something to eat. They did, however, get a few blackberries; and I looked to see if I could get some, but being unable to find more than one, which was unripe, I was obliged to make my dinner of it.

he had done, that some years afterwards, he made a second offer of his pulpit, and Mr. Wesley preached upon the eight beatitudes.

> Reprinted in *The Journal and Diaries of John Wesley*, edited by W. Reginald Ward and Richard P. Heitzenrater, vol. 22, p. 51

Samuel Johnson was acquainted with Wesley, and also with his sister Martha. His well-known verdict on Wesley was that 'his conversation is good, but he is never at leisure. He is always obliged to go at a certain hour.' Boswell records the following incident.

Of John Wesley, he said, 'He can talk well on any subject.' Boswell: Pray, sir, what has he made of his story of a ghost? Johnson: Why, sir, he believes it; but not on sufficient authority. He did not take time enough to examine the girl. It was at Newcastle, where the ghost was said to have appeared to a young woman several times, mentioning something about the right to an old house, advising application to be made to an attorney, which was done; and, at the same time, saying the attorney would do nothing, which proved to be the fact. 'This (says John) is a proof that a ghost knows our thoughts.' Now (laughing) it is not necessary to know our thoughts, to tell that an attorney will sometimes do nothing. Charles Wesley, who is a more stationary man, does not believe the story. I am sorry that John did not take more pains to inquire into the evidence for it.[3]

> James Boswell, *Life of Samuel Johnson LLD*, under the year 1778

The Gayer family of Derriaghy, between Lisburn and Belfast, came into contact with Methodism about 1772 and provided a preaching place and accommodation for visiting preachers to the village.

In the summer of 1775, when the Rev. John Wesley was on his accustomed tour through the north of Ireland, he was received, and affectionately entertained, at the hospitable dwelling of [Edward] Gayer, where he lay for several days dangerously ill by a violent attack of fever, and experienced the kindest attentions of the family. Noticing this event in his journal of that year, he writes, 'Those words ran in my mind, when I saw Miss Gayer at one side of the bed, looking at her mother on the other –

> She sat like Patience on a monument,
> Smiling at Grief.'

On this occasion many fears were entertained of Mr. Wesley's death, and much solicitude felt for his recovery. Fervent prayers were offered up for him, that God might graciously prolong his valuable life; and, as in the case of Hezekiah,[4] add to his days fifteen years; and, whilst one of the Preachers, with a few select friends, was thus engaged, Mrs. Gayer suddenly rose from her knees, and exclaimed, 'The prayer is granted.' Soon after Mr. Wesley recovered; and, it is

---

[3] Boswell met Wesley in Edinburgh the following year and asked him about the ghost, concluding, 'His state[ment] of the evidence as to the ghost did not satisfy me.'

[4] See 2 Kings 20:1–6

worthy of remark, survived from June 1775 till March 1791, a period of just fifteen years and eight months.

Wesleyan Methodist Magazine, 1834, pp. 412–13

Two quite different accounts of an accident while travelling in the Isle of Man in June 1777 help us determine the accuracy of John Wesley's reporting in his Journal.

I set out for Douglas in the one-horse chaise, Mrs. Smythe riding with me. In about an hour, in spite of all I could do, the headstrong horse ran the wheel against a large stone. The chaise overset in a moment, but we fell so gently on smooth grass that neither of us was hurt at all.

Journal of John Wesley, 2 June 1777

He [Wesley] told me when we got into the carriage that he could drive a chaise forty years ago; but, poor dear man! his hand seemed out of practice, as I thought we should be overturned several times. At last, one of the wheels being mounted on one side of a ditch, we were both pitched out in a great plain as the Lord in mercy ordered it; for had we been overset in some part of the road, it is more than probable we should have been killed on the spot. I found no bad effects from the fall at the time; but the next morning I was scarce able to stir, and felt so sore and bruised that I thought it likely I should lay my bones in the churchyard at Douglas.

The Christian's Triumph over Sin, the Devil and the Grave..., 1783, pp. 42–3

Wesley's Journal, under the date April 15th, 1779, records the resolution of a dispute among the Methodists of Halifax: 'I went to Halifax, where a little thing had lately occasioned great disturbance. An angel blowing a trumpet was placed on the sounding board over the pulpit. Many were vehemently against this: others as vehemently for it: but a total end was soon put to the contest, for the angel vanished away.' The disappearing act was rather less miraculous than Wesley's words might suggest.

For the sake either of ornament or use, a sounding board was placed over the pulpit; and several of the congregation thinking the board had a meagre appearance, hit upon a good scheme, as they thought, to remedy the defect. A subscription was opened, to which James Cooke and John Wade were the principal contributors, and an image of an angel blowing a trumpet [was] placed over the sounding board. At the sight of so noble a figure with expanded wings and a tremendous trumpet in its hand the congregation might well be astonished when they assembled for public worship the Sabbath following its erection. Without adverting to this manifestation of a depraved taste, the angel became a subject of much contention in the society, which was extended not a little by Mr. Murlin's[5] determination to preach no more under it. In the midst of this dissention, however, Mr. Wesley came to Halifax...

On the evening of the day in question, Mr. Wesley in order to settle a dispute which unhappily had been productive of no small evil, called the leaders together after service. The matter was gone into, and a lot discussion ensued, but when the votes were cast up they proved to be equal. At this juncture John Hatton of Lightcliffe, came into the room, and on the nature of the

---

[5]   John Murlin, junior itinerant in the Bradford Circuit that year.

proceedings being explained to him, gave his vote for the destruction of the angel. Eager to execute the decision of the meeting, the angel in a few minutes disappeared from the sounding board; Mr. Murlin hewed 'the dagon' in pieces, and before midnight his ashes were smouldering in the chapel yard! Mr. Wesley from his well-known antipathy against a sounding board intimated his wish that it might be removed. On the morning following, at the 5 o'clock preaching, great was the consternation of the people when they beheld the pulpit in its original plainness, being minus both the sounding board and its gorgeous appendage.

It is painful however to add, that the matter did not end here – a division ensued, several influential members left the society, and in some instances remained through life disconnected with any particular church. Mr. Wesley appears not to have been fully aware of the extent of evil which had accrued from this contention. The angel had but been erected two Sundays.

J.V. Walker, *History of Methodism in Halifax*, 1836, pp. 149–51

Adam Clarke recounts an incident which occurred as Wesley was leaving Norwich in October 1783.

When Mr. Wesley was about to depart, the poor, as usual, flocked around him, and were extremely annoying by pressing upon him. Having only as much money as would defray his expenses to the next place, he turned and said, rather sharply, when near the carriage, 'I have nothing for you; do you suppose I can support the poor in every place?' He then proceeded to ascend the steps, in doing which his foot slipped and he fell back upon the ground. Mr. Bradford, being near, raised him up; and just as he was re-ascending the steps of the carriage, he turned his head towards Mr. Bradford, who stood behind him, and bending a benignant, yet pensive eye upon him, meekly said, 'It is all right, Joseph – it is all right: it was only what I deserved; for if I had no *other* good to impart, I ought, at least, to have given them good words.'

James Everett, *Adam Clarke Portrayed*, 2nd edition, vol. 1, pp. 94–5

Many years ago, I was acquainted with an old lady, ninety years of age; she had recollections of John Wesley and was very fond of recalling them.

On one occasion, John Wesley was preaching for her father, a Dissenting minister. John Wesley dined at her father's house, and my friend, then a little girl, and her sister were allowed to go in to the dessert. Mr. Wesley, who seemed very fond of children, requested that they might be seated on either side of him.

'Just opposite,' said my old friend, 'was a dish of choice apples, which the visitor handed to me. I was a long time choosing one, finally taking the prettiest on the dish. Then they were handed to my sister, who was also long in choosing, but she was seeking the worst looking and took what she considered to be such.

'Not a word had so far been uttered, but now Mr. Wesley observed, "As this is the first time I have had the pleasure of dining here, may I be allowed to teach a lesson to my little friends?" Permission being granted, he said, "My dear little girls, *I wish you to exchange apples*."

'I have never forgotten my confusion - I had taken the best apple.

'Dear Mr. Wesley, with the kindest of smiles, but with firmness, said, "I want you to remember this my first visit;" and with such a winning manner, added, "Always think first of others and what they would like."

'We gladly exchanged our apples, and the lesson was blessed to us, for in after life, as well as in childhood, the sweet look and loving advice of our dear friend ruled many an action. Were we tempted to be selfish, a whisper came, *Remember the apples.*'

Methodist Recorder, Winter Number, 1896, p. 28

Wesley's marriage to Mrs. Mary Vazeille was a particularly unfortunate one, though scholars are still deliberating on where to lay any blame. Wesley's niece, Sally, daughter of Charles Wesley, provides one fragment of evidence. The family were then living at Marylebone; Sally Wesley was about 16 and a favourite of her uncle's.

I think it was in the year 1775, my uncle promised to take me with him to Canterbury and Dover. At that time his wife, Mrs. Wesley, had obtained some of his letters which she used to the most injurious purposes, misinterpreting expressions and interpolating words. These mutilated letters she intended publishing in the *Morning Post* – which she did. My dear father, to whom the reputation of my uncle was far more dear than his own, saw the importance of refutation, and set off to the Foundery, to induce him to postpone his journey, while I, in my own mind, was lamenting such a disappointment, having anticipated it with all the impatience natural to my years. Never shall I forget the manner in which my father accosted my mother on his return home. He said, 'My brother is indeed an extraordinary man. I placed before him the importance of the character of a minister, the evil consequences which might result from his indifference to it, the cause of religion, stumbling blocks to the weak, and urged him by every relative and public motive to answer for himself and stop the publication. His reply was: 'Brother, when I devoted to God my ease, my time, my life, did I except my reputation? No. Tell Sally I will take her to Canterbury tomorrow.'

G.J. Stevenson, *Memorials of the Wesley Family*, 1876, pp. 475–6

John Rawson was a merchant and a local preacher who, with his brother William, had introduced Methodism into Leicester.

During Mr. Rawson's residence in Leicester Mr. Wesley came to preach and was Mr. Rawson's guest. Mrs. Rawson, a lady-like and kind-hearted person of the early Methodist type, wishing to consult her guest's taste, inquired of his travelling companion Joseph Bradford what Mr. Wesley particularly liked for supper. 'Veal pie, Madam!' was the prompt reply. Accordingly the choice article was provided and placed in a cupboard near at hand, ready to be placed on the table when required. After preaching, Mr. Wesley returned with a number of friends who had been invited to meet him. When supper and worship were over, Mr. Wesley took out his watch and held it in his hand, conversing in the free-est and most delightful manner until his usual hour when he rose and, bidding all goodnight, retired to rest. After an early breakfast in the morning he left, but not without giving his hostess many thanks and his usual salute. The latter seems to have made an impression, which lit up her countenance when she spoke of it in her old age. Soon after their guest was gone Mrs. Rawson had occasion to go to the cupboard, when lo and behold! there was the veal pie untouched. They had been so taken up with their guest as to forget the special treat they had so carefully provided for him.

Methodist Recorder, Winter Number, 1895, pp. 97–8

As Wesley's travelling companion during much of the year 1780–1781, Samuel Bradburn became acquainted with many aspects of his personality and activities.

By [this] means I had an opportunity of knowing how his accounts stood; and I know that he gave away within the year, from the Bristol Conference, 1780, to the Leeds Conference, 1781, in private charities, above fourteen hundred pounds! I do not mention that year as if he never did the like before or since, but because I know he did it then. He told me in London, in the year 1787, that he never gave away out of his own pocket less than a thousand pounds a year. To enable him to do this, he had, first, the profits of the books which the preachers sold (except ten per cent, which some of them took for about eighteen years past)... He had, secondly, from London and Bristol on an average, about £150 per annum by private subscriptions. Thirdly, the Society in London gave him £30 a year, which was all the fixed stipend he had. Fourthly, every year almost there were legacies left him. Fifthly, as he went his journeys, the friends in each large society where he preached generally gave him a few pounds when he was going away. Thus, literally having nothing, he possessed all things; and, though poor, he made many rich. His manner of bestowing his charity was truly pleasing: he never relieved poor people in the street, but either he took off or moved his hat to them when they thanked him. And in private he took care not to hurt the most refined feelings of those he assisted.

T.W. Blanshard, *Samuel Bradburn*, 1870, pp. 89–90

Methodism was late being established in Southampton, partly because of the existence of a strong dissenting congregation at the Above Bar Independent chapel. Wesley had preached in the town in 1767, but did not return until August 1787, when he was on his way to the Channel Islands. A pattern maker named Fay was precentor at the Independent Meeting. His wife, a former Methodist, sometimes entertained the itinerants.

Mr. Wesley was accompanied by Mr. Joseph Bradford. Mrs. Fay invited Mr. [John] Morse to take tea in company with Mr. Wesley, hoping by this means to overcome the prejudice he had long entertained in regard to Mr. Wesley: the popular notion that the Methodist preachers were the false prophets and that Mr. Wesley was their head and leader. On entering the room, Mr. Wesley sprang from the chair to meet him, and taking him by both hands shook them earnestly, saying, 'My dear Brother, how do you do?' A reception so cordial and affectionate as this from a man whom he had hitherto viewed as a false prophet quite overcame him... Under the sermon that evening he was powerfully convinced of sin, and he rested not until Methodist preaching was regularly established in the town.

Notice of the vessel being on the point of sailing came rather suddenly, but not too much so for Mr. Wesley, who proverbially was instant in season out of season. He was never in a hurry; he was ready for the summons. Not so his *aid de camp* Bradford, who besought Mr. Wesley to tarry while he finished the operation of shaving. 'I'll wait for no man,' was his reply and [he] immediately went down to the Quay, leaving Bradford after having removed the stubble from his chin, to follow.

> John Sundius Stamp, manuscript 'History of Methodism in Hampshire', Methodist Archives Centre, Manchester

Another example of Wesley's meticulous promptness comes from his last visit to York, when he was the guest of Robert Spence (1748–1824), a bookseller and publisher who was for many years a local preacher.

The last time Mr. Wesley visited York [1–4 May 1790, according to his Diary] Mr. Spence breakfasted with him, by appointment, at three o'clock in the morning, and his carriage was ready at the door at four; as proof of the regularity and exactness of this extraordinary man, when he gave directions to the driver to be at the door at this early hour, he said to him, 'I do not mean a quarter or five minutes past.' The man obeyed his orders, and as the minster clock was striking *four* Mt. Wesley entered into his carriage. [The Diary records that he arrived in Thirsk at 8.45 a.m.]

> Richard Burdekin, *Memoirs of the Life and Character of Robert Spence*, 1827, p. 27

The following anecdote was told to Thomas Jackson by Joseph Taylor, his Superintendent in the Leeds Circuit.

One day Mr. Wesley was walking up a hill with several of his Preachers, when he was getting out of breath, which he was unwilling to confess. Then stopping suddenly, he said, 'I am surprised, brethren, at your want of taste. You are pressing up the hill, regardless of the beautiful prospect that is behind you.' Having directed their attention to the different objects in the plain below, he called upon them to sing,

> Ye mountains and vales, In praises abound;
> Ye hills, and ye dales, Continue the sound;
> Break forth into singing, Ye trees of the wood;
> For Jesus is bringing Lost sinners to God.

While they sang he recovered his breath; and then the aged man was able to keep pace with his more vigorous companions.

> Thomas Jackson, *Recollections of my own Life and Times*, 1873, p. 115

Charles Wesley died on March 29, 1788.

It is a curious incident that [John] Wesley, at the time, was preaching in Shropshire, and (as was afterwards ascertained) he and his congregation, at the very moment of his brother's exit, were singing:

> Come, let us join our friends above
>   That have obtained the prize,
> And on the eagle wings of love
>   To joys celestial rise...

Samuel Bradburn, the assistant in the City Road circuit, immediately dispatched a letter to Wesley, informing him of his brother's death; but in consequence of its being misdirected, it failed to reach him till April 4, the day before the burial. Wesley was in Macclesfield, and to get to London in time for the funeral was impossible...

Wesley had no disposition to tell the deep sorrows of his heart; but that he severely felt the departure of his brother there can be no question. A fortnight afterwards, when at Bolton, he attempted to give out, as his second hymn, the one beginning with the words, 'Come, O Thou Traveller unknown'; but when he came to the lines,

> My company before is gone,
> And I am left alone with Thee,

the bereaved old man sunk beneath emotion which was uncontrollable, burst into a flood of tears, sat down in the pulpit, and hid his face with his hands. The crowded congregation well knew the cause of his speechless excitement; singing ceased; and the chapel became a Bochim[6]. At length Wesley recovered himself, rose again, and went through a service which was never forgotten by those who were present at it.

> Luke Tyerman, *Life and Times of the Rev. John Wesley*, III, pp. 526–7, citing *Methodist Recorder*, December 5, 1861

Wesley had first taken upon himself to ordain some of his itinerant preachers for the work in America in 1784. This led to ordinations for Scotland, and eventually for England. The following is an eye-witness account of what happened at the Conference of 1790, the last to meet before his death on 2 March 1791.

The close of the Conference was very impressive. The twelve young men, or perhaps but eleven, stood on one of the benches, spoke briefly of their experience, their call to preach, & confessed their faith. After this Dr. Coke came on the fore bench with the large Minutes[7] on his left arm and delivered a copy to each, putting his right hand on each of our heads. This was ordination in every view; what else could it designate, having sworn thus to the faith and devotion to the work of the Lord? I do not recollect that this was continued in future Conferences; but am told it followed the Scottish ordinations, & though it was not called ordination, what else could it be?

Mr Wesley took no part in these proceedings; he kept his seat, but saw the Doctor deliver the Minutes to the twelve, laying his right hand in silence on the head of each. His presence sanctioned the whole; for though bound [to] him by countless [ties?], he saw and felt that half

---

6 A reference to Judges 2:4–5.

7 The 'Large Minutes' was a collection of the Conference resolutions, first published in 1753 as a summary of Methodist discipline. It became customary to present a copy to preachers when they were 'received into full connexion'.

a million people could not be kept together with[out] the bread hallowed by the Lord. The words of Peter apply here: 'What was I that I could withstand God?'

Joseph Sutcliffe, Ms 'History of Methodism'

When Helen McKenny moved with her parents into Wesley's City Road house in 1885 she found herself co-habiting with relics of the founder of Methodism. But some had already disappeared.

September 3rd [1885]. Moved here! a day of great excitement... Went upstairs and did obeisance to the Clock and the Chair and other relics.

September 7th. Today I feel I don't care a pin for the old Relics. They oppress me with their antiquity and sacredness!

September 14th. We were asking about John Wesley's bedspread and what had become of it, and [Mrs Nash] said they believed it to be in a loft in the roof, but some people believed that one of the old ministers (Rev John Scott) who came to live here, turned it out. (Afterwards we heard from a friend that a gentleman of his acquaintance had bought it 24 years ago, second-hand, curtains and all.) ...

September 13th [1887]. Met Mr Beardmore, and Rev Arthur Shipham, whose Wife was a dear friend of ours. Talking of the Wesley Relics, he said when he was at Kingswood they had Mr Wesley's gown there. It was torn up for dusters! Incredible! He secured – *stole* indeed, a bit of it, and parted it among some friends.

Helen G McKenny, *A City Road Diary, 1885–1888*, 1978, pp. 1, 2, 3–4, 72

John Wesley was buried in the graveyard at the rear of his chapel in City Road. The two anecdotes that follow relate to his reinterment. (See also under Charles Wesley below.)

Walter Griffith (c.1763–1825) was one of a number of Wesley's itinerant preachers who were buried close to him.

[Griffith's] remains were deposited in Mr. Wesley's tomb, the opening of which was an occasion of intense interest to many. It was found that Mr. Wesley's outer coffin had almost entirely disappeared, leaving the lead coffin, containing his body, exposed and bare. I observed it to be of very short dimensions. It was placed in another wood coffin of substantial material, and then in a massive stone coffin, after which the tomb was closed, with the intention that it should never be opened again till the great archangel's trumpet shall sound, summoning both the living and the dead to appear before the judgment-seat of Christ.

Thomas Jackson, *Recollections of my own Life and Times*, 1873, p. 223

An old man wished to see me on his death-bed. He had been a somewhat cranky old gentleman, and his departure was not likely to cause inconsolable regret to the church. He said, 'I want you to promise to bury me when I die!' I told him I should be most happy to do it. 'Well,' said he, 'I think I should be buried by the chief minister in Methodism in any circuit where I die, for I made the nails of John Wesley's coffin!' I told him he must be a much older man than I had supposed, for Wesley died in 1791. 'Ah, but don't you know that he was buried twice?'

I had forgotten for the moment, but it was so. Many years after his death his original grave sank. The coffin was taken out, the grave put right, and he was reburied. The old coffin was encased in another, and it was for this second that the old man made the nails. Perhaps everyone who saw the reinternment has now passed on; but the late Mrs Nash, who died a very few years ago at the age of nearly a hundred, remembered the event. She was one of the well-known Methodist family of the Gabriels.

Charles H Kelly, *Memories*, 1910, p. 163

Charles Wesley (1707–1788)

John Wesley's younger brother played a significant part in the formative years of the Methodist revival, but has been remembered first and foremost as a hymn-writer. The following anecdotes illustrate both his poetic gifts and the difference between the characters and temperaments of the two brothers.

When at the University, in early years, his brother (as he informed me) was alarmed whenever [Charles] entered his study. *Aut insanit homo, aut versus facit.*[8] Full of the muse, and being short-sighted, he would sometimes walk right against his brother's table, and, perhaps, overthrow it. If the 'fine phrenzy' was not quite so high, he would discompose the books and papers in the study, ask some questions without always waiting for a reply, repeat some poetry that just then struck him, and at length leave his brother to his regularity ... When he was near fourscore, he retained something of this eccentricity. He rode every day [from Marylebone to City Road] (clothed for winter even in summer) a little horse, grey with age. When he mounted, if a subject struck him, he proceeded to expand, and put it in order. He would write a hymn thus given him on a card (kept for the purpose) with his pencil, in shorthand. Not infrequently he has come to our house in the City-road, and, having left the poney in the *garden* in front, he would enter, crying out, 'Pen and ink! Pen and ink!' These being supplied, he wrote the hymn he had been composing. When this was done, he would look round on those present, and salute them with much kindness, ask after their health, give out a short hymn, and thus put all in mind of eternity.

Henry Moore, *Life of the Rev. John Wesley*, 1824–25, vol. 2 pp. 366–7, quoted in Frank Baker, *Charles Wesley's Verse: an introduction*, 1988, pp. 8–9

Charles Wesley was never very happy about his brother's use of lay preachers and was critical of their abilities.

Henry Moore heard the following anecdote from Charles Wesley himself. The Methodist preacher once met Dr. Robinson, afterwards Primate of Ireland, at the Hotwells, near Bristol. They had been together at Westminster [School], and were both elected the same year to Christ Church. Robinson seemed glad to see Charles Wesley and talked freely with him. He told him that he had not believed many things he had heard about the brothers, but had always been surprised that they employed laymen. 'It is your fault, my lord,' said Charles. 'My fault, Mr. Wesley?' 'Yes, my lord, your and your brethren's.' 'How so, sir?' said Dr. Robinson. 'Why, my lord, you hold your peace, and so the stones cry out.' The friends took a turn round the pump-

---

8 The man is either mad or making verses.

room in silence. Then Dr. Robinson said, 'But I hear they are unlearned men.' 'Very true, my lord; in general they are so; so the dumb ass rebukes the prophet.'[9]

John Telford, *The Life of the Rev. Charles Wesley, MA*, 1900, p. 305

John Wesley was able to claim that in forty years of travelling the roads of England he had never been robbed on the road. But his brother Charles did once encounter a highwayman, when returning to London from Oxford.

Tues., October 11th [1737]. I set out for London. In a mile's riding my horse fell lame. I sung the 91st Psalm, and put myself under the divine protection. I had scarce ended, and turned the hut on Shotover-Hill, when a man came up to me and demanded my money, showing, but not presenting, a pistol. I gave him my purse. He asked how much there was. 'About thirty shillings.' 'Have you no more?' 'I will see;' put my hand in my pocket and gave him some halfpence. He repeated the question, 'Have you no more?' I had thirty pounds in a private pocket; bade him search [for] himself; which he did not choose. He ordered me to dismount, which I did; but begged hard for my horse again, promising not to pursue him. He took my word and restored him. I rode gently on, praising God. My bags, and watch, and gold, the robber was *forced* to leave me.

Charles Wesley, *Journal*, vol.1, pp. 77–8

The pulpit at Wesley's Chapel, London was originally a 'three-decker', of which only the top section has survived.

Of his energy and earnestness in the pulpit, Henry Moore, Dr Coke, and others, occasionally related the following incident. Dr Coke had read the prayers one Sunday morning in City Road Chapel, only a short time before Charles Wesley's death. Charles Wesley always preached in his gown and bands. Before he had half finished his sermon, with the free exercise of his arms and the aid of his loose gown sleeves, the hymn book was swept off the pulpit and fell on poor Dr Coke's head in the reading desk beneath. But little hurt, though the congregation smiled, yet the preacher heeded not, and knew not what he had done. His energetic action was more enkindled, and so, turning to the front corner of the reading desk, the little doctor looked up and saw the Bible itself half over the front of the pulpit; watching and waiting, in a few moments the Bible fell also, but the prudent divine was standing with outstretched arms, and received it, without any injury either to himself or the book. On went the preacher with an outflowing eloquence and power which only inspiration could impart, quite unconscious of the loss of either of the books, till he had finished his discourse.

George J Stevenson, *City Road Chapel, London*, 1872, p. 95

Adam Clarke shared with James Everett the following recollection of Charles Wesley as a preacher in his later years.

---

9   This conversation is said to have taken place in 1748. Telford points out that Robinson did not become a bishop until 1755. In 1748 he was still Rector of Etton, near Beverley and a Prebend of York.

A singular occurrence took place in the city of Bristol, on the occasion of one of my visits there... [Charles Wesley] was expected to preach and for that purpose ascended the pulpit. I sat behind him. He gave out a hymn and prayed; but was completely in the trammels, where he had often been before. He then took a text, spoke a little, but soon found that he could not go on. He tried to relieve himself by praying; when he rose from his knees he took another text, but that also was as fruitless as its predecessor. On finding it so, he took up the hymn-book, and beckoned me to step forward. On giving me the book, he left the pulpit and retired to the rooms over the chapel. Though I had no promise of his return, I indulged a slight hope that he would not disappoint the congregation by leaving the service to me. I turned to a hymn (sixes and sevens) and gave it out: I trembled for fear. Had it been left entirely to my own judgment, I could have done well enough; but his intentions and return were alike unknown: I did not even know, till afterwards, where he was. I went leisurely on with the hymn, giving out verse after verse, till I came to the sixth; and just at the moment I was giving him up for lost to the people, he made his appearance.

J.E. - Did he make another attempt to preach?

Mr. C - He commenced by telling an anecdote about Mr. La Trobe, who was then not expected to live long; after which he exclaimed, with a strong voice, yet a little drawling: 'Believe – love – obey.' He then proceeded in the following strain: 'Who are they that believe? All true Christians. Who are they that love? All those that believe. Who are they that obey? Such as believe and love. Can a heathen be saved? Yes, if he is capable of believing, loving and obeying. But he must first be taught before he can believe, believe before he can love, and love before he can obey. Can a Mahometan be saved? Yes, if he can believe, love and obey. Can a Roman Catholic be saved? Yes, if he believes, loves and obeys. Some persons may object to their salvation; but they must first prove that they cannot believe, love and obey.' After making a few remarks in abrupt and broken sentences, on faith and obedience, he then came to love again, and said, 'We ought to love Jews, Turks, heathens, and Roman Catholics – the latter especially as brethren; for if you can prove to me that they cannot be saved, I insist upon our ceasing to love them – but then they may be saved – *ergo* they ought to be loved.'

James Everett, *Adam Clarke Portrayed*, 2nd edition, 1866, pp. 81–2

John Wesley differed sharply from his brother in his views on the consecration of churchyards. They were trenchantly – not to say sarcastically – expressed in his 'Thoughts on the consecration of churches and burial grounds': 'You say, 'This is consecrated ground, so many feet broad, and so many long.' But pray, how deep is the consecrated ground? – "Deep! What does that signify?" O, a great deal: for if my grave be dug too deep, I may happen to get out of the consecrated ground: and who can tell what unhappy consequences may follow from this?'

Charles Wesley's sacerdotal views were so strong that he refused to consent to be buried in the ground of City Road Chapel, where the dust of his great brother finds rest, or opposite in Bunhill Fields, where his mother was interred. He insisted that he must lie in 'consecrated ground'. Consequently, his grave was secured in the burial-place of Marylebone, a chapel-of-ease used before the present Marylebone parish church was erected. There he reposed in peace. But, oddly enough, it turns out that the ground never has been 'consecrated' by any bishop. It is merely a cemetery belonging to a chapel-of-ease. I was told that by Canon Barker, then Rector of Marylebone, now Dean of Carlisle. But what does it matter? Once, when Dean Stanley paid one of his occasional visits to see Wesley's Chapel and Wesley's grave, he asked the then verger, a quaint, queer old man, 'Who consecrated this ground?' and received as reply, 'Consecrated it, sir? John Wesley's bones, sir!' 'And,' said the broad-minded dean, 'a better consecration it could not have!'

Charles H Kelly, *Memories*, 1910, pp. 104–6

John Haime (1710–1784)

Before becoming one of the early itinerants, Haime had preached while serving in the British Army during the War of the Austrian Succession (1741–48). His autobiography gives graphic first-hand accounts of the Battles of Dettingen (1743) and Fontenoy and illustrates some of the fanaticism of early Methodism at grass-roots level.

The spring following, we took the field again; and on May 11th 1745 we had a full trial of our faith at Fontenoy. Some days before, one of our brethren, standing at his tent door, broke out into rapture of joy, knowing his departure was at hand; and when he went into the field of battle, declared, 'I am going to rest in the bosom of Jesus.' Indeed, this day God was pleased to prove our little flock, and to show them his mighty power. They showed such courage and boldness in the fight as made the officers, as well as soldiers, amazed. When wounded, some cried out, 'I am going to the Beloved.' Others, 'Come, Lord Jesus, come quickly!' And many that were not wounded earnestly desired 'to be dissolved and to be with Christ'...

For my own part, I stood the hottest fire of the enemy for about seven hours. But I told my comrades, 'The French have no ball made that will kill me this day.' After about seven hours, a cannon-ball killed my horse under me. An officer cried out, 'Haime, where is your God now?' I answered, 'Sir, He is here with me: and he will bring me out of this battle.' Presently a cannon-ball took off his head. My horse fell upon me, and some cried out, 'Haime is gone!' But I replied, 'He is not gone yet.' I soon disengaged myself, and walked on, praising God. I was exposed both to the enemy and our own horse: but that did not discourage me at all; for I knew the God of Jacob was with me. I had a long way to go through all our horse, the balls flying on every side. And all the way lay multitudes bleeding, groaning, or just dead. Surely I was as in the fiery furnace; but it did not singe a hair of my head. The hotter the battle grew, the more strength was given me: I was as full of joy as I could contain... Among the dead there were great plenty of watches, and of gold and silver. One asked me, 'Will you not get something?' I answered, 'No; I have got Christ. I will have no plunder.'

Lives of the Early Methodist Preachers, 1871, vol. 1, pp. 288–89

George Whitefield (1714–1770)

In February 1739 George Whitefield set the Wesleys an example by becoming a 'field preacher' in Bristol, though only after considerable hesitation. This was to be the first of many occasions throughout his ministry on which Whitefield preached in the open air, often to great crowds, on both sides of the Atlantic.

Saturday, Feb. 17. About one in the afternoon, I went with my brother Seward, and another friend, to Kingswood, and was most delightfully entertained by an old disciple of the Lord. My bowels have long since yearned towards the poor colliers, who are very numerous, and as sheep having no shepherd. After dinner, therefore, I went upon a mount and spake to as many people as came unto me. They were upward of two hundred. Blessed be God that I have now broken the ice! I believe I never was more acceptable to my Master than when I was standing to teach those hearers in the open fields. Some may censure me; but if I thus pleased men, I should not be the servant of Christ.

Whitefield, *Journal*

A few weeks later Whitefield was preparing to return to America and appealed to John Wesley to take over this open-air ministry he had begun in and around Bristol. Though with similar hesitation, Wesley eventually agreed to go.

I had no thought of leaving London, when I received after several others, a letter from Mr. Whitefield and another from Mr. Seward, entreating me in the most pressing manner to come to Bristol without delay. This I was not at all forward to do; and perhaps a little less inclined to it... because of the remarkable scriptures which offered as often as we inquired touching the consequence of this removal...

Wed.28 [March] My journey was proposed to our society in Fetter Lane. But my brother Charles would scarce bear the mention of it... Our other brethren, however, continuing the dispute, without any probability of their coming to one conclusion, we at length all agreed to decide it by lot. And by this it was determined I should go...

Sat.31. In the evening I reached Bristol, and met Mr. Whitefield there. I could scarce reconcile myself at first to this strange way of preaching in the fields, of which he set me an example on Sunday; having been all my life (till very lately) so tenacious of every point relating to decency and order, that I should have thought the saving of souls almost a sin if it had not been done in a church...

Mon. [April] 2. At four in the afternoon I submitted to be more vile and proclaimed in the highways the glorious tidings of salvation, speaking from a little eminence in a ground adjoining to the city, to about three thousand people.

John Wesley, *Journal*

Field preaching, though considered scandalous by most of the Anglican clergy of the day thus, became a major feature of early Methodism.

Whitefield's persuasive oratory was proverbial, as this reminiscence by Benjamin Franklin testifies.

Mr. Whitefield... preached up this charity [the Bethesda Orphanage in Georgia], and made large collections, for his eloquence had a wonderful power over the hearts and purses of his hearers, of which I myself was an instance.

I did not disapprove of the design, but as Georgia was then destitute of materials and workmen, and it was proposed to send them from Philadelphia at great expense, I thought it would have been better to have built the house here, and brought the children to it...

I happened, soon after, to attend one of his sermons, in the course of which I perceived he intended to finish with a collection, and I silently resolved he should get nothing from me. I had in my pocket a handful of copper money, three or four silver dollars, and five pistoles in gold. As he proceeded I began to soften, and concluded to give the coppers. Another stroke of his oratory made me ashamed of that, and determined me to give the silver; and he finished so admirably that I emptied my pocket wholly into the collector's dish, gold and all.

Benjamin Franklin, *Autobiography*, 1868

Whitefield first visited Scotland in 1741.

In one of his journeys, Whitefield was told of a widow with a large family, whose landlord had distrained her furniture... Whitefield's purse was never large, but his sympathy was great, and he immediately gave the five guineas the helpless woman needed. The friend who was travelling with him hinted that the sum was more than he could reasonably afford; to which the reply was, 'When God brings a case of distress before us, it is that we may relieve it.'

The two travellers proceeded on their journey, and before long encountered a highwayman, who demanded their money, which they gave. Whitefield now turned the tables on his friend, and reminded him how much better it was for the poor widow to have the five guineas than the thief...

They had not long resumed their travel, before the highwayman returned and demanded Whitefield's coat. This request was also granted, Whitefield accepting the robber's ragged habiliment till he could procure a better.

Presently they perceived the marauder again galloping towards them most furiously; and now, fearing that their lives were threatened, they also spurred their horses and, fortunately, arrived at some cottages before the highwayman could stop them. The thief was baulked, and no doubt was immensely mortified; for when Whitefield took off the man's tattered coat, he found in one of its pockets a carefully wrapped parcel containing one hundred guineas.

Luke Tyerman, *Life of George Whitefield*, 1876–77, pp. 525–6, quoting the *Gospel Magazine*, 1816

Thomas Mitchell (1724–1785)

While still a local preacher, Mitchell witnessed the kind of violent persecution he himself was to encounter after he became an itinerant.

One evening, while William Darnley was preaching, the curate of Guiseley came at the head of a large mob, who threw eggs in his face, pulled him down, dragged him out of the house on the ground, and stamped upon him. The curate himself then thought it was enough and bade them let him alone and go their way. Some time after Jonathan Maskew came. As soon as he began to speak, the same mob came, pulled him down and dragged him out of the house. They then tore off his clothes and dragged him along upon his naked back over the gravel and pavement. When they thought they had sufficiently bruised him, they let him go and went away. With much difficulty he crept to a friend's house, where they dressed his wounds and got him some clothes. It was my turn to go next. No sooner was I at the town, than the mob came, like so many roaring lions. My friends advised me not to preach that night, and undertook to carry me out of the town. But the mob followed me in a great rage, and stoned me for near two miles, so that it was several weeks before I got well of the bruises I then received...

On Sunday, August 7th [1751] I came to Wrangle, very early in the morning. I preached, as usual, at five. About six, two constables came, at the head of a large mob. They violently broke in upon the people, seized upon me, pulled me down, and took me to a public-house, where they kept me till four in the afternoon. Then one of the constables seemed to relent and said, 'I will go to the minister and inquire of him whether we may not let the poor man go.' When he came back, he said, 'They were not to let him go yet.' So he took me out to the mob, who presently hurried me away and threw me into a pool, of standing water. It took me up to the neck. Several times I strove to get out, but they pitched me in again. They told me I must go through it seven times. I did so, and then they let me come out. When I had got upon dry ground, a man stood ready with a pot full of white paint. He painted me all over from head to foot; and then they carried me into a public-house again. Here I was kept till they had put five more of our friends into the water. Then they came and took me out again and carried me to a great pond, which was railed in on every side, being ten or twelve feet deep. Here four men took me by my legs and arms, and swung me backward and forward. For a moment I felt the flesh shrink; but it was quickly gone. I gave myself up to the Lord, and was content his will should be done. They swung me two or three times and then they threw me as far as they could into the water. The fall and the water soon took away my senses, so that I felt nothing more. But some of them were not willing to have me drowned. So they watched till I came above water, and then, catching hold of my clothes with a long pole, made shift to drag me out.

After further torments, Mitchell was left to find his way as best he could to the home of friends three or four miles away, where he was given refuge while he regained his strength.

Lives of the Early Methodist Preachers, vol. 1, pp. 244, 248–9

John Fletcher (1729–1785)

Fletcher's first encounter with Methodism is described in an autobiographical letter to Charles Wesley, dated 10 May 1757.

Four years ago, as I was going into the country, my performing this duty [of exhorting and reproving as opportunity offered] was the cause of my finding another Christian and of hearing of a body of people among which there is several: The family [of Thomas Hill, who employed him as tutor to his two sons] had baited and while they drank tea I went to take a walk and get out of the way of the world: I soon met a poor woman who seem'd to be in distress, and asking her what was the matter I soon saw by her answers that she was a Christian. The pleasure and profit I found in her conversation made me forget that I was upon a journey, and when I returned to the inn[10] I found I had been left behind. However, taking horse, I overtook the family before it was dark and told the reason why I had stay'd behind. 'Don't go,' says a Lady, 'talking so to old women; people will say that we have got a Methodist preacher with us.' I ask'd what she meant by a Methodist and when she had told me I said that I would be one of them if there

---

10   J.S. Simon in *John Wesley, the Master Builder* p.16 locates this incident at St. Albans.

was really such a people in England. The next winter I was no sooner in town but I inquir'd after the Methodists and came to West Street and to Hog Lane every Sunday.

Proceedings of the Wesley Historical Society, xxxiii, 1961–62, pp. 28–9; corrected transcript by Peter S. Forsaith

Having occasion...to accompany his pupils to London, he determined to avail himself of that opportunity to call upon Mr. Berridge, vicar of Everton. He accordingly introduced himself as a raw convert, who had taken the liberty to wait upon him for the benefit of his instruction and advice. From his accent and manners, Mr. Berridge perceived that he was a foreigner, and enquired what countryman he was. 'A Swiss, from the canton of Berne,' was the reply. 'From Berne! then, probably, you can give me some account of a young countryman of yours, one John Fletcher, who has lately preached a few times for the Messrs. Wesley, and of whose talents, learning and piety, they both speak in terms of high eulogy. Do you know him?' 'Yes, sir, I know him intimately; and, did those gentlemen know him as well, they would not speak of him in such terms, for which he is more obliged to their partial friendship than to his own merits.' 'You surprise me (said Mr. Berridge) in speaking so coldly of a countryman in whose praise they are so warm.' 'I have the best reason (he rejoined) for speaking of him as I do – I am John Fletcher!' 'If you be John Fletcher (replied his host) you must do me the favour to take my pulpit tomorrow; and when we are better acquainted, without implicitly receiving your statement, or that of your friends, I shall be able to judge for myself.' Thus commended an intimacy with Mr. Berridge, which controversy[11] could not interrupt.

Seymour, *Life and Times of Selina, Countess of Huntingdon*, p. 236

The following facts are contained in a letter sent by the Rev. Zechariah Taft to Mr. Pearson of Gomersal. Mr. and Mrs. Taft had been spending a fortnight with Mrs. Fletcher at Madeley, when she related the remarkable intercourse she had with her deceased husband.

Shortly before her husband's death she expressed a strong wish to have some communication with him after his decease. His reply was, 'My dear, I do not know the laws that govern the kingdom of God beyond the grave, but, if it be possible and our Heavenly Father permit, your wish shall be gratified.' Soon after his death, Mrs. Fletcher dreamed that she saw her husband standing at the foot of the bed and heard him call to her by the familiar name which he used to employ when alone. 'Polly'. She answered, 'Is that thee, my dear?' 'Yes,' he replied, 'it is I, and Mr. Hay (a mutual friend) is with me, and he bids me tell thee so.' Surprised, she said, 'Is he dead?' He replied, 'Yes, and a letter is coming to thee on the subject, and by this thou shalt know it is I.' The next day a letter arrived stating that Mr. Hay had died suddenly on the preceding day.

Shortly after this, Mrs. Fletcher, wishful to be at the five o'clock preaching, set her alarum to go off at four, as it took considerable time to dress and be in time for the commencement of the preaching. She also prayed that it might please God that she might awake before it went off, and thus escape the shock to her nervous system when it awoke her out of a sound sleep. That night Mr. Fletcher seemed to rest with his head on the pillow by her side, and they conversed for a

---

[11] i.e. between the Arminian and Calvinistic branches of Methodism.

long time on various subjects, and then he pressed his finger on her arm and said, 'Let us look at our alarum.' She opened her eyes and looked at the clock, which was just ready to go off. She was surprised that the impression on her arm remained for some time, and that he should have used the plural pronoun *our*.

Soon after the *Life of Fletcher* by Benson came out [in 1806], Mrs. Fletcher dreamed that she was seated in the parlour, and that a copy of the *Life* lay upon the table. From a fear that there might be something in it that her late husband would not approve of, she had refrained from reading it. She dreamed that he came in and sat down at the other end of the table, and taking up the *Life* in his hand, observed, 'Thou hast not read this?' She replied, 'No,' giving her reasons. 'Oh! read,' he said, 'it will be a comfort to thee.' 'How has he done it?' she inquired. 'Pretty well,' he replied.

On another occasion, after conversing on various subjects, reference was made to the change of ministers that had taken place in the circuit; when Mrs. Fletcher informed him of the good impression the superintendent was making, and was greatly shocked to hear him say in a most emphatic manner, 'He's a bad man!' Mrs. Fletcher exclaimed, 'Oh! my dear, how can you say so?' 'Because,' was the reply, 'he *is* a bad man. But I shall interfere, and bring some things to light for the good of the Society.' Soon after, the superintendent decamped, carrying off Connexional money.

Methodist Recorder, Winter Number, 1895, p. 96

John Poole (c.1730–1801)

Poole was Assistant (i.e. Superintendent) of the Trowbridge Circuit from 1782 to 1784, where Adam Clarke spent the first ten months of his itinerant ministry.

My first superintendent was a man of experience. He said to me one day, 'Adam, take care of your horse.' This advice he needed not to have given, for I was always careful to see my horse cleaned and fed. On another occasion, Mr. Poole observed, 'Could horses speak, Adam, they would say to their riders – "Up the hill, spur me not; down the hill, ride me not; on the plain, spare me not; to an ostler, trust me not."'

A 'horseman' in those days, whether among clergy or laity, was an object of interest to a highwayman, especially if a pair of saddlebags happened to bolster out the top-coat, or peep from beneath its skirts. A somewhat humorous occurrence happened to Mr. Poole, which Mr. Clarke related with unusual pleasantry. The preachers, who were generally early risers, furnished themselves with tinder-boxes: Mr. Poole's was in the form of a pistol. Having to cross Sherwood Forest once, he found this innocent household utensil of considerable service. He saw a man coming towards him, whose appearance produced an unfavourable impression; upon which he took out his tinder-box, concealing the whole, except the lock, which was cocked. The man did not perceive it at first, having his eye fixed on the saddle-bags, which, from their bulk, appeared full of promise to his hopes. He passed a few paces, and then returned. Mr. Poole, seeing this, quickened his speed, which was no sooner observed by the man, than he added to the fleetness and length of his strides, and was speedily alongside of the horse; but suddenly casting his eye upon the tinder-box, which Mr. Poole still preserved in a state of full-cock, and mistaking it for a pistol, whose muzzle was directed towards him, he, with unusual presence of mind, though with a miserable excuse, said, 'Oh, Sir, I only wished to ask you the hour of the day.' 'Begone, sir,' returned Mr. Poole, 'or you shall have the contents of this.' The man instantly departed, congratulating himself, in all probability, on his narrow escape from danger.

James Everett, *Adam Clarke Portrayed*, 2nd edition, 1866, p. 75

Thomas Hanby (1733–1796)

Admitted into the itinerancy at the Leeds Conference in 1755, Hanby found himself appointed to Canterbury.

My little stock of money was nearly exhausted by the time I got to London; and though it was rather too long a journey for a winter's day, I was under necessity a necessity to push forward, not having money enough to keep me and my horse upon the road all night. It was about eight o'clock at night when I got within sight of the lamps of the city. Two men with large pistols then rushed out upon me from a narrow lane, and demanded my money. They took my watch and all the money I had in the world, which was two shillings and eightpence. (Indeed, sometimes, if a halfpenny would have purchased the three kingdoms, I had it not for weeks together.) I believe this robbery was permitted for good. It was at the time we expected an invasion from France, and the city of Canterbury was full of soldiers. They were two soldiers who robbed me, and this excited a curiosity in their comrades to hear the preacher who had been robbed; and it pleased God to convince many of them. About ten were in society before this; and when I came away, they were increased to sixty.

Thomas Hanby, in *Lives of the Early Methodist Preachers*, vol. 2, pp. 144–5

Alexander Mather (1733–1800)

Thomas Marriott was one of the earliest members of the Spitalfields society in London. He lived in Norton Folgate and was a baker by trade.

Being in want of a journeyman to serve in the bakehouse, before going to inquire the character of one of whom he had heard, he first asked guidance from the Lord by prayer. He had scarcely left his house on this errand before his attention was attracted by a decent-looking young man in an apron, dressed as a baker. Going up to him, and finding he wanted a place, he engaged him at once. The man, finding his master leave every evening, inquired of the other servants what public house he frequented, but was soon informed that he went to the preaching at the Foundery. The curiosity of the new servant was awakened at once; he also went to the preaching, got converted through a sermon of Mr. Wesley's at West Street, and became one of the most illustrious preachers in the Methodist Connexion, the friend of Mr. Wesley, and was twice President of the Conference. This was the venerable Alexander Mather.

G.J. Stevenson, *City Road Chapel, London, and its Associations*, 1872, pp. 572–3

Thomas Taylor (1738–1816)

Taylor was one of the early Methodist itinerants, who in 1765 pioneered Methodism in Glasgow in the face of formidable odds.

When I arrived, I entered on a scene which I had never witnessed before. The winter was at hand; I was in a strange land; there was no society, no place of entertainment, no place to preach in, no friend to communicate my mind to. I took a private lodging, and gave out that I should preach on the Green, a place of public resort, hard by the city... I continued to preach night and morning, when opportunity offered; and tried much to procure a place to preach in, as the winter was now come on. I believe I was disappointed in ten or twelve different places. I sold my horse; and a preacher who passed through Glasgow, to Ireland, having his horse lamed, and little money left, I spared about three guineas to help him on his way. This brought my stock into a small compass; and having everything to pay for, I was reduced to a short allowance. I paid three shillings per week for my room, fire and attendance; but I really kept a very poor house. I confess that I never kept so many fast-days, either before or since. But how to keep up my credit was a difficulty; for I was afraid my landlady would think me either poor or covetous. I frequently desired her not to provide anything for dinner; and a little before noon, I dressed myself, and walked out, till after dinner, and then came home to my hungry room, with a hungry belly. However, she thought I had dined out somewhere; so I saved my credit.

Lives of the Early Methodist Preachers, 1873, 5, pp. 27–30

George Escrick (c.1742–1805)

Escrick was one of the first Methodists in Bolton.

He was rough in temper and manners, and was fond of having his own way, but no one had a kinder heart than he. He was a true friend to the poor, and would never allow a preacher or his family to want anything that was needful. He was much esteemed by Wesley, whom George always welcomed under his hospitable roof. Indeed, his house and table were open to all that came during Wesley's stay. In one of Wesley's journeys to the North, George was informed that he had not Bolton on his plan; and hearing that he was at Liverpool, thirty-one miles distant, he set out that evening on foot, saying, 'I will neither eat nor sleep till I see him.' He got to Liverpool next morning in time for the five o'clock preaching, at the close of which he followed Wesley to his lodgings, and said to him, 'So the Devil may take Bolton for you!', repeating the words, and then withdrew. He was an extraordinary walker. He walked many times to Manchester – twelve miles from Bolton – to hear the preaching at five o'clock in the morning, and returned home to breakfast. He was nearly eighty-two years of age when he died, and a little before his death he walked to Chester – near forty miles – one day, and came back another, and only spent fourpence on the road.

Thomas W. Blanshard, *The Life of Samuel Bradburn*, 1870, pp. 50–1

Hannah More (1745–1833)

Despite her evangelical leanings, Hannah More had strong reservations about the Methodists and hesitated to associate with them.

Although unwilling to admit of Methodist help, Miss More writes [in a letter] with some indignation of the treatment they received in another parish. A Mr. Fry had gone to help open a Sunday School at Wedmore. He was attempting to teach the children to sing one of Watts's hymns, when 'Down ran one of the farmers, crying out to Mr. Fry, "Oh, sir, I am afraid this must be Methody! and, if so, I cannot give it my support."' Mr. Fry assured him it was no such thing. Miss More continues: 'He said he was glad of it, for he had a great fear of anything Methody; as once they came and preached under an apple tree of his dear mother's, and after that the tree withered and never bore any more fruit. The parish, in consequence of this, called a vestry, to see what could be done, fearing, if they continued to come, 'all the orchards in the parish will wither and decay.' They therefore agreed that the next time they came they would drive them away by throwing stones and rotten eggs at them, which they did and succeeded! ... This happened in the enlightened eighteenth century! I make no comment.'

A.M. Griffin in *Methodist Recorder*, Winter Number, 1906, pp. 72–3

Thomas Coke (1747–1814)

Joining the Methodists in 1777, Coke soon became Wesley's chief clerical assistant and travelled round the country dealing with administrative problems as well as preaching. Ramsbury in Wiltshire, where the following incident took place, had been visited several times by Wesley himself. The narrator, the Rev. William Edwards, was a native of Ramsbury who had the details from eyewitnesses in his own family.

In the centre of the village is an open square of considerable size, on the sides of which are two or three inns, the post office and some of the principal shops. In the middle of this square, and overshadowing the greater part of it, is a venerable hollow wych elm tree, popularly known in the neighbourhood as 'the witch-tree' – a name which has had the effect of keeping it free from the company of children and superstitious adults after dark. Beneath this tree Dr. Coke took his stand to preach the Gospel of Christ. As soon as he had commenced the service, he and his audience were attacked by a turbulent mob, headed by the vicar of the parish. Stones and sticks were plentifully used. Dr. Coke was violently pushed from his stand, and his gown torn into shreds. Nothing daunted, he continued the service. The vicar then thought of another expedient and gave the order, 'Bring out the fire-engine.' The mandate was obeyed, and both preacher and congregation were compelled to retire before the well-directed volleys of this liquid artillery. But, while leaving the square, the Doctor turned and remarked to the people that there were other uses for fire-engines, of which Providence might soon permit the perpetrators of this outrage to become well aware. His words were drowned by the cry of 'False prophet!' Yet within a fortnight a fire broke out which destroyed nearly all the houses in the square and extended a considerable distance down the street of the village.

J.W. Etheridge, *The Life of the Rev. Thomas Coke DCL*, 1860, p. 62

Coke is mainly remembered as the initiator of Methodism's overseas missions, and for many years he supported them by his own, largely unaided efforts in begging from door to door.

Calling one day on the captain of a man-of-war [at Stonehouse, Plymouth] he introduced the case of the negroes in such an affecting manner, as to prevail upon him to give him a sum much larger than he expected. This he gratefully received and retired. The captain, who knew nothing of Dr. Coke, happened, in the course of the day, to call on a gentleman who had long resided in the place, and to whom Dr. Coke had frequently made successful applications. After conversing together for some time, 'Pray, Sir,' said the captain, 'do you know anything of a little fellow who calls himself Dr. Coke, and who is going about begging money for missionaries to be sent among the slaves?' 'I know him well,' was the reply. 'He seems,' rejoined the captain, 'to be a heavenly-minded little devil. He coaxed me out of two guineas this morning.'

Samuel Drew, *Life of Dr. Thomas Coke*, 1817, p. 388

On Coke's first visit to America in 1784–85, Asbury saw to it that he travelled extensively through the still sparsely populated eastern States to see for himself the conditions in which the circuit riders worked. The location of the following incident was the Accotenk Creek in the neighbourhood of Pohick. Coke recalled the incident when travelling the same route in April 1791.

Wednesday, March 9 [1785]. In my ride this morning to *Alexandria, (Virginia)* through the woods, I have had one of the most romantic scenes that ever I beheld. Yesterday there was a very heavy fall of snow and hail and sleet. The fall of sleet was so great that the trees seemed to be trees of ice. So beautiful a sight of the kind I never saw before.

And now I am going to open a solemn scene indeed! May God deeply impress it on my heart. We had this day a very sudden thaw. I had two runs of water (as they are called) to cross between *Alexandria* and *Colchester*, which swell exceedingly on any thaw or fall of rain; but being earnestly desirous to get into the work, I determined to proceed on my journey. My servant, whom I had permitted to make a visit to his wife on the other side of the *Chesapeake-Bay*, had deceived me by staying with her beyond his time: and the southern preachers knew not where I was, imagining me to be in the *West-Indies*. A friend who lives in *Alexandria* came with me over the first run, and everybody informed me I could easily cross the second, if I crossed the first. When I came to the second (which was perhaps two hours after I had crossed the first) I found that I had two streams to pass. The first I went over without much danger: but in crossing the second, which was very strong and very deep, I did not observe that a tree brought down by the flood lay across the landing place. I endeavoured, but in vain, to drive my horse against the stream and go round the tree. I was afraid to turn my horse's head to the stream, and afraid to go back. In this dilemma I thought it most prudent for me to lay hold on the tree and go over it, the water being shallow on the other side of the tree. But I did not avert to the danger of loosening the tree from its hold. For no sooner did I execute my purpose so far as to lay hold of the tree, (and that instant the horse was carried from under me) but the motion that I gave it loosened it, and down the stream it instantly carried me. Some distance off, there grew a tree in the middle of the stream, the root of which had formed a little bank or island, and divided the stream; and here the tree which I held was stopped. Instantly there came down with the flood a large branch of a tree upon my back, which was so heavy that I was afraid it would break my back. I was now jammed up for a considerable time (a few minutes appeared long at such a season) expecting that my strength would soon be exhausted, and I should drop between the tree and the branch. Here I pleaded aloud with God in good earnest; one promise which I particularly urged, I remember well, *Lo, I will be with you always, even to the end of the world*. I felt no fear at all of the pain of dying, or of death itself, or of hell, and yet I found an unwillingness to die. All my castles which I had built in the air for the benefit of my fellow-creatures passed in regular array before my mind, and I could not consent to give them up. It was an awful time! However, through the blessing of my Almighty preserver (to whom be all the glory) I at last got my knee, which I long endeavoured at in vain, on the tree which I grasped, and then soon disengaged myself and climbed up the little bank. Here I panted for breath for some time: and when I recovered, perceiving the water between the little island and the shore not to be very deep, or very strong, I ventured through it and got to land. I was now obliged to walk about a mile, shivering, before I came to a house. The master and mistress were from home, and were not expected to return that night. But the principal negro lent me an old ragged shirt, coat, waistcoat, breeches, &c. and the negroes made a large fire, and hung my clothes up to dry all night. Before bed time, a man, who came to the run on a small horse, and perceived mine near the brook, concluded the rider was drowned, and wanting to cross the stream on urgent business, mounted my horse, and being well acquainted with the run, came over safe; he then perceived the footsteps of a person on the side of the water, and concluded they were made by the person to whom the horse belonged; and following the track, brought horse and bags safe to me. As he seemed to be a poor man, I gave him half-a-guinea. At night I lay on a bed on the ground, and my strength having been so exhausted, slept soundly all night. Thus was I wonderfully preserved, and I trust I shall never forget so awful, but very instructive a scene.

Journals of Dr. Thomas Coke, ed. John A. Vickers, 2005, pp. 46–8

Coke's second voyage to America in the autumn of 1786 was one of the most hazardous he experienced. The ship sustained repeated damage from violent mid-Atlantic storms, sprung a leak, and was driven with broken rigging before the gales. Coke's graphic account of the voyage is silent on the following incident.

It was during the utmost violence of the tempest, while accomplishing their perilous voyage, that Dr. Coke and his associates addressed themselves to God in prayer for the preservation of the ship, and of the lives of all on board. The captain, instead of approving their piety, or joining in their devotions, became visibly agitated, and betrayed symptoms of an approaching storm within; attributing the calamities, with which they were surrounded, to the means made use of to avert the growing danger. At first he paraded the deck, muttering in a species of audible whisper, 'We have a Jonah on board – we have a Jonah on board;' and consequently it was natural for him to conclude, that a Jonah's conduct deserved a Jonah's fate. In this condition he continued, until his fears, superstition, credulity and agitation, had wound him up to such a state of phrenzy, that he entered the Doctor's cabin, and, in a paroxysm of fury, seizing his books and papers, threw them immediately into the sea. He was about to proceed further; but on seizing 'the Jonah,' he satiated his vengeance, by grasping him with angry violence several times, and by giving loose to his passion in expressions of horrible imprecations. He did not in fact offer him any further outrage; yet on retiring, he swore that if ever the Doctor made another prayer on board his ship, he was fully resolved to throw him into the sea, as he had thrown his papers. But the gust of passion was of no long continuance. The removal of danger soothed the spirit of superstition to rest; and the cessation of the storm without, reduced to a calm the tempest that raged within.

Samuel Drew, *Life of the Rev. Thomas Coke LL.D.*, 1817, pp. 160–1

In his attitude towards the Church of England, despite being an ordained clergyman, Coke vacillated frequently. Adam Clarke's account of the Conference of 1788 shows him in his anti-establishment mood.

At the London Conference, in 1788, Dr. Coke, thinking we were in danger of losing our people, and that our avowed *connexion with the Church* hindered our work, proposed in *Conference* that 'the whole Methodist body should make a formal separation from the Church'. In this Dr. Coke was not only *earnest*, but *vehement...* After the Doctor had said what he wished at the time, Mr. Wesley rose up, and with great *calmness* said: 'Dr. Coke puts me in mind of the German proverb, which I may apply to himself, and to myself: *He skips like a flea; I creep like a louse.* He would tear all from top to bottom – I will not tear but *unstitch.*'

Letter of Adam Clarke to Humphrey Sandwith, in WHS *Proceedings*, vol. 18, pp. 25–6

Augustus William Marblestone was a Swedish waterman who joined the Methodist society in Portsmouth in 1787.

A.W. Marblestone once refused to take his boat out on a Sunday for the captain of a West Indiaman. When the captain despite this returned to him on the Monday, Marblestone asked why.

'Why,' said the captain, 'I will tell you. I once took Dr. Coke and some more of your Methodists to America, and I never saw such a change as he wrought in my crew. I am not a Methodist, but when I meet with one of the right sort, as you seem to be, I always do him all the good I can for Dr. Coke's sake.'

The Swedish Emigrant, 1852, pp. 83–4

Coke showed every sign of being a 'confirmed bachelor' until the last few years of his life, when he twice succumbed to the charms of the opposite sex. But it appears that at least once before he had been in danger of matrimony. Edward Hayes, a leading member of the Methodist society in Winchester, clearly shared the 'universally acknowledged truth' later enunciated by Jane Austen, that 'a single man in possession of a good fortune must be in want of a wife'. Eventually his sights were set on Coke and during a visit to London in 1799 he determined to offer him his daughter's hand.

He and Mrs. Hayes called to see Mr. Wesley at the new chapel and mentioned to him the business which had brought them to London, viz that they had a daughter, a very excellent young woman whom they wished to bestow on some eminent divine, and imagined no person so proper as Dr. Coke. Mr. Wesley replied, 'I believe Dr. Coke does not want a wife!' Mr. Hayes still urged his desire and wished for the favour of an interview with him, that he might see their daughter. Mr. Wesley replied, 'Oh yes, by all means,' and said that the Doctor was to dine such a day at Mr. Edwards of Lambeth who would be glad to see them, and if they thought proper they might dine with the Doctor. To this scheme they readily assented. They were introduced to Mr. Edwards and dined with the desired Gentleman. But oh the sad course of fortune and the dashing of hopes to the ground! The Doctor after staying his usual time departed, after taking leave of all in his accustomed courteous and friendly manner, and thus all the expectations respecting the doctor fell to the ground and at the expiration of six weeks the whole party returned to Winchester.

John Sundius Stamp, manuscript *History of Methodism in Hampshire* at the Methodist Archives Centre, Manchester

Bristol was one of the places where disputes between the 'Old' and 'New Planners' broke out following Wesley's death in 1791. The point at issue was whether the Methodists should continue to see themselves as members of the Church of England or as a separate denomination, with all the implications of this. The Bristol trustees were supporters of the 'Old Plan'.

On one occasion Dr. Coke went to preach at Kingswood, and found Mr. Rodda, who took part with the Trustees, in possession of the pulpit; upon which he took his stand under one of the trees and began service. This was more than some of the zealous colliers could endure. Mr. Rodda having announced the hymn beginning, 'Come on my partners in distress', some of them remarked in an unmistakable tone, 'He's no partner of ours,' and declared that they would not allow 'that dear little man to stand out of doors with his hair blowing about in the wind', and suiting the action to the word they carried the Doctor to the pulpit and displaced Mr. R.

Journal of Mary Blacker of Bristol, quoted in *Methodist Recorder*, Winter Number, 1901, p. 68

During one of Dr. Coke's visits to his native town [of Brecon] he was the guest of Squire Meredith at the Watton... His appearance one Sunday morning in gown and cassock aroused the suspicion of Lion, a very powerful and formidable house-dog. Lion's ominous growl frightened the Doctor, who precipitately sought shelter in a shed. Miss Matthews, an estimable Methodist lady ... who lived across the road, hearing a piteous voice calling, 'Miss, Miss; help, help,' crossed the road and through the trellis work saw the incarcerated divine and his gaoler Lion. He ernestly besought her protection. Assistance was immediately forthcoming, and the Doctor, with cassock literally saturated with perspiration, hurried off to church. What a scene! – the indomitable, dauntless missionary who had faced countless perils meekly invoking the protection of a maiden lady!

T. Wynne-Jones in *Methodist Recorder*, Winter Number, 1896, p. 86

Joseph Benson (1748–1821)

The following account is revealing not only of aspects of Benson's own piety but of the distinctive ethos of early Methodism. Benson was stationed at this time in the Manchester Circuit.

Jan.11 [1779]. This evening I preached on occasion of the death of Abraham Brierly, a very exemplary Christian, who, for many years adorned the Gospel. From a child he feared God and was preserved by his grace from all open sin. As he grew up, he regularly attended Church and sacrament; was honest in his dealings, and unblameable in his whole behaviour. But, notwithstanding the regularity of his conduct, he was far from being satisfied with his state; and hence he went to several Clergymen to request their directions. Still he did not find rest to his soul, but on the contrary grew more and more uneasy, till at last, having little or no hope of salvation, he was strongly tempted to lay violent hands upon himself. In this state he went to Mr. Lee, a Clergyman, who gave him some encouragement, by saying, 'I know not what advice to give you, because I never was in your state, but, I assure you, I wish I was in it, as I am satisfied that they who sow in tears shall reap in joy.' Some years after this, he had a faint hope that God would be gracious to him, but no evidence of his pardoning mercy, nor heart-felt peace and joy in believing. At length, when he was upward of forty years of age, as he went along a street one evening, he heard some people singing a hymn or psalm in a house. While he stood and listened, he thought, 'Surely these people know more of religion than I.' He afterwards, upon inquiry, learned that they were Methodists, then generally reckoned the worst description of schismatics; but this did not deter him from hearing one of their preachers, on the following Monday evening. In the course of less than a week, he heard one of them preach again. On his way to hear the second time, he was stopped short in the street by a sudden suggestion that God would be offended if he went. In this dilemma, he lifted up his heart to God, and prayed that if they were not his people, and if it was wrong to go among them, that he would prevent his going.; but if otherwise, that he would remove those fears and incline him to go forward, by giving him to feel love to them. This prayer was immediately answered; for he felt his fears dispelled, and his mind disposed to proceed; and whilst among them upon that occasion he felt that he loved them most cordially. His master, who employed him to dye fustian, learned that he went to hear the Methodists, and being much displeased with him on that account, threatened to turn him out of his employment if he went to hear them any more. He assured his master that he had received much benefit by going only twice to hear them; and as he knew they preached the truth, he was determined to hear them at all events. His master fulfilled his threatening. But the Lord made him ample amends for this outward loss by inward consolation; for within two days after he was filled with joy and peace in believing. From that happy period of his life to his latest hour, he walked in all the commandments of the Lord blameless. For the support of himself and family he submitted to drive a cart with coal; in which humble situation he continued till his last sickness confined him to his house, where, after suffering for some time, he died in the Lord.

James Macdonald, *Memoirs of the Rev. Joseph Benson*, 1822, pp. 84–6

In the summer of 1795 Benson was on a preaching tour in Cornwall and found support for a literal interpretation of the text of Genesis at a time when the nature of myth was not understood.

After dining at Camelford, Mr. Benson, accompanied by Mr. Maybin, set out for Liskeard, taking a guide with him, as he purposed going over the moors. They soon entered upon them, and for about twelve miles saw little or no cultivated ground. 'We passed,' he remarks, 'between several high mountains formed of mere rocks piled one above another, which mountains seemed evidently to have been formed by the Flood, and to have remained from that time. For while the water washed down the soft earth, on all sides, it could not wash down these rocks, but left them lying one above another in that tremendous and awkward state in which they appear. I was glad to find that there are, and have been, many other proofs of the Flood in this country. Mr. Mitchel, of Gwennap, told me he had discovered, in digging below the sea (which is often done in Cornwall) a human skull, fifteen feet beneath low water; and that different kinds of ore are generally found under the sea, and in the low valleys, washed down from the higher grounds where these sundry kinds are found in the mines; which could only have been done at the time of the general deluge.'

James Macdonald, *Memoirs of the Rev. Joseph Benson*, 1822, pp. 285–6

Joseph Bradford (1748–1818)

President of the 1795 Conference, Bradford had been Wesley's travelling companion for some years.

[Joseph Benson] related some facts illustrative of the trials through which Mr. Bradford had passed; observing that, though poor, he possessed a noble and independent spirit. When travelling with Mr. Wesley, he was once taken ill at Bristol, so that Mr. Wesley was compelled to leave him; but committed him to the care of the Society-steward, who, instead of providing for him a nurse and medical attendance, sent him to one of the city hospitals, as an object of public charity... He also stated that when Mr. Bradford was in the Colne Circuit, his wife died; and as he had not the means of meeting the expenses of her funeral, and no one offered to aid him, he was under the painful necessity of collecting the wearing apparel of his late wife, and of taking it to Manchester in the night, that by the sale of it there he might obtain the means of her decent interment. Such, I learned, were the hardships endured by the old Methodist Preachers, into whose labours I now entered: 'Godlike men, how firm they stood!'

Thomas Jackson, *Recollections of my own Life and Times*, 1873, p. 111

Samuel Bardsley (c.1750–1818)

The following incident, which sadly can be paralleled elsewhere in Methodism's history, is recorded by Thomas Jackson.

[Bardsley] left a vast accumulation of manuscripts and other documents relating to Methodism, and illustrative of its history, which came into my hands after his decease. As they were of public interest and did not properly belong to me, I felt that I ought not to retain them in my possession, greatly as I wished that they were my own; and therefore [I] sent a report concerning them to the Conference Book-Committee in London, asking their advice as to the right disposal of them. They requested me to forward them to London without delay, and with that request I promptly complied. On inquiring afterwards where they had been deposited, I had the mortification to learn that they had been placed in the hands of one of the London preachers, that he might examine and report upon them; that when he removed from the Circuit he left them in the house he had occupied; that the servant-maid of his successor – regarding them as waste paper which the owner did not think it worth his while to take away with him – had used them in kindling fires; so that not a scrap remained of the entire load which I had been so anxious to preserve for the use of some future historian of Methodism! They consisted of private letters relating mostly to the state of religion in different Circuits, and of printed circulars on Connexional affairs, embracing a period of about half a century; for Mr. Bardsley appears scarcely ever to have destroyed any papers that came into his possession.

Thomas Jackson, *Recollections of my own Life and Times*, 1873, p. 169

Samuel Bradburn (1751–1816)

Widely recognised as the most eloquent of the early Methodist preachers, Bradburn had 'an attractive personality and a pleasant voice, a ready wit and a retentive memory'. Popularly known as 'the Demosthenes of Methodism', his biographer T.W. Blanshard suggests that 'he might with greater propriety be compared to Cicero'.

He was a favourite with Wesley, though he had little money sense. Seldom was he above the poverty line, and he was frequently in want. On one occasion Wesley sent him what must have been a very welcome letter: 'Dear Sammy, trust in the Lord and do good, so shalt thou dwell in the land, and verily thou shalt be fed.' With the letter Wesley enclosed five new one pound notes. Bradburn's reply we may be sure not only amused but was relished by Wesley: 'Rev. and dear Sir, I have often been struck with the beauty of the passage of Scripture quoted in your letter, but I must confess, that I never saw such useful expository notes on it before. Your obedient and grateful servant, S. Bradburn.'

R.H. Gallagher, *John Bredin*, 1960, p. 49

The following may be an embroidering of an incident told with much less detail by his biographer. (See Thomas W. Blanshard, The Life of Samuel Bradburn (1870) pp.290–1.)

When the Rev. Samuel Bradburn entered on his ministerial career he was neither so clerical in his attire nor so polished in his manners as he afterwards became. On paying his first visit to a country place on the Saturday evening prior to his work on the Sabbath, he was met at the door of the house – a farmhouse of a well-to-do family – by the wife, who was looking out with eager expectation for the coming of the new preacher. On seeing Mr. Bradburn her countenance fell. So great was her disappointment that, instead of introducing him to her husband in a comfortable room, she sent him into the kitchen, telling him that he might sit with Jack. Venting her indignation on the Conference for sending such a raw country lad, she comforted herself by adding,

'He shan't sleep in the best bed, he shall sleep with Jack.'

In the morning she informed the preacher that Jack would show him the way to the chapel. The face of the old lady as she sat in her front pew in the gallery indicated that the cloud of displeasure had not lifted. Mr. Bradburn had not gone far in his sermon ere the rugged features of the listener relaxed, her pursed up lips became unstrung, her eyes sparkled with surprised delight. Turning to her spouse, she whispered in his ear,

'He shan't sleep with Jack. He shall have the best bed.'

As the preacher warmed to his theme, preached on in sublime strains of overwhelming eloquence, the old lady's face shone with unconcealed delight. Nudging her husband, she said almost aloud,

'Thah must buy him a new suit.'

At the close of the service she was quickly at the foot of the pulpit stairs to greet him, saying,

'Now, Mr. Bradburn, you'll come with us.'

But the preacher quietly said, 'No, thank you, I'll walk with Jack.'

Again, on reaching the house he was invited to walk into the best parlour, and when retiring for the night urged to sleep in the best bed, but both were declined. He dined with Jack and slept with Jack.

Methodist Recorder, Winter Number, 1893, p. 98

Bradburn's first wife, Eliza Nangle, was the daughter of a Dublin jeweller. But their courtship was protracted and far from trouble-free.

There is a tradition about him and a brother minister who occupied the same bed one night; and Bradburn's mind being so harassed with the perplexities of courtship, he could not sleep; and, getting up, he knelt by the bedside, and after praying for divine direction in the choice of a wife, he added with touching fervency, 'But, Lord, let it be Betsy!' His bed-fellow, whom he thought fast asleep, humorously responded 'Amen', and then broke out into a hearty laugh at poor Bradburn's expense.

Both her step-father and her step-mother opposed the marriage, but an appeal to Wesley led to a resolution of the impasse, as Bradburn himself describes.

I wrote to Mr. Wesley, entreating him to help me. He immediately sent letters to Mrs. Karr and Betsy. Mrs. Karr returned a complaisant answer, assuring Mr. Wesley that were Miss Nangle her own daughter, she would be guided by him, imagining he would return the compliment and not interfere. Instead of which, he considered the letter as a full consent and informed both Betsy and me that he had settled everything. This satisfied my beloved's mind and I gained her consent. Before Mr. Wesley's arrival I prepared everything, giving Mrs. Karr to understand our design; but she gave me equivocal answers. Contrary, however, to her expectations, Mr. Wesley invited her to breakfast with him at Mrs. King's [with whom Betsy Nangle was then living] the morning after his arrival, being his birthday; as soon as she entered he began the ceremony and married us in the parlour. Pride would not let her affront Mr. Wesley and she was forced to appear satisfied. Thus were the wise taken in their own craftiness.

Thomas W. Blanshard, *The Life of Samuel Bradburn*, 1870, pp. 65,71

Repartee was not one of the least of those things in which he excelled, and which, when preserved within due bounds, is a convenient weapon for self-defence. Something personal and untoward having taken place between himself and Thomas Olivers, it was, of course, brought up at Conference. 'Brother Bradburn,' said Mr. Wesley, 'you do not love Tommy Olivers.' 'Sir,' returned Bradburn, 'I love him as much as you do John Hampson.' It was as sudden on both sides as an exchange of shots in a duel; each felt the ball of his antagonist as it slightly grazed the chest. Mr. Wesley was a little suspicious that there was not the most cordial feeling on Bradburn's part; and Bradburn availed himself of the fact of Mr. Wesley's leaving John Hampson's name out of the Deed of Declaration, which was interpreted into a matter of prejudice and gave offence to Mr. Hampson and his friends.

Thomas W. Blanshard, *The Life of Samuel Bradburn*, 1870, p. 232

Like less able preachers, Bradburn had not on all occasions 'a good time', and it is reported that he once complained to [Joseph] Benson, after having preached what he considered a poor sermon: 'I felt confident as I ascended the pulpit stairs that I should have a successful time; but

I came down miserably disappointed.' Benson shrewdly replied: 'If you had gone up as you *came down*, you would have come down as you *went up*.' A piece of advice worth remembering, though capable of abuse.

Thomas W. Blanshard, *The Life of Samuel Bradburn*, 1870, p. 220

The following comes from 'an anonymous ministerial friend'.

A person in a state of intoxication came reeling to the door of a place in which he was giving tickets to the members of a class, insisting on admission, and with just as much sense as to enable him to say that they had no legal authority for holding private meetings. Some of the friends were for employing physical force and preventing obtrusion. 'Let the man alone,' said Bradburn coolly, and apparently unconcerned; adding, while looking at the man himself, 'Step in and sit down,' pointing to a seat and taking for the time no further notice of him, but proceeding with his work, and addressing himself separately to the respective members, saying, while looking at one of them, 'Well, my brother, you have experienced the truth of religion upon the heart.' To this the person responded, 'Yes, I bless the Lord that He ever brought me to an acquaintance with Himself.' Turning from the respondent, and waving the hand, after a partial glance at the poor sot swinging on his seat and apparently pleased with his introduction, Bradburn replied, as he again bent his eye upon the member, 'Ay, that is well; it is more than this man has experienced.' Directing his face towards another, the obtruder being a little touched and stupidly awake to the reply, Mr. Bradburn proceeded, 'Well, my sister, you have the life of God, I hope, in your soul?' 'Yes, sir,' she replied, 'I am thankful the Lord has converted me and raised me to a newness of life.' 'Praise the Lord,' returned Bradburn, again partially inclining his head to the butt of his intended remarks; 'it is more than this poor drunkard can say, for he is dead in trespasses and sins.' Addressing a third, 'Well, my brother, you have a good hope, I trust, through grace?' 'I bless the Lord I have,' was returned. Bradburn, shaking his head and with a sigh – while the bacchanalian, with something like returning consciousness of his situation and a feeling approaching to shame, manifested a degree of uneasiness – proceeded to remark, 'Ay, that is much more than this vile wretch can say; for he can expect nothing but hell.' At this the man bounced from his seat, staggered to the door and suddenly disappeared.

Thomas W. Blanshard, *The Life of Samuel Bradburn*, 1870, pp. 229–31

The following story came from a member of Bradburn's family.

A clergyman, who was a magistrate, residing in a small town in one of Bradburn's circuits, had violently opposed the introduction of Methodism into his parish. Various attempts had been made by the Methodist preachers to preach there, but without effect; the ministers having, as was common in the early days of Methodism, been driven off by the mob, headed by the clergyman. Bradburn undertook to defeat the opposition in the following novel manner. He sent to a few poor Methodists in the neighbourhood, requesting that they would make it known that a stranger would preach in the centre of the town, on a certain Sabbath day at three o'clock. They did so; and the clergyman being informed of it as usual, ordered constables and others to be in readiness at the place to arrest the preacher or drive him off. Bradburn provided himself with a new suit of clothes, borrowed a new wig of a Methodist barber, and on the day appointed he went to the place, put his horse up at the inn, attended the morning service at church, placed himself in a conspicuous situation, so as to attract the notice of the clergyman, and when the service was closed, he went up to him on his way out, accosted him as a brother and thanked him for his sermon. The clergyman, judging from his appearance and address that he was a minister of some note, gave him an invitation to his house. Bradburn respectfully declined, on the ground that he had ordered dinner, and expressed a hope that the clergyman would dine with him at his inn. He did so, and Bradburn having entertained him until dinner was over with his extraordinary powers of conversation, managed to refer to the open-air service which was to be held, and the clergyman stated his intention to arrest the preacher and disperse the congregation, and asked Bradburn to accompany him, which he did. On arriving at the appointed place, they found a large company assembled; and as no preacher had made his appearance, the clergyman concluded that fear had kept him away, and was about to order the people to their homes, when Bradburn remarked that it would be highly improper to neglect so favourable an opportunity of doing good, and urged him to preach to them. He excused himself by saying that he had no sermon in his pocket, and asked Bradburn to address them, which, of course, he readily consented to do, and commenced the service by singing part of the hymn beginning

O for a thousand tongues to sing
My great Redeemer's praise

and after praying delivered an impressive discourse from Acts 5:38,39: 'And now I say unto you, Refrain from these men, and let them alone: for if this counsel or this work be of men, it will come to naught; but if it be of God, ye cannot overthrow it; lest haply ye be found even to fight against God.' This not only deeply affected the people, but so delighted the clergyman that, although he knew as the service proceeded that he had been duped, he heartily thanked Bradburn for the deception he had practised on him, and ever afterwards, to the day of his death, showed a friendly disposition towards Methodism.

In 1806 Bradburn was appointed to the Wakefield Circuit.

When he preached crowds of people flocked to the sanctuary and were charmed with his wonderful oratory. The vicar of Wakefield – not Goldsmith's vicar, of course – meeting him in the street one day, said, 'Why dost thou put thy sickle into my standing corn?' With a pleasant smile, Bradburn responded, 'The harvest truly is plenteous, but the labourers are few.'

Thomas W. Blanshard, *The Life of Samuel Bradburn*, 1870, pp. 233–4, 264–5

At one time there was a good deal of bitterness [between members of the different branches of Methodism], and for some decades there was great aloofness. This was characteristic of nearly all the offshoots from the mother Church; most of them seemed to be against her, great virulence being displayed on the part of some. But the mother had not always set a good example to her daughters. Shortly after the Rev. Richard Watson, a great theologian and a mighty preacher, left the New Connexion and became a Wesleyan Methodist minister, he had to preach on a special occasion at Irwell Street Chapel, Salford. On the Sunday preceding, this was announced by Samuel Bradburn, an Ex-President, and one of the greatest pulpit orators of his day. Having announced the fact, he paused, and said sarcastically and slowly, 'They say this dog barks well – but – he comes from a dirty kennel!' Such a thing has long been impossible. It was as vulgar as it was brutal.

Charles H Kelly, *Memories*, 1910, p. 190

Sammy Bradburn's power of repartee is well known. One day a lawyer who resided in Sammy's circuit was out riding with a legal friend from London, when in front of them was to be seen Bradburn quietly jogging along to his appointment on the 'circuit horse'.

'Ah!' said the local man, 'yonder is the Methodist preacher. They say he is a bit of a wag. Let's have some fun out of him.'

Riding on, they soon overtook Bradburn and rode one on either side. After introductions were over, the lawyer said, 'Mr. Bradburn, how do you find time to make your sermons when you travel about so much?'

'Oh! I make them on my pony's back very often, and when I am walking about; in any way I can.'

'But you must often make mistakes if you prepare them in that way?'

By this time Bradburn clearly saw they were trying to 'pull his leg', so he answered with a dry significance, 'Yes, I do make mistakes. The other day I wanted to quote that passage about liars having their part in the lake that burneth with brimstone and fire, and I said, "All *lawyers* have their part," &c.'

'Of course you corrected a mistake like that?'

'No,' said Bradburn, 'I thought it was so near the mark that I might let it go.'

'I see you are more of a knave than a fool,' said the London man.

'Well,' replied Sammy, giving a shrewd look on either side of him, 'it may be that *I'm between the two.*'

Methodist Recorder, Winter Number, 1906, pp. 101–2

Henry Moore (1751–1844)

Because of the numbers that flocked to the Methodist Communion services, especially in London and Bristol, some control over admission became necessary. Members of Society presented their class ticket, while others might be given a note of admission.

Mr. Moore was in 1789 the Superintendent of the City Road Circuit. One gentleman, who usually had received the Lord's Supper at the New Chapel, had been with his family to the theatre. Mr. Moore objected to his coming to the sacrament for that reason; and not being a member of the Society, he had to obtain from Mr. Wesley a note of admission. The gentleman had called upon the Rev. John Richardson[12], and got from him a promise to apply to Mr. Wesley, when he returned to London, for the note desired. Mr. Wesley had preached, he went into the vestry, and Mr. Moore, having shortly followed him, saw Mr. Wesley writing the note, and about to hand it to Mr. Richardson, when Mr. Moore, addressing Mr. Wesley, said, 'Sir, do you mean to give a

---

[12] An ordained clergyman who had joined the Methodists and was employed by Wesley as a curate at City Road Chapel. Relations there between clergy and itinerants were never easy.

note of admission to the holy sacrament to Mr. ---?' Mr. Wesley replied, 'Yes, Henry; I have reason to believe that the report of his conduct is a mistake.' 'I have fully examined into it, sir,' rejoined Mr. Moore, ' and I find it is no mistake; and if you give him a note, I shall not take the sacrament myself.' Looking earnestly at Mr. Moore, Mr. Wesley said, 'I would take the sacrament if the devil himself were there.' 'And so would I, sir,' rejoined Mr. Moore, but not if you gave him a note of admission.' Mr. Wesley immediately put the note into the fire and returned into the chapel.

G.J. Stevenson, *City Road Chapel, London, and its Associations*, 1872, p. 376

George Holder (c.1751–1836)

Thomas Jackson recalled the introduction of Methodism into his native village of Sancton, Yorkshire in 1786–87.

Two aged men, whom I well remember, one of whom, Robert Hudson, was a retired shepherd, and the other, Thomas Wallis, a superannuated schoolmaster... resolved to invite some Methodist Preacher to visit them regularly and proclaim the Gospel in Thomas Wallis's cottage. There were, however, difficulties in the way. Thomas lived alone. He had no wife, and no housekeeper; he had only one bed, which stood upon the mud floor of his humble dwelling. Robert Hudson's accommodation for the entertainment of the stranger was deemed not equal even to this. Yet they ventured to carry their scheme into practical effect.

The Preacher whom they invited was the Rev. George Holder. When they had expressed to him their wishes, they told him that they could give him some refreshment in the evening of his arrival; that he should have Thomas Wallis's cottage to preach in; half of Thomas's bed for the night, provender and shelter for his horse, and a breakfast for himself the next morning; adding, with an expression of regret, that they could not give him a dinner. He received their offer with all readiness, in the true spirit of his Lord, telling them that he would visit them once a month, on the Friday, which he observed as a weekly fast...

The place of preaching was not inviting. Thomas Wallis's cottage was low, like nearly every other in the village; it was covered with thatch; it had but one storey; the floor was much lower than the street; and the entrance to it was by a descent of two or three steps. Mr. Holder fulfilled his engagement, and opened his commission in this humble sanctuary. His word was made a blessing to the people who attended to hear, among whom was my mother.

Thomas Jackson, *Recollections of my own Life and Times*, 1873, pp. 23–4

Robert Carr Brackenbury (1752–1818)

Mr. Brackenbury was a man of family and fortune; he was educated at the University of Cambridge, and in early life was brought to a saving knowledge of God. He formed an intimate friendship with Mr. Wesley and became a fellow-labourer in connexion with him... In the pulpit his address was calm, but impressive; his sermons were polished, instructive and edifying... He was somewhat nervous in his temperament, and occasionally, when he was engaged to preach, thought himself unable to perform the duty; and then the footman was required to take the pulpit, and the disappointed congregation heard the man instead of the master, who was mourning in secret over his infirmities. One Sunday evening, at Raithby [Brackenbury's Lincolnshire estate], I remember, he was sorely troubled on account of the imperfect manner in which he had that day ministered the Word of life, and said he thought that he would never attempt to preach again. Mrs. Brackenbury, a shrewd and sensible person, who knew that in these seasons of depression words of condolence and sympathy only increased his grief, replied that indeed he was not qualified to preach, and would do well never again to enter a pulpit, but leave the people to find the way of salvation as best they might, or perish in their sins. This roused him from his despondency; and after observing that she resembled 'Job's comforters', he dropped the subject.

Thomas Jackson, *Recollections of my own Life and Times*, 1873, pp. 74–5

William Myles (1756–1828)

Myles was an Irish preacher who wrote one of the earliest histories of Methodism.

Though lacking the advantage of an early and systematic education, he had given both to his mind and his manners the best culture of which they were otherwise capable... The respect universally felt for him did not prevent his friends from practising on his good nature. A brother asked him one day, 'Who was the father of Zebedee's children?' Myles pondered well the question, and replied, 'I believe it is not revealed.'

Thomas P. Bunting, *The Life of Jabez Bunting*, 1887, p. 142

John Barritt (c.1757–1841)

Mr. and Mrs. Brackenbury had an unconquerable aversion to the fumes of tobacco, and would on no account tolerate smoking in their mansion. Mr. John Barritt, who was entertained as a Preacher at Raithby Hall, and knew the law of the house, did not like to forego the use of the pipe. He was found by one of the servants to have secreted this article and his tobacco in his bedroom, which was in the third storey. To punish the transgressor, the servant filled the pipe with tobacco, mixing with it a few grains of gunpowder; a dangerous experiment, though meant only as a joke. In the evening, after supper and family prayer, Mr. Barritt retired to his room for the night, thinking that he should enjoy his pipe without discovery. He therefore placed his chair before the fire, put his feet upon the two sides of the grate, leaned back, and began to draw and emit his narcotic fume with his accustomed zest, when an explosion took place; which was so sudden and unexpected that he lost his balance and fell backwards upon the floor. The noise alarmed the family; the Squire rushed into the Preacher's room to know what was the matter; when the truth was disclosed and the offender was compelled to confess his fault and ask forgiveness. He had, however, paid the penalty of his offence, and Mr. Brackenbury was not vindictive.

Thomas Jackson, *Recollections of my own Life and Times*, 1873, pp. 75–6

Michael Fenwick (died 1797)

Described by Charles Atmore as 'a very eccentric character' - 'he had a weak head, but his most intimate friends generally supposed him to possess a good heart. He travelled some time with Mr. Wesley, but his eccentricities were so great that he was dismissed from that post.' Fenwick's complaint that Wesley had never named him in his Journal is said to have led to the following entry.

Monday, 25 July 1757. I left Epworth with great satisfaction, and about one preached at Clayworth. I think none was unmoved but Michael Fenwick, who fell fast asleep under an adjoining hayrick.

Fenwick's death, in Bridlington, was as unusual as his life.

It pleased God to take him hence in a violent storm of thunder and lightning, in the year 1797. But he was observed for some time before to have drank very deep into the spirit of holiness. His conversation was in heaven, and he frequently expressed his earnest desire to depart and be with Christ. The day before, or the day on which he died, he spoke of <u>sudden death</u> as very desirable, and also observed, 'if the Lord called <u>him suddenly</u> he was ready to go!' So that there was good reason to believe that to him, sudden death was sudden glory! It is perhaps not unworthy of remark, that a pious woman in that neighbourhood dreamed the night before Mr. Fenwick was killed by the lightning that she was standing at her own door, and looking up she saw the heavens open and two angels descending to the very place ... and in a short time she saw them ascend towards heaven again with a glorified spirit accompanying them; and as they ascended, she distinctly heard their voices singing <u>hallelujah</u>, and she exclaimed, 'it is the voice of Mr. Fenwick which I hear!' This dream she related to several persons previous to the awful circumstance occurring; so that this puts it beyond the possibility of being fictitious.

Charles Atmore, *The Methodist Memorial*, 1801, pp. 124–5

William Bramwell (1759–1818)

Bramwell was a particularly effective evangelist, known for his reliance on prayer.

He prayed about everything, and with the most manifest results. A friend called to see him on the way to Leeds and poured into his ear his woes and distresses about business. He had sold no cloth for six weeks and was at his wits' end. 'Let us pray,' said Bramwell. He prayed with earnestness, he kept at it till they both had an assurance of being heard, and then his friend went on his way rejoicing; he says, 'I had not been more than a quarter of an hour in the cloth-hall before a merchant, with whom I had never before traded, came to me and purchased all the goods which I had on hand.'

Sometimes Bramwell started to pray for dying people, and seemed literally to pray death off the scene altogether. He prayed about tenancies, about journeys, about family troubles. And he seems to have had a sort of second sight. One of the members at Liverpool was starting for Jamaica. The day before she was leaving Bramwell called to say farewell. He talked about the voyage, and then knelt down to pray. After a while he suddenly stopped, and then said, 'My dear sister, you must not go: God has just told me you must not go.' He bustled about to get her luggage off the boat and was no doubt thought to be very meddlesome and troublesome. The girl did not go, but the ship was lost with all hands. Once he went to pray with a dying man. For some time he was silent. Then he broke out: 'All is not right here! There is something amiss.' Then he turned to the woman who had fetched him and said, 'This man is not your husband. You were never married to him.' He had hit the target. On another occasion he met a woman who was making herself very active among the Methodists. After a time, Bramwell startled everybody by saying, 'Woman, you are a hypocrite,' and he proceeded to details. There was a scene, but Bramwell was right. Another day it was a man who tried to deceive this terrible seer. But soon the bolt fell on him too. 'Man, is there not a bastard child in this case?' And there was.

C.W. Andrews, *William Bramwell*, 1909, pp. 94–5

Sarah Wesley (1759–1828)

Charles Wesley's daughter had literary talent and a lively wit, but was not keen on socialising. As a child she had been physically attractive, but smallpox had left her features badly scarred.

Miss Wesley was as interesting a companion in the social circle, when she could be prevailed upon to appear there, as she was by the contributions of her pen. She shrunk from appearing in company, partly from a natural aversion, and partly from the terribly severe marking which the smallpox left upon her face in childhood. Before that affliction she was handsome: afterwards, quite the opposite. Yet her manners and conversation bore testimony to her ladylike habits and cultivated mind.

Once at an evening party where some were present, not her personal acquaintance, she overheard an unfortunate remark heedlessly made, by one who was crooked in form, of the masculine gender: 'That she would have been a bewitching creature if she had not been so horribly ugly.' Retiring for only a few moments, Miss Wesley presented a slip of paper to the gentleman, on which she had written these impromptu lines:

Malice and envy in one point agree,
That the outside is the worst part of thee:
Small is the censure as it stands confest,
Bad as it is – thy outside is the best.

G.J. Stevenson, *Memorials of the Wesley Family*, 1876, p. 485

Charles Atmore (1759–1826)

When Charles Atmore came to the Halifax Circuit [in 1793] I walked from Greetland to hear his first sermon, and when I seed him walk up t'pulpit stears I thou't I'd neer seen such a praed Methody pracher i' all me life, and I sed to mesel, 'I'll trie thah, lad, when thah cooms to aar plaes.' His appointment came on soon after, and it so leet that he had to stay wi' us. So I sed to my wife when I was starting for chapel, 'We'll ha porritch for dinner.'

She gave me an inquiring look, and sed, 'Nout else?'

'Nay, nout else,' I sed.

After the preachin' I took Mr. Atmore woam, and we found the dinner just ready. A pleat o' porritch, a spooin, and a porringer o' milk i't middle o't teable. I sed, 'Naah, Mr. Atmore, yoe ax a blessin,' and we all fell to, each takin' a dab o' porritch, and then a dip o' milk. But I needn't tell yoa folk how we eat Yorkshire porritch; yo all know that weel enough.

Mr. Atmore watched us, took up his spooin and cleared his pleat. I watched him closely, but there warent a louik or a word that he waer in the least annoyed or dissatisfied. But ah, friends, waren't I ashamed of mesel'! I should think I wor. I never set porritch before Mr. Atmore again. We always gave him the best we could get. It wor a life-long lesson to me never to judge a man by looking only on the outside.

Yorkshire local preacher, quoted in Methodist Recorder, Winter Number, 1893, pp. 96–8

Adam Clarke (c.1760–1832)

The young Adam Clarke, encouraged by John Wesley, set out from Londonderry in 1782 to meet him at Kingswood. Travelling via Liverpool and Birmingham, he reached Bristol, with his resources reduced to three halfpence, only to find anything but a warm reception by the Simpsons who were at that time in charge of the school. This was a disheartening start to what became an outstanding ministry in the early decades of the nineteenth century.

Quitting the inn at an early hour, he walked out to Kingswood, which he reached about seven o'clock, when preaching in the chapel was about to commence. He entered with the crowd and heard the preacher discourse from 'Woman, why weepest thou? Whom seekest thou?' Making a personal application of the text to his own case, he says, it proved a word in season, for he now began to be very heavy and jaded in mind, having a presage of some approaching distress. When service was over, young Clarke was introduced to Mr. Simpson, the head master, to whom he delivered Mr. Wesley's letter. Mr. S. appeared surprised, declared 'he had heard nothing of it, and that they had no room in the school for anyone; that Mr. Wesley was now in Cornwall, but was expected in a fortnight,' and added, 'you must go back to Bristol, and lodge there till he comes.' This was appalling tidings! Adam had travelled several hundred miles by sea and land in quest of a chimerical *Utopia* and *Garden of Paradise*; and now all his hopes and expectations were blasted. With a heart full of distress, Adam ventured to say, 'Sir, I cannot go back to Bristol; I have expended all my money and have nothing to subsist on.' Mr. Simpson said, 'Why should *you* come to Kingswood? It is only for preachers' children, or for such preachers as cannot read their Bible; and it appears from this information, that you have already been at a classical school, where you have read both Latin and Greek authors.' Adam rejoined, 'I am come to improve myself in various ways by the advantages which I understand Kingswood could afford.' Mr. S. replied that it was not necessary; and that 'if I were already a preacher, I had better go out into the work at large, for that there was no room for me in the school, and not one spare bed in the house.' Poor Clarke said to himself,

> *Hei mihi! quanta de spe decidi!*
> 'Alas for me! – from what elevated hopes have I fallen!'

The rest must be given in his own words:

'At last it was agreed that there was a spare room at the end of the chapel where I might lodge till Mr. Wesley should come home from Cornwall; but that I must stay in that room and not come into the house. I was accordingly shown to the place, and was told one of the maids should bring me my daily food at the stated times. As soon as I was left alone, I kneeled down and poured out my soul to God with strong crying and tears. I was a stranger in a strange land, and alas! *among strange people*, utterly friendless and pennyless. I felt also that I was not at *liberty*, except to *run away*; this I believe would have been grateful[13] to the unfeeling people into whose hands I had fallen. But I soon found why I was thus cooped up in my prison house... Mr. Simpson that day took an opportunity to tell me that his wife suspected I might have the itch, as many persons coming from my country had;[14] and that they could not let me mingle with the family. I immediately tore open my waistcoat and shirt and showed him a skin as white and clean as ever came across the Tweed; but all to no purpose. 'It might be cleaving some where to me, and they could not be satisfied till I had rubbed myself, from head to foot, with a box of Jackson's itch ointment which should be procured for me next day.'

'It was only my strong hold of God that kept me from distraction. But to whom could I make my complaint? Earthly refuge I had none. It is utterly impossible for me to describe the feelings, I may justly say the *agony* of my mind. I surveyed my apartment; there was a wretched old bureau wainscot bedstead, not worth ten shillings, and a flock-bed with suitable bedclothes, worth not much more; but the worst was, they were very scanty, and the weather was cold and wet. There was one rush-bottomed chair in the place; and besides these neither carpet on the floor, or at the bedside, nor any other kind of furniture. There was no book, not even a Bible in the place; and my own box, with my clothes and a few books, was left in Bristol; and I had not even a change of linen. Of this I informed them, and begged them to let the man (as I found he went with a horse and small cart three times a week) bring out my box to me. To this request, often and earnestly repeated, I got no definite answer; but no box was brought.'

The odiferous unguent was brought, certainly, and poor Clarke was compelled to anoint himself before a large fire, the first and last which he saw while he remained there, and which they had ordered to be lighted for the purpose... 'The woman that brought my *bread and milk*, for breakfast, for dinner, and for supper, for generally I had nothing else, and not enough of that, I asked to let me have a pair of clean sheets; but in vain: no clean sheets of any kind were afforded me. I was left to make my own bed, sweep my own room, and empty my own basin &c. &c. as I pleased. For more than three weeks no soul performed any kind act for me. And as they did not give orders to the man to bring out my box, I was left without a change of any kind till the Thursday of the second week, when I asked permission to go out of my prison-house to Bristol for my box: which being granted, I proceeded thither and carried my box *on my head*, a distance of four miles, without assistance of any kind.' Under these circumstances it was no loss that his wardrobe was not more extensive. He begged and entreated that he might be indulged with a little fire, the season being unnaturally cold, both day and night; but it was denied him, although coals were raised within a few roods of the house and very cheap; but had it been otherwise, they were not at *their* expence, being paid for out of the public collections. 'One day, having seen

---

13 i.e. 'pleasing'.

14 The author here adds as a parenthesis: 'this was excellent from *Scotch* people, for such they both were'.

Mr. Simpson walking in the garden, I went to him and told him I was starving with cold, and shewed him my bloodless fingers. He took me to the hall, shewed me a cord which was suspended from the roof, and to the end of which was affixed a cross stick: he told me to jump up and catch hold of the stick and swing by my hands, and that would help to restore the circulation. I did so: and had been at the exercise only a few minutes, when Mrs. S. came and drove both him and myself away, under pretence that we should dirty the floor! From this woman I received no kindness, a more unfeeling woman I never met. She was probably very clever, all stood in awe of her; for my own part, I feared her more than I feared Satan himself. When nearly crippled with cold, and I had stolen into the kitchen to warm myself for a few moments, if I heard her voice in the hall, I have run as a man would that was pursued in the jungles by a Bengal tiger.'

> William Jones, *Memoirs of the Life, Ministry and Writings of the Rev. Adam Clarke*, 1838, pp. 82–5

Clarke was received into full connexion at the Bristol Conference of 1783, ten months after he had been first sent into circuit.

His name had not yet appeared upon the minutes, in consequence of his having gone out[15] after the Conference; and this year also it was on the point of being omitted. 'Mr. Wesley,' he observed, 'was, as usual, in the chair. The list was read; my name was not mentioned, owing to the list having been made out from the year preceding. Mr. Rankin, not having heard it, directed his eye to the chair, and asked, 'Are there any objections against brother Clarke?' Mr. Wesley instantly perceived the omission and replied, 'I know of none'; and the name was immediately inserted.'

One of the questions put to the candidates was, 'Are you in debt?' On the morning of that day he had borrowed a halfpenny of another preacher, as they were walking in the street, to give to a beggar. The preacher had gone out of town without being paid. Adam felt himself in a difficulty, as he could not conscientiously say he was not in debt, while to say before the assembly that he owed a halfpenny might excite a laugh. Just as the question was put, in an instant he thought of an answer, 'Not one *penny*' – which saved both his credit and his conscience.

> James Everett, *Adam Clarke Portrayed*, 2nd edition, 1866, p. 81

In 1786 Clarke was appointed to Jersey and was accompanied by his newly-wedded wife Mary, the daughter of a devout Anglican family from Trowbridge.

Mr. Clarke was extremely particular in his person and habits; and was therefore still less able to bear the dirt and slovenliness of the islanders, and the irregularity and confusion with which they were mixed up. Yet in both (for they generally support a twin existence in the same person) his patience and forbearance were often called into exercise. 'One of Mr. Wesley's mottoes,' said he, when speaking upon the subject, 'was 'Cleanliness is next to godliness.' When I went into the Norman Isles I found French dirt – the worst of all dirt... After my marriage, and on Mrs. Clarke's arrival on the islands, she found it equally difficult with myself to be comfortable or silent in the presence of dirt. On one occasion she took courage to speak to a good woman whose

---

[15] i.e. been stationed.

children appeared never either to have had their faces washed nor their hair combed. 'Do you think,' said she, placing the subject in the least objectionable form, by proposing a question, 'Do you think your children are as orderly as they might be?'

'*Woman* - 'Indeed they are.'

'*Mrs, Clarke* - 'Would it not be better to wash them?'

'*Woman* - 'Oh! away with your English pride.'

'*Mrs. C.* - 'Does not Mr. Wesley say that cleanliness is next to godliness?', hoping, by this reference, as she knew the woman entertained great respect for him, to win her over to compliance with more agreeable habits. 'Thank God!' exclaimed she in return, as though cleanliness had been viewed as an intolerable burden, and deliverance from it a blessing; 'Thank God, that it is not written in my Bible!'

James Everett, *Adam Clarke Portrayed*, 2nd edition, 1866, p. 115

Clarke was elected to the Presidential Chair three times. On the first occasion, at the Conference of 1805, he accepted the honour with the utmost reluctance.

July 28th. This morning our Conference began... After breakfast, as I had heard from all quarters that they designed to put me in the chair, I addressed the Conference and, having told them what I had understood, proceeded to give reasons why I could not go into the chair, and begged that no brother would lose a vote for me, as my mind was fully made up on the business. This produced a conversation I little expected. All the old preachers insisted on it that I was at present the proper person, and entreated me not to refuse. I insisted upon it that I would not, and solemnly charged every one who intended to vote for me to give his suffrage to some other. I then wrote [mine] for Mr. Barber, and showed my paper to those about me, who all followed my example. I trembled till this business was concluded: and what was the result? I was chosen by a majority of one half beyond the highest! I was called to the chair in the name of the Conference, and refused, begging that the next in number of votes might take it. We were thrown into a temporary confusion, during which Mr. T. Taylor and J. Bradford lifted me up by mere force out of my seat and set me upon the table! I was confounded and distressed beyond measure and, against all my resolutions, was obliged to take the seat.

J.W. Etheridge, *Life of the Rev. Adam Clarke*, LL.D, 1858, p. 211

The following story was recounted by the wife of Jabez Bunting to the members of the Wesley's Chapel Friday Sewing Meeting.

When Dr. Clarke was going to open Oxford Chapel, there was a young woman in the coach with him and Mrs. Clarke, who was going to the opening. She was talking about it to them, and asked if they knew Dr. Clarke. Dr. Clarke replied he had heard something of him. She said she believed he was not a very good preacher, but he was put first because he was an old man. She advised them to go and hear him, telling them it would be no disgrace to go into a Methodist Chapel. As they went up the town and passed the place where the martyrs were burnt, she said it would be well for them to have that religion they could burn for. The next day in the chapel she saw Mrs. Clarke, and told her she hoped she had brought the old gentleman with her. When she saw him ascend the pulpit she was struck with astonishment. She said she had been used very ill, and they ought not to have carried it so far. In the afternoon Mr. Watson related the circumstance to a large company, not knowing the young woman was present, and it so affected her that she fled the company. Dr. Clarke admired her zeal, but was grieved that she should be so hurt.

Methodist Recorder, Winter Number, 1904, p. 22

John Hamilton (c.1764–1825)

Hamilton was an eccentric Irish preacher who served as an itinerant missionary from 1794.

On one occasion, having preached the previous evening in a cottage where he lodged, he prepared to proceed to another part of the circuit. The good woman prepared an oaten cake and put it before the fire to bake for his breakfast. He wished to have prayer before breakfast, to save time; three neighbouring women came in to prayer, each having an infant in her arms. During prayer one of the women became so distressed in her soul, she could not take care of her child; John, still on his knees & praying, took it from her and laid it on a shakedown of straw, when it was quiet. Another of the women became affected in like manner, and John took her child in the same way. The third became equally troubled in soul, and John still praying took charge of her infant also. He then perceived by the smell that the cake was burning; knowing there would be no other provision for his breakfast, he turned it. He continued praying till the three women successively found peace, keeping the children quiet meantime, and had the cake nicely baked also.

Manuscript diary of Elijah Hoole, at Drew University, Madison, New Jersey

Edward Towler (c.1765–1822)

Dr. Benjamin Gregory tells this story of his maternal grandfather.

At the Conference of 1820, my mother's father, a devoted Wesleyan-Methodist minister, worn down by his three years' superintendence of the then large and laborious Boston Circuit, had felt himself unequal, for the present, to the strain of the Itinerancy, and had obtained leave to seek, in partial retirement, the renewal of his strength. He settled at Spilsby, in the centre of a large circle of friends; and, as he was but fifty-five years of age, was blessed with a robust constitution, and was withal comfortably circumstanced, no doubt was entertained of his speedy restoration. He had no definite ailment, his symptoms were wholly those of exhaustion through overwork. But that had befallen him which comes to many who suddenly exchange varied and engrossing preoccupation for a comparatively monotonous leisure. He had sunk into a state of morbid depression. This had happily passed away; he had regained his habitual brightness; and he was in an every way hopeful condition.

Such was his case when, at daybreak on January 4th 1822, my mother lay awake with me, her babe of thirteen months, by her side; my father being away on one of his Circuit-rounds. She heard the sound of fire-irons and of crockery as my eldest sister was preparing breakfast in the room below. She was just about to rise, when suddenly the bedroom door opened and in walked her father, dressed just as he used to be when leaving home for District-Meeting or for Conference. She started up, exclaiming, 'O father, whoever thought of seeing you?' He advanced to the bed and kissed her. She said, 'I'll be down in a few minutes; you must want your breakfast.' 'No, child,' he replied – his habitual way of addressing his daughter – 'I must not stay; I am going a long journey, but I wanted to see you first.' He bade her 'Goodbye', kissed her and her babe, and walked out of the room. His appearance was so lifelike that until he turned to go, no thought of the supernatural ever crossed her mind. She immediately rose, threw on her dress, hurried downstairs, and eagerly asked her daughter what her father said. She had seen no one. On hearing this, my mother fell into a deadly fainting-fit, from which she was with difficulty brought back. On recovering, she was so alarmingly ill that it was necessary to fetch my father from the country place at which he was planned. A letter was at once despatched to Spilsby, anxiously enquiring as to my grandfather's health; but before an answer could arrive, a letter was received announcing his death at the very hour at which my mother saw him.

Benjamin Gregory, *Autobiographical Recollections*, 1903, pp. 2–3

Richard Reece (c.1766–1850)

Reece entered the ministry in 1787 and was twice elected to the Presidential chair.

Richard Reece was the last Methodist preacher to keep up 'the Private Bands' and the five o'clock morning service. Both these institutions he held in the highest estimation, though he could not always persuade his colleagues to sustain them. When he was Mr. S.D. Waddy's superintendent in Sheffield, he said to him: 'Oh, Mr. Waddy, if you would attend the five o'clock preaching every morning, it would *lengthen your days.*' 'Of course it would, Sir,' he replied, 'but then it would proportionately shorten my nights.' Mr. Reece was more indulgent than another early Methodist preacher who ernestly advocated these healthful exercises. This brother, in conducting a five o'clock service in the Morning Chapel, City-road, London, chose his lesson from the Psalms, but on reading the words: 'I meditate on Thee on *my bed,*' he paused, and exclaimed: 'Lazy creature! why couldn't he get up to meditate?'

Methodist Recorder, Winter Number 1892, p. 33

William E. Miller (1766–1839)

Inheriting musical and artistic talents from his father, Miller was a gifted but somewhat eccentric character, as the following anecdote shows. He entered the Wesleyan ministry in 1799 and in 1803 found himself appointed to the Sheffield Circuit, under the superintendency of the Rev. Walter Griffith.

A somewhat curious anecdote is told respecting Mr. Miller's scruples of conscience with regard to riding on horseback. Because his blessed Master rode an ass, he doubted whether he, the servant, ought to be elevated above him in the use of the more noble animal. After turning over this case of conscience with his usual sincerity and singleness of eye, he made known his perplexity to his kind and affectionate Superintendent. The issue was a grave consultation between the brethren and the circuit stewards on the question; but as they were not quite prepared to go all lengths with Mr. Miller, they agreed to compromise on the matter and procure a mule. This anomalous steed carried the preachers to their places once or twice pretty well; but either on his second or third journey with Mr. Griffith, the self-willed animal took it into his head to stop short on the road. Neither kind nor severe treatment could make him stir in advance. He was willing enough to go back, but had no inclination to go forward. The place being distant, no remedy could be discovered to meet the difficulty, and the poor people were disappointed. This was deemed too serious a matter to be overlooked; itinerancy could not be interrupted. Poor *Mulo* was disposed of, and his place taken by the more noble and tractable horse.

James Dixon, *Memoir of William E. Miller*, 1842, p. 111

John Oxtoby (1767–1830)

Oxtoby, known as 'Praying Johnny', left the Wesleyans in 1819 for the Primitive Methodists. He preached mainly in the Yorkshire Wolds and in 1823 initiated a revival among the fishermen of Filey.

His most memorable achievement was the re-missioning of Filey. The work there had been fruitless and the [Bridlington] Quarterly Meeting was contemplating withdrawal. Questioned in the meeting as to his opinion, it was given in characteristic fashion: 'What do I think?' he retorted. 'I think the Lord has a great work to do at Filey, and if you will send me, I will go, and live upon potatoes and salt, and lie on a board if necessary, before it shall be given up.' It was decided to give the place another trial and Oxtoby was sent. He set out a few days later. Asked where he was going, he replied: 'To Filey, where the Lord is gannin to revive his work.' When he came in sight of the town he fell on his knees behind a hedge, and there pleaded with God for hours for the success of his mission. A miller passing by overheard the strange prayer: 'Thou munna mak a feal o' me. I told them at Bridlington Thou was gannin to revive Thy work, and Thou mun dea so or I shall never be able to show my face among them again, and then what will the people say about praying and believing?' At length the assurance came, and rising from his knees, he exclaimed: 'It is done, Lord! it is done! Filey is taken! Filey is taken!' And Filey was taken forthwith. A great revival began, which completely revolutionised the moral condition of the place and laid the foundations of a powerful church, which abides to this day.[16]

Joseph Ritson, *The Romance of Primitive Methodism*, 1909, pp. 114–15

Oxtoby's faith in the power of prayer was expressed in a sermon of 1824 on the text Hebrews 11:3, in which the second of his three points was 'By faith we understand that Driffield Chapel was built.'

Some of you here can remember that after you began to build this place you were brought to a dead stop. There was a tree on the next piece of ground, and one of its largest branches grew right out where your wall was to be, and when you got so far you could go no further. You asked Mr. ... to allow the branch to be sawn off, but he refused to let it be touched.

After you had appealed to him again and again, without avail, you met to consider what was to be done. At last you said, we must send for Johnny Oxtoby, and you sent for me, and I came. You talked about going to the owner, but I said, you have done that over and over again, and all to no purpose, we mun gan to the Lord. You remember we had a prayer-meeting, and asked the

---

16 A similar, and more familiar story is connected with the launching of the Primitive Methodist mission in Berkshire in 1830 by John Ride and Thomas Russell.

Lord to remove the obstacle, and while we were praying the Lord sent a great wind and blew the branch clean off, and you went on with your building. So by faith the walls of this chapel went up as truly as by faith the walls of Jericho fell down. Praise the Lord!

Then some of you remember that when you got the walls up, and all ready for the roof, the builder wanted £250 according to contract, but you had no money, and nobody would lend you any. You tried here, and you tried there, but all of no use. Then you said, 'We must send for Johnny Oxtoby again.' And I came a second time. You wanted me to go round begging, but I said, 'Nay, I'll go to the Lord first.' So we held another prayer-meeting, and told the Lord we wanted the money, and we must have it. And you know as well as I do, the next morning Miss ... came to my lodgings with exactly the sum we wanted, and gave it to me for the Trustees, and said she could not sleep all night, and that it had been impressed upon her mind that she must bring the money to me as the Lord had need of it. She knew nothing about the matter, but, bless the Lord, He knew all about it, and sent her with it.

George Shaw, *Life of John Oxtoby*, 1894, pp. 49–50

In 1825 'Johnny' visited Bridlington Quay, and, as usual when there, he made his home with Mr. Stephenson, who was one of the most influential persons in the place. He was engaged in the shipping business, and carried on a considerable trade at home.

In 1825 Mr. S had a ship which had gone on a long voyage to foreign parts, and had not returned at the time expected. He and his wife anxiously waited for news, as not only was the vessel their own, but they had a son on board, for whose safety they were greatly concerned.

During Mr. Oxtoby's stay with him, he became pained to witness their increasing anxiety, and as day after day passed without any tidings of the missing vessel, he at length resorted to special fasting and prayer on their behalf. After spending many hours in deep travail of soul, he came downstairs one day with a countenance beaming with smiles, and informed his friends that the vessel would return with all on board safe and sound. High as he stood in their esteem, and exalted as was their opinion of his extraordinary piety, and the power and prevalency of his prayers, and notwithstanding his calm and positive assertions, they could scarcely venture to believe that such good news was true. He smiled, however, at their doubts; reiterated his expressions of confidence, and told them that God had shown him the ship while he was at prayer, and that he was as certain of her safe return as if she were then in the harbour.

As he had never seen her, this was surprising, and they wondered how his predictions would turn out.

Time rolled on. One day John was pursuing his work in a country village about ten miles from Bridlington, when a man drove up in a gig and informed him that he must return with him to the Quay at once. On his reaching Mr. Stephenson's, that gentleman said: 'John, should you know my vessel if you saw her?' 'I should,' said John, 'God so clearly showed her to me that I could distinguish her among a hundred.' They then walked on to the pier. On their left were a number of vessels of different kinds at anchor in the beautiful bay, some near and some at a considerable distance. Oxtoby, after scanning the fleet, pointed to a vessel and said: 'That's the ship God showed me while I was at prayer! I knew she would come home safely, and that I should see her.' It is scarcely necessary to add that he was correct.

George Shaw, *Life of John Oxtoby*, 1894, pp. 95–97

Richard Treffry (1771–1842)

According to Treffry's fellow Cornishman, Dr. George Smith, 'His manner was rough, and sometimes approached harshness and austerity; yet he possessed great tenderness of feeling and kindness of heart.' It was the first of these aspects of his character which Benjamin Gregory recalled during the brief time Treffry served as House Governor of Woodhouse Grove School following the death of the Rev. George Morley in 1831.

One cause of Mr. Treffry's unpopularity at the Grove was his hostility to the favourite game of marbles. 'Playing marbles,' he says, 'I think seriously objectionable, because it is unfavourable to health, as it requires no muscular exercise, as it places the body in a position inclining to prostration; and what, perhaps, is worse, it often awakens irascible passions and fierce contentions among boys, and leads to trick, artifice, and deception.' To declare *taws* to be *contraband of war*, and make a Grove lad empty his pockets of all his store of *potties* – plain or painted – *stonies* and *alleys*, was looked on as a more Visigothic act than the deportation of the Elgin marbles from Athens to the British Museum. What an important part marbles played in Grove life may be guessed from the fact that when 'Jerry Thompson', years after he left school, touched at the Cape, *en route* for India, as he leaped ashore, ran up against another Grove lad, J.P. Archbell, his immediate salutation was: 'Eh, Jerry, let's have a game at *taws*!' Whereupon Archbell brought out from his pocket a handful of marbles, and describing a circle on the ground, the two fell into 'a position inclining to prostration' and gave themselves up to a game at 'ring-taw'.

Benjamin Gregory, *Autobiographical Recollections*, 1903, pp. 100–102

Hugh Bourne (1772–1852)

Here is a recollection of the Primitive Methodist leader in his later years. The writer, John Simpson, was a young preacher in the Huddersfield Primitive Methodist Circuit between 1845 and 1847. Bourne was persuaded to give his support to the evangelical work there. The following incident was the more remarkable from the fact that he was known to have no natural affinity with or affection for children.

We were carrying on very interesting revival services at Honley; and to increase their efficiency, we had an open-air service, whenever the weather permitted. One night our singing had attracted an unusually large number of boys and girls, who drew up to the stand from which I was delivering what [Bourne] called a 'five minutes' sermon'. No sooner did his eyes fall on the group of capless boys and bonnetless girls, than he began to manifest symptoms of uneasiness: I saw he was afraid I should 'talk them tired', so making my short sermon a little shorter, I stepped from the stand, took my place at the head of the procession, and looked about for my venerable companion. He was nowhere to be seen. On we went without him, in the direction of the chapel – I wondering what had become of him. My wonder was soon appeased: I was about to form the procession into a ring, at the corner of a lane, for the purpose of giving a word of exhortation to the people there assembled, when I was suddenly arrested by his well-known voice uttering in its loudest pitch, 'Go on there, will you? You'll have the childer starved.' I looked down the street up which we had processed, and there he was, at the tail end of the crowd, behind fifty or sixty children, of both sexes and all ages, whom he was urging forward to the chapel with the promise of a sermon if they would go; and shepherdlike, endeavouring to intercept any lamb which seemed disposed to break away from the flock. Soon we got to the chapel, when, perceiving that the adults were securing seats nearest the stove, he peremptorily ordered me to 'clear the benches for the childer', whom he placed in rows on each side of the stove, and in front of the reading desk from behind which our addresses had to be delivered. This done, he shouted to me, 'Get on with the service, if you please.' ...

At our previous meetings we had had invariably a course of prayer before preaching; and seeing no reason on this occasion to depart from a plan which had answered so well, I called upon an intelligent brother to engage in prayer. The brother this night prayed lengthily – not inordinately so, but too much for the impatient Hugh Bourne, who every now and then came to me and said, much excited, 'Bless me, that man's never going to give over.' 'Sing him down, sing him down, will ye!' 'The childer will be tired; won't you bring him down?' And then, feeling no longer disposed to leave the meeting in my management (for he saw that I had no inclination to stop the brother), he knelt down and – being unable to sing him down – he prayed at the top of his voice. This soon silenced the long-winded brother, which the venerable man no sooner perceived, than he also desisted, and rising and getting behind the reading desk, he delivered his favourite sermon to the children.[17]

J. Simpson, *Recollections and Characteristic Anecdotes of the late Rev. Hugh Bourne*, 1859, pp. 13–15

William Dawson (1773–1841)

Dawson was a very popular local preacher from Garforth, Yorkshire, though he never entered the itinerancy.

How disdainfully some people look upon young preachers. We have known people walk out of the chapel on seeing a beardless youth enter the pulpit. Dawson, when young, was sent to supply the place of a very popular preacher. The steward, on seeing him, sarcastically remarked, 'Oh, you are come, are you?' 'Yes,' replied Dawson. 'Well, you are better than nobody.' Dawson stood by the official and said, 'Yes, I know my place; I am next to nobody.' Speaking to a person who had the character of a 'snarling critic'. he said, 'I passed some geese, when the old gander stretched out his neck and hissed at me; you are just like him, for you can do nothing but *hiss*.'

One day he heard a hearer criticising his sermon. 'Ah,' said the preacher, 'you critics are just like flies! You settle on the bad places on the horse's back, and you leave all the sound parts untouched.' This reminds us of a fine criticism once given upon a funeral sermon preached by the Rev. Dr. Dixon on Dr. Bunting. The preacher lamented that God was taking away the best

---

[17] Text: Matt.13:43.

men from the Wesleyan body, and leaving none behind. An old woman rose from her seat in the gallery and cried out, 'Bless the Lord, that's a lie.'

David Whiteley, ed., *Illustrious Local Preachers*, Bradford, 1891, p. 41

Benjamin Gregory (c.1773–1849)

A contributor to the Winter Number of the Methodist Recorder, 1906, p.81, wrongly attributed this anecdote to Gregory's better-known son of the same name.

Robert Jackson[18] was here yesterday. He told me some capital and most characteristic anecdotes about my father. One of his tales was that a Baptist minister once undertook in my father's presence to prove that all the elect had been baptized by 'immersion, overwhelming, plunging over', and only the reprobate by sprinkling. Father having heard all his arguments, took the directly opposite proposition that the elect had been baptized by sprinkling, the reprobates by 'immersion, overwhelming, plunging over'. He took first of all Noah and his family, quoting the text from 1 Peter 3:20,21, and showed that they if baptized at all must have been sprinkled by the rain from heaven when the world of the ungodly were 'immersed, overwhelmed, plunged over'. He then brought Moses and the Children of Israel of whom Paul says, 'They were *baptized* in the *cloud*,' which must have been by sprinkling; whereas Pharaoh and his army were 'immersed, overwhelmed, plunged over'.

Benjamin Gregory, *Autobiographical Recollections*, 1903, p. 405

Thomas Stanley (C.1773–1832)

His wit was ready; and when it was necessary, he could administer an effective rebuke to insolence and folly. A man in Leeds, whose name I forbear to mention, was expelled from the Society for bad conduct; and yet used to force his way into the love-feasts and other private meetings, to the great annoyance of the people. One Saturday evening, when Mr. Stanley had just pronounced the blessing at the close of the band-meeting, the intruder exclaimed, 'Mr. Stanley, I accuse you before these people of having taken away my character!' 'Have I taken away your character?' responded Mr. Stanley. 'You have, Sir,' rejoined the man. 'I am glad to hear it,' answered Mr. Stanley; 'it is the best thing that could have ever been done for you. I hope the next character you get will be a benefit to you.'... He told me that once, when he was preaching at Sheerness, a sailor was in the congregation, and feeling that the sermon did not proceed with due rapidity, exclaimed, 'Come, Sir, crowd a little more sail there!' Mr. Stanley, who was not ignorant of nautical terms, promptly answered, 'I will, as soon as I have weathered this point.'

Thomas Jackson, *Recollections of my own Life and Times*, 1873, pp. 118–19

---

[18] Brother of Thomas Jackson, entered the ministry in 1823; died 1881.

Jabez Bunting (1779–1858)

In 1807 the Buntings moved to the Sheffield Circuit, where at first they lodged with the Holy family. The wife of Robert Newton, one of their colleagues, recalled the first occasion of her first meeting with Mrs. Bunting.

Soon after their arrival, I made my first call, and with more interest than I usually felt on such occasions. Shall I tell you of our first introduction – so perfectly characteristic of your dear mother? Mr. Bunting had his foot on a chair; and she was stitching a loop that had failed in his black silk stocking, on his then remarkably finely formed leg – much admired in those days, when trousers were worn only by seamen. The footman announced my name; and Mrs. B. desisted from her work for a few moments and we shook hands. Then, with one of the looks peculiar to her, half droll, half serious, she said to me, 'Do you mend your husband's stockings?' Of course, I answered in the affirmative. 'Oh well, then,' she said, 'I will finish my job'; and in a few minutes Mr. Bunting and she were conversing with me, rather as old friends than as those so newly introduced to my acquaintance. On parting, I said, I hope we should meet often; and your mother replied, 'I have no objection to be very thick with you.' Such was our first meeting.

> T.P. Bunting, *Life of Jabez Bunting*, 1887, p. 310

Bunting was first appointed as a secretary of the Wesleyan Methodist Missionary Society in 1833, playing a prominent part in its development until his retirement in 1851.

At the May anniversary of the Missionary Society in [1852], he was prevailed upon to preach the annual sermon in the great room at the Centenary Hall. He apologiszed for reading his discourse, 'a practice,' he said, 'which I have not been accustomed to recommend or to follow.' Several times, however, the manuscript was laid down and he spoke with all his wonted freedom and fervour. Those who were present can never forget the scene when, having noted various circumstances in which the *name* of Christ was of peculiar preciousness to the believer, ending with the mortal crisis and its prayer, 'Lord Jesus, receive my spirit,' the old man said, 'Brethren, I confidently appeal to your own experience. Is not the name of Jesus essentially associated with everything holy and happy? You have often sung,

> Thy mighty Name salvation is,
>   And keeps my happy soul above.

I wish you would sing it now;' and then, his voice trembling with emotion and broken with tearful pauses, he gave out the verse:

> Thy mighty Name salvation is,
>   And keeps my happy soul above:
> Comfort it brings, and power, and peace,
>   And joy, and everlasting love:
> To me, with thy dear name, are given
> Pardon, and holiness, and heaven.

With an instant response of perfect sympathy, the assembly caught the same spirit of glowing tenderness. They rose and sang. At first the music faltered, and almost sobbed; then, growing steadier and fuller, swelled into a great rapture of adoring praise. After this the preacher resumed his sermon.

T.P. Bunting, *Life of Jabez Bunting*, 1887, pp. 723–4

Chris Green, a Wesleyan local preacher in Horbury, near Wakefield, was 'a man of mark and individuality' and in politics a Liberal.

On one occasion rumour had it that Dr. Bunting expressed himself in the Conference in deprecation of the Democracy. The Liberal instincts of our hero were stirred and he went to the Superintendent, the Rev. William Atherton, demanding,

'Were you at the Conference, Mr. Atherton?'

'I was, Mr. Green.'

'Did Dr. Bunting say anything about the Democracy?'

'He did.'

'What?'

'He said Methodism was opposed to a rabid Democracy next to sin and the Devil.'

'Did you hear that?'

'I did.'

'And what did you say?'

'Nothing, Mr. Green.'

'Nothing! I'm surprised.'

'What would you have said, Mr. Green?'

'I should have said, 'Mr. President, that's Dr. Bunting's Methodism, but it's not mine. My Methodism is opposed to a lavish aristocracy and a similarly lavish priesthood, not only next but *equal* to sin and the Devil.'

Joshua Haigh in *Methodist Recorder*, Winter Number, 1899, p. 60

John Howe (1780–1839)

Howe entered the Irish itinerancy in 1802.

John Howe, when preaching in some part of Ireland near a market was disturbed by a ruffian who opposed the Gospel. The preacher, being a powerful man, seized his antagonist by the collar and the breech and taking him to the market hung him on one of the hooks of the market by his waistband of his leathern small clothes, and then concluded his sermon.

He subsequently lost his piety. While in this state, in a fit of sickness, a Romish priest came to visit him. When he was announced, 'Show him in,' said John. The priest entered & after a friendly conversation was about to depart. 'Stay,' said John, 'you will not go without praying with me.' 'Why,' said the priest, 'I had no expectation of being called to perform that service and i have not brought my book.' 'Oh well, then,' replied John, 'kneel down and *I* will pray for *you*.' The priest did as he was desired, & John raising himself in bed uttered a prayer in his own energetic style. When he had concluded the priest rose and assured him that it was the best *sermon* he had ever heard in his life. 'Well, but,' said John, 'I now want you to anoint me. You profess to be successors of the Apostles and to have the same power, and you anoint sick people in imitation of them. Now they anointed the sick to cure them & I want you to cure me. My pain is here,' pointing to his side, 'and if you cure me I will become a Catholic – and if not,' pointing to the pistols that hung in his room, 'I will shoot you as an impostor.' The priest was terrified. John disarmed his fears, talked to him seriously on his character & professions. The man was affected by what he said; he drooped and three months afterwards died. It was thought his death was occasioned by the pain & fears of his mind.

Manuscript Diary of Elijah Hoole, at Drew University, Madison, New Jersey

Michael Thomas Sadler (1780–1835)

The social reformer grew up under the influence of Methodism and knew Jabez Bunting during his ministry in Leeds Circuit, 1813–1815.

'Mr. Bunting,' said Michael Thomas Sadler, 'I have been thinking of the difference between us Methodists and other people. They talk of 'our venerable Establishment', or of 'the cause' at such or such a place; but we always talk of Methodism as 'the work of God'.'

T.P. Bunting, *Life of Jabez Bunting*, 1887, p. 398

William Clowes (1780–1851)

In his early years the future leader of the Primitive Methodists attended his first love-feast. His experience throws interesting light on grassroots Methodism at the beginning of the 19th century. The following incident took place the day before his conversion on 20 January 1805.

The deliverance of my soul from the heavy sorrows that oppressed it was preceded by a circumstance in which may be traced the finger of God: it occurred about a fortnight prior to my conversion. In taking up the prayer-book to read, that passage in it powerfully struck my attention: 'They that eat and drink the Lord's Supper unworthily eat and drink their own damnation.' This made a deep impression on me at the time, and I resolved that, wicked as I was, I should never do this thing; for I conceived this to be the sin against the Holy Ghost which was unpardonable. The Sunday following, a neighbour of mine called upon me, and asked if I would accompany him to Burslem, to a preaching. Well, thought I, it is dark, I shall not be seen; accordingly I assented to the proposition of my neighbour, and went with him. After preaching was concluded, and the congregation was dismissed, it was announced that there would be a love-feast immediately, and that the members of the Society would be admitted to the meeting by presenting their Society tickets to the door-keepers. The individual who was my companion on this occasion asked me if I should like to go into the love-feast. I inquired of him what the meeting was for, and what the people did; for I was totally ignorant of such matters. The man, however, replied that if I wished to go in, he would go home, and I should have the ticket which he had borrowed of his mother-in-law for the purpose of getting in.

So, feeling inclined to see this meeting, and my curiosity being thus excited, I took the ticket, and with it directions how to act, in order to gain admission. The person told me, in showing the ticket to the door-keeper, I was to cover the name written upon it with my thumb, and just let him see the alphabetical letter[19], and thus I should be allowed to pass on into the chapel. Accordingly, we both went up to the chapel door, and my companion, observing that the door-keeper, instead of giving a rapid glance at the presented tickets, took them out of the hands of the individuals and examined them minutely, said to me, 'Come, we must go home; I see neither of us can get in.' But, at the moment, I neither felt any disposition to return, nor to give my friend his ticket back; and, just as I stood in this undecided state, a puff of wind came and blew the door-keeper's candle out. In a moment, I presented him my ticket; but on taking it into his hand, he called for another light; and just as he was going to read the ticket, another puff came and away went the light a second time. The man, being fluttered and disappointed, hastily pushed back the ticket into my hand, saying, 'Here, here, move on.' So I passed into the gallery of the chapel. I was no sooner seated than I felt disturbed with a variety of thoughts. I thought, 'What shall I do here? How must I act amongst this people?' I, however, concluded in my mind, that I would sit still when the people did, kneel when they knelt, and regulate matters as well as I could in this way, taking care to be always on the watch. The service had only proceeded a short way when I observed, to my uncommon surprise, certain individuals going round, and handing bread and water among the congregation. Immediately the thought struck me like lightning - 'This is the sacrament!' – and what I had read in the prayer-book respecting eating and drinking it unworthily rushed in upon my mind, and shook me from head to foot. I glanced rapidly round on the people to see if there were any that did not receive; that if there were, I should do as they did, and thus I would escape the damnation threatened; but to my anguish and distress I observed every individual partook. At last I thought, 'Well, if I take it as these people do, and never commit sin afterwards, but serve the Lord, it will not be eating and drinking unworthily.' So I prayed to God in my heart, that if this was a good thought, he would give me peace of mind. I therefore received the bread and water in the love-feast, persuaded that, if I sinned after this, I must be damned to all eternity. So ignorant was I, at this period of my life, of religious things. From this time, however, I became conscious of a stronger power working in my soul, and I resolved, with my besetting sins, to give up my wicked companions, and to attend religious meetings.

William Clowes, *Journal*, 1844, pp. 18–20

Returning from preaching in Longnor, on the Staffordshire/Derbyshire border, Clowes found himself lost on the moors north-east of Leek. His companion was another preacher, John Wedgwood.

As I had feared and intimated, we found ourselves utterly lost on the common, in the darkness of the night. We knew nothing in what direction to proceed, for we found we were up to our

---

[19] Class tickets were issued quarterly, the date being indicated by a letter of the alphabet.

knees in moss[20] and ling. We tried to grope our way with our sticks, but after wandering for some time we came to the edge of a large sheet of water, called the Blackmere of Morridge. I perceived we were now in considerable danger. We went on in a straight line until we came to a stone wall, and then we proceeded along until we came to a gate, over which we climbed, and there Brother Wedgwood lay down, intending to remain all night, as he despaired of finding the way till morning; but I would not lie down because the ground was very wet... I therefore began to cry, 'Lost! Lost!', and in a short time, in the distance, we saw a light and shortly heard the tramping of feet and the barking of a dog. I shouted again, but no answer was returned: we began to conclude that enemies were advancing upon us; we therefore took to our heels and ran. We soon reached a wall over which I climbed and fell down a considerable way on the other side, and Wedgwood came after me. I arose and as we ran we heard the dog, and some persons pursuing. In a short time we came to another wall. I tried to get on top of it, but it gave way and down came the wall and I together... Onwards we ran... At last, when nearly exhausted, we found ourselves in a farm-yard and having conversed with the people we found them to be relations to my wife. Never did my heart feel more thankful than for this deliverance. We were told that we had certainly escaped destruction, for the precipices and moss-pits were numerous, and where we first saw the light, there was a house the inmates of which would have either robbed or murdered us, had they caught us.

William Clowes, *Journal*, 1844, pp. 113–4

Talking one day to good old Mr. Freeman of Somerby, I said, 'Did you ever meet William Clowes?'

The old man's eyes trembled with a happy smile. 'Yes,' he replied, 'I will tell you how it was. One morning while lying in bed asleep, I was awakened by someone singing. I listened. A clear, beautiful voice rang out:

'Stop, poor sinner, stop and think,
    Before you further go:
Can you sport upon the brink
    Of everlasting woe?'

'Hark!' I cried. 'Missis, that's one of them ranter preachers.'

'Hush,' she said. 'Go to sleep, it's only four o'clock. It's no preacher.'

'I listened again, and once more I heard the clear voice sing:

'Once again I charge you stop,
    For unless you warning take,
Ere you are ware, you'll drop
    Into the burning lake.'

'It's no use, missis, I'm sure it's one of them ranter preachers.' I rose and went to the window, and there, on the road, was a solitary man. He cried out in a voice that seemed to set all your

---

[20] i.e. peat-bog.

nerves a-tingling, 'Come, ye good people, awake from your slumber. Come and hear the Word of the Lord. I am going to preach on the village green. Come and hear what the Lord has done for my soul.'

'I dressed myself quickly and hurried to the green. It was harvest time and the men were going to work. We all stood round and listened. At the close the preacher said he would preach on the same spot, God willing, a month from then. The men passed on to work and the preacher was left alone. I said to him:

'Mister, have you had your breakfast?'

'No,' he answered.

'Well, what are you going to do for it?'

'I don't know,' he responded.

'Oh, well, if that's it, you might as well come with me.'

'I brought him into my cottage, kindled the fire, and made him some tea. Having ended his frugal meal, he said, 'Let us pray.'

'As he passed out of the door, I said:

'You might leave me your name.'

'My name,' he replied, 'is William Clowes.'

'What brings you here so early?' I asked.

'I finished my day's work last night at ten o'clock by preaching in the street at B. Having no friends and no money, I went into a cart shed to sleep. But the night was so cold I could not sleep, so I thought I would begin this day's task a little earlier.' That,' said Mr. Freeman, 'was my first meeting with Mr. Clowes.'

James Flanagan, *Scenes from my Life, both Grave and Gay*, 1907, pp. 169–70

Richard Hampton (1782–*c*.1856)

Hampton, known more informally as 'Uncle Dick' or even 'Foolish Dick', was born in Porthtowan, near Redruth. His short, thickset figure and heavy slouching walk, together with his eccentricities, made him a well-known figure in the neighbourhood and beyond. His preaching, especially in the open air, involved him in travels, mainly on foot, throughout Cornwall.

It was easier for him to gain the confidence of the ministers than to gain access to their pulpits. Physically, except as to height, 'Uncle Dick' was built on gigantic lines. Unfortunately he was born into an age of lean preachers and narrow pulpit doorways. The Rev. Walter Lowry, the pioneer missionary in the South Seas, tells how he once met our friend at the Lizard and said to him, 'You must preach for me tonight, Uncle Dick.' He replied, 'No, my dear, I am come to hear you preach.' However, he was ultimately persuaded to mount the pulpit stairs and promptly stuck fast in the doorway to the great amusement of the congregation. At last he managed to get in. With most preachers the difficulty is not getting into the pulpit, but finding something suitable to say when there. Once 'Uncle Dick' was safely in the Lizard pulpit his difficulty was over till the time came for leaving. When the service was over, and he had wriggled out of his temporary prison, throwing a comical glance back to the scene of the struggle, he said, 'You shan't catch me in that trap never no more – all open doors aren't safe ones.' It was in connection with the pulpit difficulty that some humorist suggested to 'Uncle Dick' that he should preach on the text, 'Be ye also enlarged.'...

The 'Pilgrim Preacher' was wont to set out in apostolic style on his journeys. He was as little cumbered with silver and gold, or scrip and coats as the first disciples. No doubt he made himself as much at home amongst the people and partook of their hospitality in the same spirit, knowing that the workman is worthy of his hire. On some few occasions when he met people who were more ready to hear the Gospel than to provide food for the preacher, he would employ a subtle but effective method of remonstrance. Coming to a farmhouse where he was appointed to dine, and seeing the housewife take one egg only to boil for his dinner, he said, 'Please don't boil but three eggs for me. If you were to boil a dozen I should only eat three.' Of course he had three, and was worthy of them. If he could have been Wesley's companion instead of John Nelson, our revered Founder would never have had to dine on blackberries in Cornwall.

John Martin in *Methodist Recorder*, Winter Number, 1904, pp. 66–7

Thomas Jackson (1783–1873)

William Wray was born in the same Yorkshire village as Thomas and Samuel Jackson, the noted Victorian Wesleyan ministers, and remembered their parents, Thomas and Mary Jackson. The Rev. Thomas Jackson's own account of his parents is found in his Recollections of my own Life and Times (1873) pp.6–11.

For very many years Thomas Jackson – he was a farm labourer – worked for Mr. James Marshall, and afterwards for his son Thomas. Not long before [the latter] died, he said to me, 'Thomas Jackson always did our work by *measure*, whether harvesting, turnip hoeing, or anything else. He always set his own price, measured his own work, made out his own account, and we never had any reason to complain of his chargers; he was always fair and honest.'... Everybody knew that the name of Thomas Jackson was synonymous with truth and honour.

I have many a time heard my mother tell of a very hard winter, when poverty was keenly felt by nearly all working people. At a parish meeting someone said, 'Thomas Jackson must be badly off, though he never asks for help.' It was resolved to send him two shillings and sixpence a week as long as the hard weather lasted. The messenger took the half-crown, and Mrs. Jackson received it with many thanks. When her husband came home she told him the good news. He immediately said, 'Thou must take it back. I have never been beholden to the parish, and I never shall.'

The evening of his life was not only calm and untroubled; it was bright, beautiful, happy... His noble sons, Thomas, Samuel and Robert. saw all his temporal wants bountifully supplied. In his old age he was, in the best sense, a retired gentleman. He dearly loved reading, and his sons put it in his power to revel in literature. It was a fitting close to a good and noble life.

William Wray in *Methodist Recorder*, Winter Number, 1896, pp. 92–3

Thomas Jackson was received into 'full connexion' at the Conference meeting in Bristol in 1808.

At Birmingham we found the Bristol coach pre-engaged; so we took the coach to Bath, where we arrived late in the evening of the next day and remained all night at the inn. It became known, by some means or other, that a company of Methodist preachers, on their way to the Conference, had arrived by the Birmingham coach, and we all received a pressing invitation the next morning to breakfast at the house of two brothers, the Messrs. Shum, Germans by birth, then resident in Bath, members of the Methodist Society, and examples of Christian godliness. We accepted the invitation and were hospitably entertained; and after praying with the family, and expressing our sense of obligation, we returned to our inn, to pay for our suppers and accommodation for the night, and prepare for our departure to Bristol. To our surprise, we found that one of the good men whose hospitable abode we had just left had been to the inn during our absence and discharged all our obligations there. After the lapse of more than sixty years, I feel a pleasure in recording this act of kindness, thus delicately performed.

Thomas Jackson, *Recollections of my own Life and Times*, 1873

Mary Porteous (*c.*1783–1861)

Mary, as one of the women preachers of early Primitive Methodism, endured considerable deprivation as a wife and mother.

She earned a precarious living for some years by keeping a school and taking in needlework. Entire consecration to, and dependence upon, God may be said to have been the keynote of her life... The answers to prayer which often brought her deliverance when she and her children were reduced to the last extremity of want are among the most striking on record. One instance must suffice. Placed upon the plan as a local preacher, her gifts and graces and usefulness soon brought her a call to our ministry. She spread the matter before the Lord, saying: 'Let not man have his way in this matter; let not me have mine; but let Thy will be done in me and by me in all things.' The divine will was made clear, and she consented. She owed £1.5s for rent, but believed God would provide the needed cash. A gentleman soon afterwards called at her door and said: 'Did I not hear you preach the other Sabbath?' and then put into her hands the exact sum needed. He immediately departed and she never knew who he was. For the cold weather and rough mountain journeys of her new sphere of toil she needed her wardrobe replenishing. The list of articles required she spread before the Lord, and soon after there came two parcels containing every article she had named in her list.

Joseph Ritson, *The Romance of Primitive Methodism*, 1909, pp. 139–40

Joseph Newsome (*c.*1783–1849)

Remembered as an eccentric local preacher, Joseph Newsome of Staleybridge was married three times. His first wife was Martha Bray of Deighton.

This first wife was a crusty, crabbed, cantankerous woman. She had no sympathy with Joe or with his Methodism. Report says she sometimes tumbled him over when he was knelt down saying his prayers, and in a variety of ways annoyed him. Joe went to the superintendent minister and, telling his troubles, resigned his plan as a Methodist local preacher, so that he might be free to use his best endeavours to restrain the violence of his wife. This done, he gave her to understand that he would endure her jibes and jeers no longer, and that if she did not behave herself he would give her a good thrashing. She found that Joe, *off the Plan*, was not to be trifled with. Joe the local preacher and Joe the ordinary member were two very different husbands. So she went to the superintendent minister and begged him to restore Joe to his place on the plan, solemnly promising that she would behave herself for the future.

George Gelder in *Methodist Recorder*, Winter Number, 1896, pp. 88–9

Alexander Mackey (c.1785–1865)

A native of Antrim, Mackey was an outstanding Wesleyan preacher who retired from the ministry after running into debt through over-enthusiastic chapel building in the Carrickfergus area.

My grand-uncle, the Rev. Alexander Mackey, was held in very high esteem in Methodist circles in the last generation, exercising a wide influence throughout the Connexion. He was the intimate friend of Dr. Adam Clarke, with whom he corresponded for many years... After retiring from the active ministry he settled in his native town of Antrim.

In my frequent visits to his home I saw many relics and curios which he possessed... But nothing interested me so much, as a young lad, as an old blunderbuss with a brass barrel, flint lock and curious design, which he possessed. I questioned him many times about it, but he always refused to give any information on the subject. Several of his friends to whom I addressed similar questions were quite unable to solve the mystery.

Prior to his entering the ministry Mr. Mackey was engaged in the linen trade. He had a factory, beetling works, &c., near Antrim, and a trout stream ran through the land.

A man in the service of a gentleman of the district had come on several occasions with fishing rod and equipment, and without making any request for permission to fish on private ground, he had followed the sport – or the poaching.

One day Mr. Mackey noticed the man so engaged, and said to him, 'You are aware that this is private ground, and no one can fish here without permission. If the privilege is worth having, it is worth asking for.'

The man looked at him fiercely and, with a threat of revenge, walked away.

The night after this occurrence Mr. Mackey was in his bed, when he heard a slight noise on the stair leading to his room. While he listened a man entered his room and advanced toward the bed on which he was lying. Mr. Mackey, who was then young and vigorous, immediately sprang up, seized the man, and wrenched from his hand a weapon which he held. In the struggle he threw the intruder on his back, and had sufficient light in the room to recognise the man who had at the trout stream on the previous day uttered the threat of vengeance.

Mr. Mackey, while holding him with a powerful grip, said to him, 'You came here to take my life. You are in my power now, and I could take yours; but I will return good for evil, and I will let you go. While you live I will not mention this to anyone.'

With this he dismissed him, keeping the weapon, which turned out to be a blunderbuss heavily loaded with slug shot.

Mr. Mackey was as good as his word; he gave information neither to the authorities nor to anyone else, and kept the secret for several years.

One day Mr. Mackey was dining in the house of his sister, the late Mrs. Henry McLonnan, of Antrim. The tolling of the bell of the parish church near at hand announced that someone was being laid in his last resting-place. Mr. Mackey paused for a moment or two, listening to the bell, and then said, 'I can speak now about the old blunderbuss.'

He then narrated the incident above mentioned, and added, 'The man who is now being buried was the one who made the attempt on my life. I am no longer pledged to silence, and you now have the story of where and how I got the old blunderbuss.'

A.M.P. in *Methodist Recorder*, Winter Number, 1906, p. 91

Thomas Marriott (1786–1852)

A member of a well-known London Methodist family and an early collector of Wesley manuscripts, Marriott had a redeeming sense of humour, of which the following examples are recorded.

He had a few sparks of mirth in his nature and delighted to relate anecdotes of old Methodism. He more than once related how good old Mr. Vasey[21], when he had lost his teeth, and found articulation difficult, added to the oddness of the service by administering the Lord's Supper at City Road Chapel with a brown paper plaster soaked in vinegar on his forehead, to allay the swelling from a bruise which an accident had raised just before commencing the service. Visiting the home of an old Methodist in the days of King George IV, when 'spencers'[22] were greatly in vogue amongst the preachers, instead of greatcoats, addressing his friend and pointing to his legs, he observed, 'It is as the poet says –

_____

[21] One of the Anglican clergy appointed by Wesley to preach and administer the Sacrament at City Road Chapel.

[22] A short. close-fitting jacket.

Man wants but little here below,
Nor wants that little long.'

G.J. Stevenson, *City Road Chape, Londonl and its Associations*, 1872, p. 575

Sir Robert Peel (1788–1850)

The father of the future Prime Minister was a Lancashire cotton manufacturer who himself entered Parliament in 1790.

When the first Sir Robert Peel was solicited to give ground for a Wesleyan chapel at Tamworth, he said to the applicants, some of whom were his own workmen, 'My lads, do not build your chapel too large – people like to go to a little chapel well filled better than a large one half full. I often go into your chapels at Manchester, Liverpool and London, and have no wish to find myself alone in a large pew, and pointed at as Sir Robert Peel.' He also added, 'I have left most of my works in Lancashire under the management of Wesleyans; they make most excellent servants.' Also, 'When I resided in Lancashire, I asked Mr. Wesley at one of the Manchester Conferences to come to breakfast with me. He agreed on condition he might bring some of his children, and he brought thirty-six preachers with him!'

Wesley Banner, 1850, p. 114

Hodgson Casson (1788–1851)

A native of Workington, Casson became widely known as a fervent evangelist whose colourful methods often bordered on the eccentric – a kind of northern Wesleyan Billy Bray. He once slid backwards down the pulpit rail to illustrate 'backsliding'. His first appointment as a probationer was to the Ayr and Kilmarnock Circuit.

He surveyed the peculiarity of his position, and felt himself in the midst of a people who required arousing. The mere stated performance of a certain quantum of religious duty, in a dry, formal way could never satisfy that longing desire which glowed within him to promote the salvation of those that heard him. He saw that something out of the ordinary way must be attempted, and his peculiarly witty and inventive mind hit upon a plan to excite the people. Taking a chair upon his shoulder, he sallied out into the public street at Kilmarnock, and proceeding along, proclaimed, at the top of his voice, 'A roup! a roup! At... (mentioning a certain part of the town). The people turned out: the crowd continually increasing, till they reached the spot; when he mounted his chair and, directing the attention of his auditory to the first verse of the 55th chapter of Isaiah, he invited them to come and buy wine and milk at a price to which none could object – 'without money'. At the close of the service, he invited his audience to attend the regular performance of Divine Worship at the Wesleyan preaching-room; and, singular as this expedient might be regarded, the end contemplated was answered in a good increase of regular hearers...

His love to the souls of men, and his jealous concern for God's glory, would not allow him to see his brother sin and pass on without rebuking him. One Sabbath morning, as he was proceeding to his appointment across one of those barren moors so common in that wild and romantic neighbourhood [Westmorland], he espied a man hard at work in digging turf, generally used there for the poor man's fire. Mr. Casson remonstrated with him on the sinfulness of his conduct, in violating the day of the Lord, but with little effect; the man attempting to justify his proceeding on the plea of his having a large family, and that he had to work hard through the week, and they must have fuel for the winter. Finding the man proof against arguments, he changed his mode of attack, and looking at him rather more sternly, he rejoined, 'But let me tell you, this ground belongs to my father; you have no business here, to cut peat without his leave: come along with me, and we will see whether he will grant you leave to cut turf on Sunday morning.' The man was obliged to desist, and throwing his spade over his shoulder, tamely followed, concluding him to be the son of the proprietor of the common. As they trudged along, Mr. Casson renewed his remonstrances on the sin of violating the Sabbath, and then more pointedly dealt some home-truths on the guilt and danger of his spiritual state. The heart of the conscience-stricken sinner began to melt, and the tears of contrition to trickle down his cheeks. Upon arriving at a convenient spot, Mr. Casson made a sudden pause, saying, 'Now God Almighty is my Father; we will kneel down and ask Him if it be right to cut peat on a Sunday.' He prayed; the man trembled and united with him in fervent supplications for mercy, and obtained a sense of pardon. It is said that he took him along with him to the place of preaching, and rejoiced to exhibit to the people a trophy of saving grace...

Going one evening to his appointment, he overheard a man uttering some awful imprecations; he boldly went up and accosted him thus: 'Then you are praying, are you? Now let me make a bargain with you – never to pray more as long as you live, and I will give you five shillings' (meaning that the man should never *swear* more). The swearer accepted the offer: Mr. Casson gave him the money, saying in a very solemn tone, 'Now, remember it is a bargain; and I will meet you again before the bar of God.' Mr. Casson left him to ruminate on this strange adventure. The more the man thought about it, the more deeply he became alarmed, until the conviction fastened upon his mind, that the strange personage who had appeared to him so unexpectedly was no other than the devil, to whom, for the paltry sum of five shillings, he had now sold himself. Under these alarming apprehensions he hurried home to disburden his distress to his wife, to whom he related all the particulars of the appearance of the tall stranger clothed in black, and this desperate bargain. She listened with amazement and fully coincided with him in the conviction that he was a lost man. She would have nothing to do with the money, 'the price for which he had sold himself, body and soul'. In deep distress he found his way to the Methodist chapel and heard Mr. Casson preach: the arrow of conviction pierced his soul, and he rested not till he was made the happy partaker of the sovereign efficacy of that blood which makes the wounded whole...

We may relate in this place the remarkable conversion, effected through his instrumentality, of a poor but wicked man who had, like others, been induced to come and hear the strange preacher, of whom he had heard so many wonderful accounts. The individual was lame and earned a precarious living by carrying coals with two donkeys, from the [Durham] pits to the city. The poor animals suffered many an unmerciful beating at his hands, a huge staff being carried for that purpose and used amidst volleys of oaths and imprecations. This man, however, obtained mercy, and for some years 'walked in the fear of the Lord and in the comforts of the Holy Ghost'. Mr. Casson meeting him one day after his conversion, kindly saluted him and inquired, 'What has religion done for you?' The man, looking to the companions of his daily toil, who now met with a different course of treatment, significantly replied, 'Ask my donkeys there!' The reply, it is said, afterwards furnished a new and extended idea to the preacher in illustrating that passage, 'Godliness is profitable to all things.' This humble individual began to rise in the world: the two donkeys disappeared to make room for a pony and cart; and, had he continued faithful, he would no doubt have realised to a greater extent the blessedness of true religion.

> A. Steele, *Christianity in Earnest, as exemplified in the Life and Labours of the Rev. Hodgson Casson*, 1881, pp. 28, 41–2, 127–8, 142

Casson was appointed to the Gateshead Circuit in 1827, under the superintendency of the Rev. Joseph Mann, described as 'a severe, serious, sober-minded colleague'.

Mr. Casson was known for his unconventionality. He had been known when preaching in a village chapel, and a man had come in late – and all eyes wandered to the door to see who this latecomer was – to hold up his hand and say, 'Don't be frightened, friends; don't be frightened. Never mind the door. If anybody comes in that shouldn't, I'll put him out again.'

There was much more freedom of speech in those days, and much more familiarity indulged in by certain people, both in their mode of addressing the Deity and their way of speaking of the Devil, than would be considered at all proper today. Mr. Casson belonged somewhat to that school, and sometimes greatly shocked the more sensitive and refined. It was after one of these sallies that he met his senior colleague in Gateshead High Street one Monday forenoon.

The colleague was troubled. An old lady had called on him that morning to complain of Mr. Casson's language in the town pulpit the evening before. He had prayed that the Lord would make the devil bankrupt and sell him up. She hoped Mr. Mann would speak seriously to Mr. Casson on the subject, and Brother Mann had promised to expostulate with him on the very first opportunity. And here was the sinner coming straight towards him with hand stretched out and a genial smile, and his cheery, 'Good morning, Brother Mann' cleaving the air before him.

But Brother Mann drew himself up stiffly, and while he took the hand, he looked severely on the young man's face and said, 'Mr. Casson, I'm sorry to have to speak to you again.'

'What is the matter this time, Brother Mann?' said Mr. Casson quietly, with none of the penitence which should have marked his tone.

'Well, I have been greatly troubled, Mr. Casson, greatly grieved, I may say, to hear that in the town chapel you prayed that the Lord would make the devil bankrupt and sell him up. Now you know, Mr. Casson, you know that will never do.'

'Are you a partner in the concern, sir?' asked Mr. Casson, with an eager enquiring look, in an earnest tone, with a mock-serious face, and about the corners of his mouth the faint flickerings of a wicked smile.

Brother Mann tried hard to keep his gravity, but the serious look gradually faded from his face and the severe expostulation failed.

The miners in one colliery village had sworn to drive out any Methodist preacher who came there, and a widow living in a particularly roomy cottage declared that she would have no Methodist preacher under her roof.

Mr. Casson had heard of these things, and said nothing to anyone. But one evening, just as darkness was coming on, he walked into the village in such a dress as no one would ever expect a 'Methody chep' to wear. He walked straight up to the widow's cottage. It chanced that the door was open and she was stirring the fire. Unheard by her he walked in, and when she turned round and looked at him, he said, 'Could you lend us a bit of rope, missus, please? I'll not keep it. You shall have it back.'

Yes, she had a bit of clothes line, if that would do.

'Just the thing,' he said... He took it from her and began to tie knots in it, so as to make a noose. He tried the loop - yes, the cord ran freely through it. Then he put it round his neck and drew it close. He carried the other end in his left hand and began looking all round the cottage walls and up at the beams overhead. He seemed to be looking for a staple or a nail. The widow began to get scared. What was the man going to do? She watched until his back was turned and then she slipped out at the open door. She rushed into her neighbour's, crying, 'Eh! hinney, Mrs. Robson, come an' help us. Here's a man clean oot of his heed. He's come into ma place, an' a believe he's gannin' te hang hissell. Had away hinney, luk sharp, a wadden't hev a murder i' my hoose, no, not if the man did it hissell.' The news flew from house to house, and in a few minutes the cottage was full. Most of the miners were down the pit, so the little crowd was mostly women. There was the man, sure enough, standing on a chair with a rope round his neck, and the other end in his hand, and trying the strength of a big nail in the wall with the other. 'Hi! Mistor!' cried an old man who had just come in – and the stranger turned round and faced them. He saw they were mostly women, and the room was full. He looked at them strangely and said, 'What's the news? What's the news? Wherever you go, everybody ask you what's the news? Now if you'll all sit down, I'll tell you the best news I ever heard. There's the long settle, some of you can sit on that, and if one of you will pull the form out from under the table, some of you can sit on that. The men can sit on their 'hunkers', and the rest can sit on the table. It won't hurt it and I'll tell you the news.' And as soon as they were seated, he began: 'The best news ever I heard was 'Christ came into the world to save sinners.'...

[After preaching to them, he began to sing and everyone was moved to tears.]

When he came down from the chair and shook hands with every one of them, and said 'Goodnight', there was not one of them who had not become his slave. They asked him to come again. They were said to be the most violently wicked people in all the countryside – and that was saying much in those days – but from that night Mr. Casson was their pet and their idol. They would have knocked down any man who laid a hand on him in anger, and he called them his lambs. He took them with him as his body-guard when he ventured into other notorious villages. He could have had none better, and they were happy and proud.

Cleadon Meadows in *Methodist Recorder*, Winter Number, 1904, pp. 56–7

James Dixon, DD (1788–1871)

James Dixon was one of the outstanding figures in mid-Victorian Wesleyanism. Dr. Frederic Greeves as a young preacher had known him in the Bradford Circuit. This was the age of lengthy sermons!

He was then blind; but his face was as beautiful as chiselled marble, and the long white hair streaming over his shoulders gave him an appearance both picturesque and patriarchal... He told me once, 'When I preached my Centenary Sermon at Manchester, Hamilton of Leeds' (the late Richard Winter Hamilton) 'heard me but he had to leave before I had done. About a year after they wrote and asked him to preach in the same chapel; and what do you think he said? He said, 'The last time I was in that chapel my friend Dr. Dixon was preaching and I heard him for an hour and a half, and it seemed to me it would go on for ever. If you can assure me he has *quite done*, I will come.'

> *Methodist Recorder*, Winter Number 1892, pp. 3–4

James Rhodes (1790–1847)

Rhodes, a local preacher in Bradford, 'was a self-taught man' and an avid and wide-ranging reader.

As a local preacher his services were more than 'acceptable'. It may be doubted whether there was a minister in the town whose discourses were more distinguished for correctness of expression, sound doctrine, lucid exposition, and tenderness of appeal; or were more generally appreciated by thoughtful and intelligent hearers than were his.

It was not his privilege, however, to witness such visible results to his labours as not unfrequently followed the pulpit efforts of inferior men. And this fact was at once a mystery and a trouble to him. In conversation one day with John Rowsby, a good, earnest man, and something of a 'Revivalist', he asked,

'How is it, John, that you scarcely ever preach without having the joy of reaping? In the prayer meetings held at the close of your pulpit addresses penitents are heard crying aloud for mercy, and from time to time souls are added to the Lord. Whereas I, who may be supposed to know more about the Scriptures than you do, and at the same time am equally sincere, seldom, if ever, have such a joy accorded to me.'

'Oh,' said John, 'I'll tell thee how it is. Thah sees, James, thah allus sticks ta th' text. Ah doant. Thah begins be sayin, '*First of all*, dear friends, I will direct your attention ta so-and-so.' Nah, that's like telling 'em wheer thah't going ta shooit, an' they all get aht o' t' road. That's just wheer I think thah maks a mistak'. *Ah* nivver tell 'em which way *ah'm* going ta' shooit. *All my shot goes willop-wallop, in an' aht - it's shure to knock somebody dahn!*'

> John Rhodes in *Methodist Recorder*, Winter Number, 1893, p. 47

William Mason (1790–1873)

Before he became a Bible Christian, Mason had been the champion wrestler of Devon. He had no lack of physical strength or courage, and needed both for the life of an itinerant preacher of those days. His story has been told by his great-grand-daughter.

The next year [1819–20], in the Camelford area of the Michaelstowe Circuit, William's courage was put to the test again and again. Many of his successes were achieved by the exertion of both spiritual and physical strength. It must be left to each reader to interpret the records in his own modern way. The preachers knew nothing of psychology by that name, but if psychology is 'organised common sense', they practised it nevertheless.

Visiting a man who was popularly supposed to be possessed of a devil, Mason found him so furious that his wife and children could not approach him. The preacher himself immediately received a blow that produced a black eye.

Mason requested the wife and children to leave the house, and then shut himself in with the maniac for a whole day. Getting no visible results, he visited him a second and a third day; always binding the man with cords when he left the house.

At last he spent a whole night there, and after a great struggle against almost inhuman rage, Mason saw the man collapse into insensibility, which was followed by complete meekness.

'The preacher took him out of bed, shaved and washed him, for he was as helpless as a child. He afterwards met in class as a changed man... and was found dead one morning on his knees by the side of his bed.'

There is a less terrible story of William Mason's efforts which has been passed down through two widely separated branches of the family.

After holding a meeting on a village green, Mason arrived late one evening at a farm where he knew he could have a night's rest and a meal. As it was fine, he did not knock up the farmer, but went into the stackyard, where he found a haystack with a piece cut out, halfway up. He settled himself on the shelf of hay and slept.

During the night he was wakened by a shaking of his bed, and found a man below, helping himself to hay. William grasped the man by the shoulder, and this conversation took place:

'What are you about, my man?'

'Sorry, sir, sorry! I have been here before, but I wanted a bit of hay for my donkey.'

'Have you had permission to take this hay?'

'Oh, no! I won't take any if you will let me go – but my poor donkey's starving.'

'Kneel down, my friend, and we will pray about this.'

I would like to think that, after the prayer, William Mason allowed the man to take a little hay for the donkey, but the story, as related, did not cover that point.

Lois Deacon, *So I Went My Way*, 1951, pp. 50–51

Thomas H Squance (1790–1868)

Squance was one of the young missionaries who sailed for Asia with Dr. Coke in 1814 on his last voyage. He served in Ceylon until returning to the English work in 1822.

I heard Mr Squance preach on the Conference Sunday of my ordination. I was to have been the guest of the Town Clerk of one of the boroughs on the Tyneside, a Quaker; but, on arrival, was told on the railway-station that, as fever had broken out in his house, arrangements had been made for me to be entertained by a retired sea-captain. This old gentleman, a bluff, jolly old sea-salt, gave me a hearty reception.

'We are glad to see you. We are not Wesleyans; we are United Frees; at least my wife is a United Free – whatever that is – and I go with her.'

On the first Sunday morning the captain said, 'I'm not going to be a United Free today, wife; I'm going wherever Mr Kelly goes!'

I looked on the Conference Plan to select the most suitable preacher for the old captain, and was delighted to find that the Rev T.H. Squance was appointed to preach at a chapel not far off. He had the reputation of delivering only one missionary speech. What did that matter? Everyone liked to hear it, however many times he had heard it before. So, it was said, he always preached the same sermon at Conference. He could not have acted more wisely. It was about 'shaking the nations'.

So I took my good host, the captain. I felt sure he would be greatly gratified, and I knew I should be. When the patriarchal preacher took his text, it was all right – just as I expected: 'You will find the words of my text in Haggai, second chapter, seventh verse: "I will shake all nations, and the desire of all nations shall come: and I will fill this house with glory, saith the Lord of hosts."'

The preacher had a rare good time; he had what used to be called 'liberty'. He had a loud voice, and used it; he 'made the deaf to hear'; he stamped the pulpit floor; he thumped the pulpit sides. There was no namby-pambyism. He was far from being like one of Madame Tussaud's wax figures. He had something to say, and he said it. There was a decided difference between the utterance of old Father Squance that morning and the exquisite, well-groomed, well-hair-oiled lads who mumbled, 'Let him that hath yaws to yaw, yaw'!

When we left the chapel the captain said, 'There, that's what I call preaching. Can't he shout? Lor'! what a noise he could make on a quarter-deck!'

When we reached his house he told his wife he did not know why they were United Frees; he had never heard such a sermon before, and did not believe he ever should among the United Frees.

C H Kelly, *Memories*, 1910, pp. 107–9, 67

John Ride (1790–1862) and Thomas Russell (1806–1889)

The first Primitive Methodist preachers came into southern England in the 1820s, working mainly in the villages. In 1828 John Ride, known as 'the apostle of Wiltshire' began to mission the downland villages east and south-east of Swindon. He was joined the following year by Thomas Russell and a meeting of these two ardent missioners early in 1830 led to the extension of the mission southwards across the county boundary into Berkshire and Hampshire. The scene of the following occurrence was Ashdown, on the Berkshire Downs between Ashbury and Lambourn.

It is a dull, cheerless day in the month of February, 1830. 'Two men of solemn mien and dressed in the garb of peasant preachers, are to be seen approaching Ashdown Park Corner, where the treeless, rolling downs are varied by a coppice or small wood. The younger man had already that morning walked ten miles across the downs to meet his companion for prayer and counsel, and they were now returning together. Reaching the wood they had to part, as their destinations lay in different directions. They had already shaken hands. But no; they must not, should not part until it had been fought out on their knees whether their mission was to prosper. 'Let us turn in here and have another round of prayer before we part,' was the remark of one of them, and turning aside into the coppice and screened by the underwood, and being far away from any habitation, no more secluded spot for communion with God could be found. Oblivious of the snow, and of personal considerations, they throw themselves upon their knees, and in an agony they pour out their souls to God. The success of their mission, which is for God's honour, and the salvation of souls, is summed up in the burden of their prayer, 'Lord, give us Berkshire! Lord, give us Berkshire!' The pleading continued for hours. At last the younger one receives the assurance, and rising to his feet, exclaims with an outburst that betokens a new-found possession, 'Yonder country's ours, yonder country's ours! And we will have it,' as he points across the country, the prospect of which is bounded by the Hampshire hills some thirty miles distant. 'Hold fast! I like thy confidence of faith' is the reply of the more sober pleader. They now part with the assurance that 'Yonder country is ours.'[23]

> H.B. Kendall, *Origin and History of the Primitive Methodist Church*, vol. 2, p. 320, quoting the *Primitive Methodist Magazine*, November 1886

John Hannah (1792–1867)

Hannah was appointed the first Theological Tutor at the Theological Institution in Hoxton in 1834. He moved to Didsbury College, Manchester when it opened in 1842.

Dr. Hannah was the Theological tutor during the whole period of my residence [at Didsbury]. He was a remarkable man, a sound Evangelical theologian, and earnest and often eloquent preacher, noticeable in appearance, peculiar in deliver, very sensitive, very touchy. It was a great trouble to him if students did not ask questions after a lecture. Who that ever heard it does not remember his plaintive cry, 'Are there no questions?'

---

23 John Ride's own account of this incident is rather less dramatic and does not include the claim, 'Yonder country is ours!' (Thomas Church, ed., *Gospel-Victories, or Missionary Anecdotes* (1851) p.87).

Once it caused a scene and grief; that great wag, Theophilus Pearson, nudging the innocent man sitting next to him, said, 'Ask him how Mrs. Hannah is.'

He did. The Doctor was aghast, pronounced the Benediction, and there was a dispersion.

Sometimes the lectures were not strong. There was one on 'Truth'. The upshot was nothing more than that 'Truth is truth.'...

The good old Doctor was very touchy. If he thought the men were inattentive he was pained. Once, rightly or wrongly, he had the idea that one student – ah, me, now a venerable supernumerary – was writing a letter during the lecture. He flew into what would be called a passion if an unregenerate had shown it, and ordered him out of the classroom. I see him going now...

Mrs. Hannah was a striking personality. She was the monarch of the house. But the love those two old doves had for each other was as beautiful as it was strong. Once when she was very poorly the unworldly old man, wishful to help her, asked if he could not do her shopping. The idea was absurd, but she yielded by saying, 'Well, you can order a leg of mutton.'

That seemed so simple; he trotted off, but turned back and said, 'My dear, you did not tell me whether it was to be a front leg or a hind one.'

Who does not remember that although sometimes the lecture itself was not great, when through some question he was led out to an extemporaneous utterance or some exposition, he poured forth a torrent of eloquence with a spiritual fervency that made him seem to be inspired. Peace to his memory! Grand old man!

Charles H. Kelly, in *Methodist Recorder*, Winter Number, 1902, p. 72

Mark Guy Pearse, when a student at Didsbury College, objected to the strict rule of those days against the use of tobacco. The theological tutor of the time was Dr John Hannah. At the beginning of the autumn term Dr Hannah told the students that he had formed a new resolution. 'You must know,' he said, 'that in the past I always smoked one pipe of tobacco before retiring to bed. Mrs Hannah filled the pipe and brought it to me every night. But it so happened that I stayed in a home at Conference where my hosts strongly objected to tobacco smoking, and so I was deprived for three weeks of my nightly pipe. On the first night of my return, Mrs Hannah, as usual, filled my pipe. 'No, my dear,' I said, 'I have done without a pipe for three weeks without discomfort, and now the pipe and I will part company for ever.' 'Does that apply all round, sir?' said a young student. 'Why do you ask that question, Mr Pearse?' 'Well, sir, did you say to Mrs Hannah, 'My dear, I have been separated from you for three weeks without discomfort, let us part company for ever?' ' The boy was the father of the man.

J Ernest Rattenbury, quoted in Mrs George Unwin & John Telford, *Mark Guy Pearse: Preacher, Author, Artist*, 1930, p. 30

John Scott (1792–1868)

My maternal grandfather, John Scott, was the son of a farmer at Copmanthorpe, near York... Endowed with deep devotion, great dignity of character, and remarkable sagacity, he early became a trusted lieutenant of Dr Bunting, exercised a moderating influence in the painful controversies of 1849, and was twice President of the Conference – in 1843 and 1852... His most eminent services were in the sphere of Education... By his efforts Westminster College was built, and he became its Principal throughout the eventful years when Wesleyan Day Schools were being founded in all parts of the country...

Matthew Arnold was the Government Inspector of the College, and was in close contact with my grandfather. Only a few years ago an educationalist who was engaged in searching out the history of Elementary Education in the Early Victorian period, inquired of me whether I was related to John Scott; and when I told him that I was his grandson, he informed me that, in searching the records at the Board of Education, he found what a great part John Scott had played, and that, whenever a suggestion was made either by or to Matthew Arnold, he had been accustomed to remark, 'I must consult Scott about it.'

J Scott Lidgett, *My Guided Life, 1936,* pp. 8–10

Sammy Brindley (1792–1875)

Brindley, a nail-maker and local preacher of Audley, Staffordshire, had a natural gift for the homespun, but telling, expression.

Dealing with the question of sincerity, he said, 'Oi know a woman, an' as good a woman as yow can foind in this warld, an' she's moi woife, an' her's offen gien hersel' a poor character as a Christian. Won day her wor complainin' abawt hersel', an' sayin' how unworthy an' unfaithful she wor, little better than a hypocrite, when Oi quietly anserd, 'Aoi, moy wench, Oi've heerd so.'

Her got loively in a minnit an' ast, 'Whoy, who's bin sayin' so? Who's bin spakin' evil abawt me? Oi's ha' thei knaw ut Oi'm as good as them us tellt thei.'

'To which Oi anserd, 'Thou'st tellt me thissen, but Oi thowt tha didstna mane it, an' naw Oi'm sure tha didstna. Tha shud allus moind what tha says, an' be sincere.'

[A chance acquaintance shared with Thomas Wareham his recollection of the one occasion on which he heard Brindley preach.]

'He preached the opening sermon at the first Wesleyan preaching place in Crewe – a poor little shed of a place it was, too... I remember one thing very well... He was speaking about different passages of Scripture and he said: 'Friends, dun yo know what Oi do when Oi come across one o' these hard texts? Oi'll tell yo. Oi do just loike Mester Wesley's hoss did. Yo know Mester Wesley was once travellin' in Cornwall, wheere there's stone wa's instid o' aar bonny green hedges. Mester Fletcher was with him, an' they were both on hossback. By-an-bye Mester Wesley says, 'John, whoy does my hoss look over this stone wall?'

Mester Fletcher couldna guess, so he gen it up.

'Well,' said Mester Wesley, 'he looks o'er it, John, because he canna see through it.'

'Nah,' said Sammy, 'that's just what Oi do wi' these hard texts. When Oi canna see thru' 'em. Oi look o'er 'em.' '

To 'look o'er' with us in Staffordshire meant to overlook, to ignore, to disregard. Is not this a bit of genuine philosophy? Only this morning I happened to be glancing over Matthew Arnold's *Essays in Criticism* and I came on these words in the essay on Joubert: 'We ought to lay stress upon what is clear in Scripture, and to pass quickly over what is obscure'; a saying based on the recognition of the same set of facts, but not half as memorably said, especially for the half-taught folk, as in Sammy Brindley's idiosyncratic fashion.

Methodist Recorder, Winter Number, 1900, p. 30; 1906, pp. 41–2

Billy Bray (1794–1868)

This Bible Christian preacher is remembered as an eccentric character who called himself 'a King's son'. Like many of his Cornish contemporaries, he had a lively sense of the Devil as a real person. In his own words:

Friends, last week I was a-diggin' up my 'taturs. It was a whisht poor yield, sure 'nough; there was hardly a sound one in the whole lot. An' while I was a-diggin', the devil come to me, and he says, 'Billy, do you think your Father do love you?' 'I should reckon He do,' I says. 'Well, I don't,' says the ould tempter in a minute. If I'd thought about it I shouldn't ha' listened to 'en, for his 'pinions ben't worth the least bit o' notice. 'I don't, says he, an' I'll tell 'ee what for; if your Father loved you, Billy Bray, He'd give you a pretty yield o' 'taturs; so much as ever you do want, and ever so many of 'em, and every one of 'em as big as your fist. For it ben't no trouble to your Father to do anything; and He could just as easy give you plenty as not, an' if He loved you, He would too.' Of course, I wasn't goin' to let he talk o' my Father like that, so I turned round 'pon 'en. 'Pray, sir,' says I, 'who may you happen to be, comin' to me a-talkin' like this here? If I ben't mistaken, I know you, sir, and my Father, too. An' to think o' you comin' a-sayin' He don't love me! Why, I've got your written character home to my house.; an' it do say, sir, that you be a liar from the beginnin'! An' I'm sorry to add, that I used to have a personal acquaintance with you some years since, and I served you faithful as any poor wretch could; and all you gave me was nothing but rags to my back, and a wretched home, and an achin' head, an' no 'taturs, and the fear o' hell-fire to finish up with. And here's my dear Father in heaven. I have been a poor servant of His, off and on, for thirty years. An' He's given me a clean heart, an' a soul full o' joy, an' a lovely suit o' white as'll never wear out; and He says that He'll make a king o' me before He've done, and that He'll take me home to His palace to reign with Him for ever and ever. An' now you come up here a-talkin' like that.' Bless 'e, my dear friends, he went off in a minute, like as if he'd been shot – I do wish he had – and he never had the manners to say good mornin'...

At a friend's house in Truro, the mistress read the account of the temptation of our Lord at family prayer. Billy listened quietly till the verse was read in which Satan promises the Saviour all the kingdoms of the world, and the glory of them, if He would only fall down and worship him, when he started to his feet exclaiming, 'The ould vagabond! the ould vagabond! he give away all the kingdoms of the world when he never had an old 'tatur skin to call his own, the old vagabond!'

A suspiciously similar saying is recorded of the Lancashire preacher Sammy Hick. One of his hearers, William Lancaster JP of Burnley, remembered him commenting on Satan's offer: 'Lyin' devil! He never had as much as a hedge-stake to give!'

F.W. Bourne, *The King's Son, or a Memoir of Billy Bray*, new and revised edition, 1898, pp. 110–111, 114; cf. *Methodist Recorder* Winter Number, 1892, p. 47

At a chapel anniversary Billy once said: 'I went into Truro to buy a frock for the little maid, and coming home I felt very happy, and got catching up my heels a little boit, and I danced the frock out of the basket. When I came home Joey said, 'William, where's the frock?' I said, 'I don't know, es-en-a in the basket?' 'No,' said Joey. 'Glory be to God,' I said, 'I danced the frock out of the basket.' The next morning I went to the class-meeting, and one was speaking of his trials, and I said, 'I've got trials too, for yesterday I went into Truro and bought a frock for the little maid; coming home I got catching up my heels a little bit, and I danced the frock out of the basket.' So they gave me the money I had paid for the frock; and two or three days afterwards someone picked up the frock and brought it to me; so I had two frocks for one. Glory!' And he closed his narration with one of his favourite sayings when persons opposed and persecuted him for singing and shouting so much: '*If they were to put me into a barrel, I would shout glory out through the bunghole!* Praise the Lord!'

Methodist Recorder Winter Number, 1892, pp. 46–47

Billy Bray built as many as six chapels, largely with his own hands and sometimes with very little support from his fellow Bible Christians.

In the neighbourhood where I lived there were a great many dark-minded, wicked people, and chapels were few. The Lord put it into my mind to build a chapel... When my mother gave me the ground, I began to work as the dear Lord told me, and to take away the hedge of my mother's field, and to dig out the foundation for a chapel, or a house to worship God in, which was to be called *Bethel*. Many will have to bless God for ever that Bethel Chapel was built, for many are in heaven already that were born there. In that day there was but one little chapel in our neighbourhood, at a place called *Twelveheads*, which belonged to the Wesleyans. Our people had a little old house to preach in, which would hold only twenty or thirty persons... I had not only the wicked against me, but a little class which was held in the house where we preached; most of them turned against me, and tried to set the preachers against me. But with all they could do, they could not hurt me, though they made me uneasy at times...

When I had taken down the field hedge, cleared out the foundation, had got some stone home to the place where the chapel was to be built, when the masons had put up some of the walls, and I had £1.15s given me by friends, the devil entered into some of my classmates, who said that the chapel ought not to be built there; and when my classmates saw that they could not stop me, they went to the superintendent of the circuit and told him that he ought to stop me from building the chapel there, for that was not the place; it ought to be built at *Twelveheads* or at *Tippett's Stamps*. Our preacher came to me, and told me that the members had been to him to stop me from building the chapel where I had begun. Then I told him that the Lord had put it into my mind to build the chapel there, and I showed him what I had done already towards building it. It was the preaching night; and he asked me whether I would be willing to cast lots whether the chapel should be built where I had begun it or in another place. 'Yes,' I said, 'I was willing; for I did not want to build the chapel there unless it was the Lord's will.' In the evening we went to meeting, and most of our little class were there, and the men who were against me. After preaching, our preacher wrote three *lots* – for *Twelveheads*, *Tippett's Stamps*, and *Cross Lanes*, which was the place where I had begun my chapel. When they drew lots the lot came for *Cross Lanes* to be the place for the chapel. They then said they would help me to get on with it by raising stone; but telling about it that night was all they did to help me. The following day one of them came to me and said, 'We shall not help you, for *Cross Lanes* did not ought to be the lot.' So I was as well off as I thought I should be.

I went to work and raised stone, and got mortar, and set the masons to work. And the dear Lord helped me, for I was very poor, and had no money of my own. But the dear Lord raised me up friends, who sent me money to pay the masons; we got the chapel walls up, and timber for the roof; and then got it sawed and put up. But we had not timber enough by one principal; and I asked my Heavenly Father to send me some timber, or money to buy some. That morning there was a Wesleyan local preacher home praying; the Lord said to him while he was on his knees, 'Go down and give William Bray a pound note.' At that time there were no sovereigns; there were one pound notes drawn on the banks. After he had taken his breakfast he came down to me by the chapel, and said to me, 'What do you want a pound note for?' and I replied, 'To buy timber to put a principal up on *that* end of the chapel.' He said he never felt such a thing in all his life, 'fore while I was home praying this morning it was always coming into my mind to go down and give you a pound note, and here it is.' So I had the note, went to Truro, bought a principal, put it up on the chapel, and there it is to this day. When the timber was on the chapel, I went round and got two pounds towards covering the chapel. At that time we had young children, and the youngest of them was taken very ill.

When my little maid was taken ill, Satan tempted me that it would take seven pounds to cover the chapel, and I had but two pounds, and our little one would die, and it would take one pound to bury her, and then I should have but one pound left. The devil tempted me very much on that point; for if I wanted it I had a right to take it, for the dear Lord and 'me' in this place kept but one purse; and I paid any money that I earned at the mine to the chapel, when I wanted it. So I had but one to give my account to, and that was the dear Lord, the very best comrade that man can ever have. So the devil tempted me that the child would die. While I was thus sore tempted, it came into my mind that I should be paid for building this chapel, and it was applied to me, 'Because thou hast built this chapel, I will save thy child's life.' And I said, 'Where is this coming from?' And it was aid to me, 'I am the God of Abraham, Isaac and Jacob, be nothing doubting, it is I, saith the Lord;' and I believed it; and it was so. When I went home I told my wife that the child would not die, for the Lord had told me so. She replied, 'Don't say so; for all the neighbours say she will die, she is so very ill.' I then went to the mine to work; when I came home the child was not any better, and had not eaten any meat. On that night the child was very ill, and got no better all the forenoon of the next day. She was very ill when I came home to dinner. That day I was afternoon 'core' at the mine'; and ever since the Lord converted my soul I always felt it my duty to pray with my wife and children before leaving my home to go to work. We knelt down to pray; the child was lying in the window seat; we had for dinner what was very plentiful at that time, fish and potatoes; and in my prayer I said, 'Dear Lord, Thou hast said that my child shall live, but she has not eaten any meat yet.' And she began to eat meat there and then. She is living now, and is the mother of ten children; so the Lord made the devil a liar once more.

The devil did not do me any hurt; he only made me bolder. I had only two pounds; and the cost would be seven pounds by the time the roof was on. I borrowed a horse and rode ten or twelve miles from where I lived, up among the farmers, and asked one of them whether he had any reed to sell, for I wanted three hundred sheaves. He told me he had, and that it was two pounds for a hundred. So I told the farmer to bring three hundred sheaves to me as soon as he could, and some spears for them. But I did not tell him that I had only two pounds. He brought down one hundred first and some spears. I had three pounds when he came; so I paid him for the hundred of reed and the spears; and had a few shillings left. I asked the farmer to bring down the rest of the reed as soon as he could, but didn't tell him I had not money to pay for it. And it wasn't necessary that I should, for by the time the other two hundred sheaves were sent a friend gave me money to pay for it. Then I put a man to work to cover the roof, and that would cost one pound ten shillings, with a little other work besides; and when the man came to be paid I had but one pound; so I wanted ten shillings more. The Lord put it into my mind to go into a high-road near where a great many people went up and down to work; and the first man I met was P.B. I said to him, 'You have not given me anything yet towards my Father's house.' And he said, 'No; nor do I intend to.' I replied, 'What, are you "amind" for the Lord to say to you in *that* day, "You saw me hungred, and you gave me no meat: thirsty, and you gave me no drink: a stranger, and you took me not in: naked, and you clothed me not?"' And he said, 'Well, I don't mind if I do give you ten shillings.' I said, 'That is just the money I want.' So he gave me the ten shillings; and I went home and paid the thatcher.

After that I wanted timber for the door and windows and forms. A mine had lately been stopped; and they were selling off the timber. There was a bargain in timber for one pound six shillings; but I had not money to buy it. To a friend who asked me whether I had been to the mine and bought any timber, I said I had not, because I had no money. Then he gave me one pound, and with that and some other sums the Lord sent me from other places I was able to buy what I wanted. As the timber had to be brought home to the dear Lord's house, I wanted a horse and cart. One of our neighbours had a horse, but he said she would not draw anything. I asked him to lend her to me. He told me I might have her, but she would not draw; but I took the mare and put her in the cart, and brought the timber home. I never saw a better horse in my life; I did not touch her with a whip or stick, though we had steep hills to come up over. When I took back the mare and told my neighbour, 'I never saw a better mare,' he said, 'I never saw such a thing; she will not draw with anyone else.' That mare was working that day for a very strong company, Father, Son and Holy Ghost, whom horses, angels, men and devils must obey. If there had been no one there more powerful than Billy Bray, she would have been as bad with him as with anybody else. But bless and praise the name of the dear Lord! He said, 'The horse shall work, for the timber is to seat my house;' and what the dear Lord says shall be obeyed...

They named my chapel Bethel. We had preaching there every Sabbath, afternoon and evening, and class-meeting in the morning. The Lord soon revived His work, and we gathered a great many members.

F.W. Bourne, *op. cit.,* pp. 47, 50–57

Billy Bray's second chapel was at Kerley Downs. The following account may owe something to the fact that it is in the words of Mark Guy Pearse, but there are no grounds for doubting its basic authenticity.

When the little place at Kerley Downs was up, Billy began to think where the pulpit could come from. At last, as he looked about among some furniture at an auction sale, his eye fell upon an old three-cornered cupboard.

'The very thing!' cried Billy, 'the very thing. I can cut a slit down the back of un, and strengthen the middle of un, and put a board up in front of un, and clap a pair o' steers behind un, and then the preacher can preach out of un pretty.'

With much glee he turned to someone near him and asked, 'What do 'e think they'll want for that there cupboard?' The man looked and gave it as his opinion that it would go for six shillings. Billy told him what he meant to do with it, and the man said, 'Why, you're Billy Bray. Here, I'll give 'e six shilling to buy it.'

After a while the cupboard was put up. Billy knew nothing of auctions. All eager to have his pulpit, he cried, holding out his hand, 'Here, Mister Auctioneer, here's six shillin' for un; I do want un for a pulpit.'

Of course, there was a great laugh at Billy's expense. As it passed away the auctioneer cried, 'Six shillings, going for six.' A nod from behind Billy was quickly caught. 'Seven,' said the auctioneer, 'seven shillings'.

'No,' cried Billy, 'tis on'y six; there's the money.'

Of course, down went the hammer, and much to Billy's astonishment the cupboard was not his.

'Well, Father do know best,' said he in a rather disappointed tone; 'but anyhow I must give the man back his six shilling.'

The man was gone, nor was Billy likely to see him again. This was a new and even greater trouble.

'I'll be gone down and tell Father about it,' said Billy as he started off for his little chapel.

With faith renewed, and a comfortable assurance that it would be all right, he was coming from the chapel, when he saw the cupboard going up the hill in a cart.

'I'll follow un, anyhow,' he whispered, 'an' see the end.' They carried it to a house, and tried to take it inside, but it was just too big to get in. They twisted and turned, they pulled and pushed, but it was no use.

'Here's a mess,' said the purchaser angrily; 'I've given seven shillin for un, an' shall have to skat un up for firewood.'

Then, as his eyes twinkled, Billy stepped over and put his hand on the man's shoulder as he stood, hat in hand, wiping his forehead. 'I'll give 'e six shillin' for un, if you'll carry un down to my little chapel.'

'That I will,' said the man, pleased at being so well out of it.

'Bless the Lord!' cried Billy, 'tis just like Him. He knew I couldn' carry un myself, so He got this man to carry un for me.'

F.W. Bourne, *op. cit.*, pp. 67–69

Billy Bray was a firm believer in both the virtue of generosity and divine providence, as his own account of the following incident demonstrates.

At one time I had been at work the whole of the month, but had no wages to take up when pay-day came; and as we had no bread in the house, 'Joey' [his wife] advised me to go up and ask the 'captain' to lend me a few shillings, which I did, and he let me have ten shillings. On my way home I called top see a family, and found they were worse off than myself; for though we had no bread, we had bacon and potatoes, but they had neither. So I gave them five shillings and went towards home. Then I called on another family and found them, if possible, in greater distress than the former. I thought I could not give them less than I had given the others; so I gave them the other five shillings, and went home. And Joey said –

'Well, William, have you seen the captain?'

'Yes.'

'Did you ask him for any money?'

'Yes; he let me have ten shillings.'

'Where is it?'

'I have given it away.'

'I never saw the fellow to you in all my life. You are enough to try any one.'

'The Lord isn't going to stay in my debt very long,' and I then went out. For two or three days after this Joey was mighty down; but about the middle of the week, when I came home from the mine, Joey was looking mighty smiling, so I thought there was something up. Presently Joey said –

'Mrs. So-and-so has been here today.'

'Oh!'

'And she gave me a sovereign.'

'There, I told you the Lord wasn't going to stay in my debt very long; there's the ten shillings, and ten shillings interest.'

Coming home one Sunday evening from his appointment through a dirty road, Billy stuck in the mud, and in extricating one foot, he tore off the sole of his shoe. Holding it up, now almost useless, he said, 'Here, Father, thou knowest that I have worn out these shoes in Thy cause, and I have no money to buy new ones; help me.' The Lord heard him in this time of need, and sent speedy relief. A friend the next week said he wanted Billy to accompany him to Truro; and on their arrival he took him first to a shoe shop and bought for him a pair of shoes, and then to other shops to get some needed articles of clothing...

His facetious remark on a similar occasion was, when a good friend said to him, 'The Lord has told me to give you a coat and waistcoat, but I do not know whether they will fit you,' 'If the Lord told you to give them to me, they will fit me all right, *for He knows my size exactly*.' It is right to state that it was Billy's opinion that almost all the garments which he had given to him fitted him so well because 'he and fashion had once quarrelled,' and the breach had never been made up.

F.W. Bourne, *op. cit.*, pp. 102–104

Drinking and smoking were among the indulgences of his early years which Billy Bray gave up after his conversion and he was critical of preachers who failed to set their hearers a good example in such matters.

Billy and a preacher of somewhat the same type of character were holding a missionary meeting at F.... Billy opened the meeting with prayer, and the preacher and others fervently responded to many of his petitions. Observing this he began to be more minute and pointed in his requests. 'O Lord, help the people to give up their idols.' The preacher said, 'Amen.' 'May Thy children be saved from the love of the world's fashions.' 'Amen,' again said the preacher. 'Help Thy people to give up their ribbons and feathers.' 'Amen,' was still the response of the preacher; and again 'Amen' when he added, 'And their cups and drinks.' 'And their pipes and tobacco,' but to this there was no 'Amen' from the preacher. Billy at once said, 'Where's your Amen, Brother B...? Why don't you say 'Amen' to the pipes as well as to the cups? Ah! you won't say 'Amen' to the pipes!' He then proceeded with his prayer. And what would be irreverent in most persons did not appear so in him. But the preacher afterwards found fault with Billy for thus rebuking him in public. He justified himself by saying, 'You were hearty and loud enough with your 'Amens' for others to give up their idols; but you are not willing to part with your own. Bless the Lord! I have given up *all* for my Saviour.' '

F.W. Bourne, *op. cit.*, pp. 123–4

Thomas Hepburn (1796–1864)

'Tommy' Hepburn was a leading figure in the early trade union movement among the miners of Durham and Northumberland.

'He was formed by nature for a leader. He was an eloquent speaker, had a voice of great compass, was thoroughly unselfish, and was completely trusted.' At Shadon's Hill, on the Black Fell, a place where perhaps more miners' meetings had been held than anywhere in the County Durham, an incident occurred in 1832, which illustrates Mr. Hepburn's coolness, and exhibits the ready obedience of the miner to his words. [Mr. Richardson's father] had just finished speaking when a company of cavalry was seen approaching the gathering at full gallop. Some of the miners were armed, it is said, though what with we are not told. They closed their ranks round the platform as if to protect their leaders. The cavalry, with a coal owner, the Marquis of Londonderry, in command, had reached the confines of the crowd. A conflict seemed inevitable, when a ringing voice from the waggon, where the miners' leaders stood, called out, 'Make way for His Majesty's troops.' The voice was that of Thomas Hepburn... The tumult was hushed as if by magic. The men made an opening for the cavalry, and a collision of forces that might have ended in a massacre was averted. The Marquis addressed the men at considerable length, Richard Fynes tells us, and promised to meet their delegates at Newcastle to talk matters over; but so inflamed were the passions of some of the men at what they, no doubt, regarded as an unwarranted interference with their rights of public meeting, that, as one account puts it, 'they would fain, had they dared, have had a rub with the redcoats'.

John Oxberry, *Thomas Hepburn of Felling*, 1933, pp. 14–15

John Bowers (1796–1866)

Charles H Kelly was a student at Didsbury during Bowers' Governorship.

Mr Bowers, the Governor, was every inch a gentleman of the old school. He had old-world manners; and he was punctiliously polite. He was a dramatic preacher. He was genial and kind, but the most incurably unpunctual man I ever knew. He was always late at meals, and greatly provoked generation after generation of students by this bad habit. He had much power in prayer, but was always too long. In class he often kept us on our knees for twenty minutes; and at Dr Bunting's funeral service in Wesley's Chapel, City Road, he prayed fifty-seven minutes. Dr Liefchild said of that prayer that it gave him the most lively sense of eternity he ever had. And yet, despite all these things, he was a rare, fine man, a sincere Christian, and a true gentleman...

I never had a free Sunday until late in my third year, and then I had to beg hard for it. I wanted to hear the Governor preach. He greatly disliked to have students in his congregation, and flatly refused to leave me without appointment; but he ultimately consented. I went over to Bowdon, where he was advertised to preach one of the sermons at the opening of the new church. The congregation was small; the Governor was not gratified. He beckoned me after service to the vestry, and said, 'Verily, to see the nakedness of the land art thou come.'

C H Kelly, *Memories*, 1910, p. 60–61, 67

One of the most awkward prayers I ever heard was in the Barlow Moor School, near the college. There was a week of special services. The Governor wished to prevent any excesses. He was supposed not to favour the 'penitent-form'. Interest rather dropped. An earnest revivalist student, Alfred Barber, troubled in his soul because of the coldness in the after-meeting prayed: 'O Lord, there is some hindrance to Thy work; remove it, we beseech Thee!' 'Amen! Amen!' said some of the brethren. Again he prayed, 'Remove the hindrance!' Mr Bowers, the Governor, was kneeling next to me, and whispered, 'Do you think he refers to me?' I replied, 'I am afraid he does, sir!' He immediately closed the service by pronouncing the benediction.

C H Kelly, *op. cit.*, pp. 70–71

Samuel Dunn (1797–1882)

William Griffith was the youngest of the three ministers expelled by the Wesleyan Conference in 1849 for refusing to sign a declaration that they were not involved in the publication of the anonymous 'Fly Sheets'. Many years later he told the Rev. Featherstone Kellett the following story, describing Dunn as 'impracticable and hopeless' and even 'pig-headed'.

The last occasion on which I saw him was not a little remarkable. It was near the close of the Agitation. Everett, Dunn and I had been speaking at Bradford-on-Avon, and next day we drove together towards Bath, where we were to hold another meeting. On the way Dunn began to talk. He said:

'I should like to broach a matter that has long been on my mind. It is time for us to gather up the fragments that have been broken off from the old denomination and to organise our new Societies. It is hopeless, even if we wished it, to approach Conference with a view to reconciliation. It is evident that, notwithstanding all our exertions, Conference will never make concessions on our lines. We must, therefore, resolve to form our followers into some kind of Church. Now I have long been of opinion that Episcopacy is the best form of Church government.'

We listened, I need hardly say, in astonished silence.

'I consider,' he went on, 'that John Wesley made a great mistake in not organising his Societies on an Episcopal basis. This being the case, it only remains to decide who shall be the Bishop of the new Church. Now you, Mr. Everett, are too old for the post. Your work is nearly done. And you, Mr. Griffith, are too young. I think, then, that the Bishopric would most suitably fall to me. What do you say, Mr. Everett?'

Everett, with calm irony, replied, 'This is a Court Martial. Let the youngest officer speak first.'

'Very well,' said Dunn, 'what do you think, Mr. Griffith?'

'Do you really want my unbiassed opinion?' said I.

'Your unbiassed opinion.'

'Well, then,' I answered, 'since you will have it, I will tell you. I would rather go and knock at the door of the Conference and petition it for mercy on my bare knees, confessing all my ecclesiastical offences and begging for forgiveness, than take a position of subordination under the Episcopal authority of Samuel Dunn.'

[Kellett asked what was Dunn's reply.] He turned to Everett and asked for his opinion. Everett answered: 'Have you not had enough?'

'No,' said Dunn, 'I should like to hear what you have to say.'

'Then, said Everett, in a tone which I despair of reproducing for its concentrated scorn, 'have I, during the whole course of my ministerial life, been labouring, and have I even suffered expulsion, striving against this very thing in the person of Jabez Bunting, in order to see it reappear in the person of Samuel Dunn? It was respectable in Jabez Bunting; but a Bishop in the person of Samuel Dunn is to me most ridiculous, despicable and unendurable.'

During the remainder of the drive, Dunn said not another word. When we reached our destination, he merely stipulated that he should speak first at the meeting. He came on the platform bag in hand, said his say, and vanished without shaking hands or uttering a word of farewell. And from that time down to the present, I have neither seen him nor heard from him.

William Griffith, quoted in *Methodist Recorder*, Winter Number, 1899, pp. 21–2

Sammy Styles (1797–1885)

Despite being blind from an early age, he was a skilled carpenter and was well known in the Sherborne Circuit as a popular, if eccentric, local preacher from Holwell. He was reputed, despite his blindness, to have 'walked five hundred miles alone every year in all kinds of weather for about forty years'.

Once a number of carpenters at Yetminster, sitting round a table at a public house, were guessing the wood of which the table was made. The publican, who was also a carpenter, told them they were all wrong and that even a blind man could tell them what the wood was. He sent for Samuel Styles, telling him of the chat they had had. He felt the table all over, and then surprised the company by correctly naming the wood of which it was made...

One Sunday he was preaching in a village and, calling at the house which was to be his 'home', he soon said, 'What time is it? I don't hear the clock?'

'No,' was the reply, 'it will not go.'

'Why not? Where is it?'

He was led to it.

'It is all on one side; no wonder it is stopped. But I'll tackle it tomorrow, and you shall see whether it will go or not.'

So on Monday morning the blind man took the clock to pieces, cleaned it, set it upright and it went all right for many years...

He relates an interesting experience which he had at Winterbourne near Poole[24], which shows his quickness of wit and cleverness in dealing with an opponent. He was to preach in a house which had not been licensed for preaching. On getting near, 'I was informed that the clergyman, who was a magistrate, had sent down two constables to stop me from preaching. There were crowds all round anxious to hear me; many of them could not gain admittance on account of the people who had already taken possession of the room. I forced my way through them, when the constables informed me that I must not preach; they had been sent there to prevent it, and if they allowed it the magistrate had vowed he would prosecute them. So I said, 'We can sing and pray, licensed or not,' and gave out a hymn, prayed, and continued as usual in Methodist services until I had to announce my text.

'Then I said, 'If this house had been licensed for preaching I should have preached from Isaiah 21:11,12, and I should have opened my subject in this way:... So I gave my introduction and my divisions one after another, going through the sermon as on other occasions, until I came to the conclusion, finishing with singing and prayer. Then I sent my compliments to the clergyman, saying how gladly I would have preached if he had not interfered.'

---

[24] Perhaps Winterborne Zelstone or Winterborne Kingston

The constables went back and reported that Samuel Styles had not preached!

W.J. Chant in *Methodist Recorder*, Winter Number, 1904, p. 54

Peter Duncan (1798–1862)

Duncan entered the ministry in 1819 and was Superintendent of the Edinburgh Circuit from 1841 to 1844, i.e. at the time of the Great Disruption in the Scottish Kirk. He served in the West Indies from 1819 to 1832, so was nowhere near Edinburgh in the late 1820s, when the notorious grave-robbers and murderers Burke and Hare were apprehended. This anecdote therefore illustrates the unreliability of oral tradition, rather than the operation of divine providence!.

In early life [Peter Duncan] was an evangelist in Edinburgh, and in that capacity would go into the low parts of the city and talk to the people and distribute tracts. One evening, while so engaged, he offered a tract to a rough-looking man, who refused to accept it, saying, 'I do not want your tract.' Pointing across the road, he added, 'But there's a man, leaning against that post, who will have one.'

Mr. Duncan went across the road and gave the man a tract. He seemed pleased to receive it, told Mr. Duncan where he lived, and invited him to visit him the next evening.

Mr. Duncan promised that he would do so, and at the time appointed found his way to the court where the man lived. After climbing two or three flights of stairs he came to his door and was on the point of knocking when his courage entirely failed. He felt that he dared not knock. He could not understand it and said to himself,

'What a coward I am; I have come up here on purpose to see this man on his own invitation, and now I am afraid to meet him.' He came down the stairs and went home.

The next morning he was in the neighbourhood again and saw a great crowd. In the midst were policemen with a man in custody. Mr. Duncan recognised the prisoner as the man who had invited him to his lodgings. Asking what it all meant, he was told that the notorious murderer, Burke, had been captured.

This man and an accomplice named Hare were in the habit of enticing victims to their lodgings and then murdering them by putting a pitchplaster over their mouths – afterwards selling their bodies to medical men for anatomical purposes. They were discovered, convicted and executed, and their wax figures have for years been exhibited in Madame Tussaud's 'Chamber of Horrors'.

Had Mr. Duncan entered that man's room, the probability is that he would never have left it alive again. God was watching his servant. He gave his angels charge concerning him.

Charles Harrison in *Methodist Recorder*, Winter Number, 1901, p. 90

Francis A. West (1800–1869)

West preached his first sermon in the Halifax Circuit in 1839.

A Sowerby Bridge man had heard a sermon on the text, James 1:12. So great was the blessing that he prayed to hear another sermon on the same words. One night in a dream he found himself in a service, and the preacher announced the text in question, but the dream died with the opening day. The next Sunday morning, however, on a friend telling him that he was going to hear the new minister at South Parade, he agreed to accompany him. Immediately on seating himself he recognised the chapel of his dream. He whispered this to his friend, and added, when the preacher appeared, 'Why, this is the very man!' When the time for the sermon came the text, too, was the text of the dream!

J. Edward Harlow, in *Methodist Recorder*, Winter Number, 1900, p. 83

William Lea (1800–1870)

Lea was a Primitive Methodist minister who served through the middle years of the 19th century, mainly in northern circuits. His first appointment, in 1823, was to the widespread Liverpool Circuit.

In the town of Ormskirk we did not see much effect, the ground seemed hard and dry. And at St. Helens we succeeded but little better. Our labour here was like to the siege of a city, slow, cold, hungry and exposed. As an illustration of this I will give the particulars of one day's labour and fare. After a very middling night's lodging and a scanty breakfast, I walked eighteen miles to this place, having nothing by the way except some berries that I gathered from the hedge, and some whey or sour milk that I begged at a farm house. I arrived at the house, not of Martha and Mary, but of a professed friend, the patron of our mission at the time in St. Helens; it was about one o'clock. Dinner was over, but the table was not cleared. I was received with the wordy compliments of the day, but alas, for me I wanted something more substantial; but I soon perceived that I was doomed to disappointment. The table was cleared of dishes and cloth in my presence, and not the slightest move was made to relieve my hunger. I tried to solace myself with the hope of an early tea. Being scant in pocket I was obliged to abide the time. I counted the hours as they passed and anticipated the usual hour - four, as the hour of my relief; but to my painful disappointment, five o'clock passed, and six came before I saw the least sign of relief for my almost fainting frame. I was then favoured with some tea which somewhat satisfied my hungry appetite; and about seven o'clock I mustered the best force I could in the open air, and gathered a numerous congregation of young persons who had just come out of the factories. I preached unto them Salvation in Jesus' name and apparently with some effect. And when I closed the service which might be about half past eight o'clock, my friends bade me Good night, and I walked to Liverpool, twelve miles, for my supper and bed. I was quite ready for both when I arrived there.

Autobiography of the Reverend William Lea, edited by Sheila Gibbs, 1996, pp. 19–20

Thomas Church (*c.*1800–post-1821)

Church was for a short time a Primitive Methodist itinerant, about whom little seems to be otherwise known. The following incident occurred before he joined the itinerancy. Although it is clearly related from one point of view only, it vividly illustrates a number of features of Primitive Methodist witness in its earliest days.

Jan.12, 1818. Being Plough-Monday, a number of men, who traverse the streets on that day carrying a plough, and begging money from house to house, came to my house at Sileby. I refused to give them any money, which they use in a drunken revel, but embraced the opportunity to say something for my Master. 'Oh,' said they, 'you're a Ranter by your talk.' I asked them if there were any Ranters at Syston? 'No!' they replied, 'and if they come there, we'll kill 'em.' This passage was applied with force to my mind, 'Fear not them that can kill the body.' I felt it powerfully impressed on my mind to go, and consulted one of the preachers. He advised me *not* to go. I therefore gave up all thought of going, till the time of preaching at Sileby on Sunday, January 18. In the morning preaching, a young woman, who stood next to me, was told by her brother-in-law that her father went into a shop, dropped down, and died in an instant. I thought this a loud call for me to go to Syston. Consequently, mustering up all available strength, after dinner, I set off with about twenty-six persons, who accompanied me. We all went in good spirits, till we reached the village, which is large, respectable, and populous. But when we began to sing, one deserted to the right, and another to the left; some stopped behind, and others ran before, till they all left off but six. I confess I was here put to an extraordinary trial; but the Lord said, 'Fear not, I will be with thee.' Almost the instant we reached the green (which is a large piece of ground, surrounded by respectable houses), hundreds were collected together. After I had sung, and prayed, I heard a noise at a distance, and a cry of 'Make way! make way!' After some time (for they had a difficulty in getting through the crowd of people), three persons – a clergyman, a gentleman, and a lawyer – thus accosted me:

Clergyman. Who sent you *here*? We don't want you, I'm sure.

Preacher. Why, sir, are *all* the souls in Syston converted to God?

Clergyman. There is preaching in the chapel, and twice, and sometimes three times in the church, and there is no room for you; so get you off about your business, for we won't have you here.

Preacher. You will let me preach first?

Lawyer. Have you got a licence?

Preacher. No. Nor have I need of one.

Lawyer. How is that?

Preacher. Because no magistrate has required me to take the oaths; and no person is liable to consequences, till he refuses after such notice is given him. Besides, in giving such notice, the magistrate cannot compel him to go more than five miles.

Clergyman (to the Lawyer). *Is that the law*, sir?

Lawyer. I believe it is, sir; but it is a point of the law with which I am not now fully acquainted.

Lawyer (to the preacher). Well, if *you* have no need of a licence, the *place* where you preach has, and I am sure this green has not been licensed.

Preacher. You are wrong again, sir. This is not a place in the eye of the law you refer to.

Lawyer. The d...l it is not!

Preacher. No, sir, it is not; for the object of the law, respecting secrecy in places of Divine worship, says, 'No places held for Divine worship shall be bolted or barred (viz., places that are so licensed, as you call them), that the ecclesiastical court might have a right to inspect the proceedings at any time.' And very right, too. But this green has neither bolts, bars nor building, but is public property, and I am not liable for trespass, but only for nuisance. If you think the Word of God is a nuisance, you may prosecute. But stop and hear, and if I say anything against the doctrine of the Church of England, or against the laws of the land, take me up, and I will answer for myself.

A conversation then took place between the clergyman and myself, respecting the forgiveness of sins, the witness of the Spirit, and the sensible perception of the love of God in the heart. The three opposers went away, after pulling me about, and insisting on my going home. A local preacher, standing on an eminence, said, 'Mr. Handford, stand firm.' I gave out a hymn, and began to preach. I had not proceeded far, before there was cry all round me, 'The constable is coming, sir; the constable is coming!' I replied, 'Be patient.' The people having made way for the constable, he said, 'I have orders to take you up, sir.' 'For what?' I said. 'Mr. M..., the lawyer, has ordered me.' 'Well, where is your *warrant*?' He did not speak, but went to Mr. M..., and said, 'Sir, he says I must have a warrant.' 'O,' replied the lawyer, 'd..n him, he knows the law.' Mr. Dolly, an eminent doctor of physic, here interposed, and most likely warded off any other proceedings against me that day. I therefore *preached* and felt very happy. Every soul seemed inspired with courage, and we sung down the street,

'Turn to the Lord, and seek salvation.'

Thomas Church, ed., *Gospel Victories, or Missionary Anecdotes*, 1851, pp. 22–4

Dr William H Rule (1802–90)

Charles Kelly, Rule's junior colleague at Aldershot, declared, 'Taking all things into consideration, I regard him as the most remarkable man with whom I ever came in contact...'

There is no doubt that Dr Rule was a very striking personality both physical and mental. His perseverance and power of will were marvellous; his courage was tremendous; his doings were sometimes startling and amusing... The rank of the officer would not dismay the brave little man.[25] He went to call on the commanding officer of an infantry regiment that had arrived in camp during the week, and to arrange for the Wesleyan service to be put into regimental orders.

---

[25] Rule was little more than five feet in height.

The colonel was a marquis. He was surrounded by officers at the moment, and seemed to be amused when he saw this parson of long beard and very short stature. He had never been on a station before where Wesleyans were paraded for their own worship. When Dr Rule, with his punctilious politeness, had paid his respects and made his request, his lordship said rudely that there would be no such entry in orders, 'for I know nothing about either Westlians or Eastlians'. Making one of his never-to-be-forgotten polite bows, Dr Rule replied, 'My lord, a little literature from headquarters will be instructive to your lordship, and I will at once apply for it to be sent to you.' It was so sent, in the shape of emphatic orders, and the Wesleyans of the regiment were duly marched out to service on the next morning. We had no further trouble from that gallant, noble lord.

C H Kelly, *Memories*, 1910, pp. 112–14

Sir Francis Lycett (1803–1880)

Lycett was a highly successful business man whose London firm was particularly celebrated for the making of black kid gloves. The phrasing of Perks' account below was characteristic of the late Victorian age and I have not chosen to emasculate it in the interests of political correctness.

I remember an amusing incident which took place when Sir Francis Lycett was the lay speaker at the annual May meeting of the Wesleyan Foreign Missionary Society in the Exeter Hall, Strand, where the yearly meetings of the great Missionary Societies and other religious and philanthropic societies used then to be held. It occurred to Sir Francis that he might lend some colour and force to his speech by producing on the platform a real black negro lad, and so illustrate the necessity of educating the coloured races in their youth. Knowing that his friend, and brother Methodist at Highbury, Jenkins, was a shipowner trading on the African coast, he inquired if on any of his ships then in the Port of London, he had such a thing as a young nigger lad; for, if so, he wanted to take him to Exeter Hall with him. Fortunately Jenkins had, so on the morning of the meeting Sir Francis took with him to Exeter Hall the small nigger, some ten or twelve years old, whom he gave into the charge of the Hall attendant with instructions to keep him safely in the vestry until he came for him.

When Sir Francis was called upon to speak he slipped down the platform stairs into the vestry where the nigger boy had been kept waiting. In a few minutes Sir Francis again appeared leading the lad up the stairs to the platform, where he stood before the great audience with one hand in his breast coat and the other on the lad's head – a manifest and standing proof of the effect of Christian Missions. Unfortunately some humorous Methodist in the far gallery directly he saw the small nigger yelled out at the top of his voice, 'Black Kids'. The audience roared with laughter at this too evident hit at Lycett's trade.

Sir Robert William Perks, autobiographical notes, 1936, pp. 32–3

Samuel Dousland Waddy (1804–1876)

Waddy was Governor of Wesley College, Sheffield from 1844 to 1862 and President of the Conference in 1859. Early in his ministry he had raised eyebrows by wearing a gown and bands in the pulpit at Hull.

At the Conference in Liverpool, 1868, someone sent a letter to the President complaining that Dr. Rule persisted in wearing a surplice when he read either the funeral or the marriage service. Dr. Rule, on being appealed to, said with considerable warmth of feeling, 'Then I will neither marry nor bury!' The Rev. William Arthur and others tried to tone matters down; then Dr. Waddy rose, and his speech was listened to with eager and breathless interest. He referred to his own experience, and to his having worn a gown in the pulpit of Waltham Street Chapel, for which he was censured by the Conference. He observed that it was a matter not worth quarrelling about. Then turning to the President he said, 'I have often thought, Mr. President, what a singular thing it was that this Conference should censure me for wearing a gown at Hull, and should then send me to Sheffield and compel me to wear one for eighteen years!'... The loud and prolonged laughter which greeted this sally settled the complaint brought against Dr. Rule.

Methodist Recorder, Winter Number, 1893, p. 100

The 'circuit horse' provided in the early days for the preachers' travels around the circuit was often a broken-down nag. Cleadon Meadows remembered his father declaring, 'It was no use getting anything better for them. If you got one preacher who knew how to ride, you got a dozen who knew no more about a horse than a haystack, and any tinker's nag was good enough for them... And then for one who knew how to feed him, or groom him, or look after his comfort, you would get a score who didn't, and who never gave the poor animal a thought from getting off his back at night to getting on again next day.' The following anecdote is not altogether easy to reconcile with Waddy's statement in a letter dated January 2nd, 1830: 'We have a good horse, and are out about twelve nights in six weeks'; i.e. the three preachers spent six days in turn visiting the outlying societies.

When young Mr. Waddy came to Gateshead[26], this was the kind of horse he was given to ride. He knew something about horses, and he didn't like it. He hated to ride this rough, shaggy-looking beast, especially when he met a man on a horse decently fed and decently groomed, and noticed how he looked down on him and smiled.

At last he thought he saw a way out of the trouble. It was just when a few people had begun to clip their horses. The practice was mostly confined to hacks and hunters, and horses of that class, but notwithstanding this he hoped to persuade his senior colleague [Joseph Mann], who had to ride the same horse every alternate week over the same ground, to have him clipped. And so after one of his country journeys he broached the subject. He pointed out that often the horse wasn't groomed. The dirt was not even scraped off his belly or his legs, and they must mount him in the morning with all the mud he had gathered the day before hanging like so many dirty icicles from the long hair under his belly. Sometimes this went on for a whole week,

---

[26] In 1829. Waddy was the junior colleague of the Rev. Joseph Mann and Hodgson Casson.

and for himself he was ashamed to come riding into town at the end of the week in such a state, and he proposed that they should have him clipped.

He was astonished at the severe rebuke administered by his colleague. He was asked if he did not think he was indulging in the sin of pride and reminded that it was pride which cast Satan out of Paradise.

He was asked if he knew what kind of persons had their horses clipped, and if he considered what the Methodist people would think if they saw their preacher riding into the village on a horse fit only for a huntsman or a groom. He was asked if he thought such a giving in to worldly customs and worldly ways was befitting a preacher of the Gospel, and if he remembered that his Master rode on an ass.

Young Mr. Waddy left the house crestfallen and surprised. He had expected some opposition, but nothing so severe as this. Still he was a young man and had some resource. Besides, he possessed the grace of humour, which often saved him from too great depression when things were going wrong. He wasn't in a hurry, so he let another week go by, and another, when he took the journey again, and then, when it was the week for his colleague to ride again, he paid him another visit on the subject.

He said, 'About the clipping of that horse, sir?'

'Now, Mr. Waddy,' said his colleague very sternly, 'I thought I made you understand about the matter the first time you raised it. I don't want to hear another word on the subject. I hope you'll never mention it again.'

'Very well, sir,' said Mr. Waddy. 'I only wished to tell you that I have had my half of the horse clipped. You can do what you like with your half!'

Cleadon Meadows in *Methodist Recorder*, Winter Number, 1904, p. 56

At Wesley College Waddy proved himself a firm disciplinarian, but there was another side to his personality.

He was a joker and wit whose sayings lingered for many years. On one occasion he went onto the school cricket pitch and bent down to tie his bootlace. A boy came up and gave him a terrific smack with a bat. When the Governor straightened up, the boy, realising who it was, burst into profuse apologies, saying, 'I thought it was Carruthers, sir.' The answer came: 'Even if you had thought it was Carruthers, you needn't have hit him so hard,' and the matter was dismissed. (Harsh Victorian discipline?)

J. L. Waddy, *The Waddy Family*, 1982, p. 84

Joseph Kipling (1805–1862) and Frances Kipling

Rudyard Kipling's grandparents knew from experience the austere life of a Wesleyan itinerant.

During the course of their married life Frances bore her husband eight children, all but two of whom lived to old age... The rearing of a family, consisting of two boys and four girls, without falling into debt, involved strict economies on the part of Joseph and Frances and their 'life-style', at all times, called for 'plain living' as well as 'higher thinking'... John Wesley used to say that he read the newspapers in order to see what God was doing in His world and it seems that Joseph Kipling wished to do the same: his problem was how to afford it. The report of the Poor Law Commissioners for 1834 had described the price of a newspaper as 'an insurmountable obstacle to the education of the poor' and whilst the lot of the Kiplings could not be compared with that of the town and country labourer they were always strangers to anything approaching affluence.

As a result the Revd. Joseph developed the habit of snatching a glance at the newspapers which the better-off members of his flock could afford, an exercise in which he used to engage whilst on his pastoral rounds. According to the family traditions, the day came when he was caught 'red-handed' whilst engaged in this particular ploy. He had immersed himself in *The Times* when Frances heard their host approaching. She snatched away the newspaper and sat on it, but when the owner asked if Mr. Kipling had read Mr. Bright's recent speech in the House and *The Times* could not be found, a blushing Mrs. Kipling was forced to admit she was sitting on it!

Arthur A. Ankers, *The Pater*, 1988, pp. 7–8

George Browne Macdonald (1805–1868)

Let me mention... an instance of touching humility of which I have heard my father speak, and to which he referred with deep feeling. It was in Wakefield, and the incident occurred in my childhood. It was a time of religious awakening, and some very thoroughgoing transgressors were converted. One of these, a rough labouring man of the lower class, was in great anguish of soul, and nothing that was said seemed to give him light or help. So my father brought him into the house, that he might have him by himself, and explain to him the 'comfortable words our Saviour Christ saith unto all that truly turn to Him'. He then knelt by his side and prayed, while the poor fellow sobbed in unrelieved distress. After a while they rose from their knees. The man was utterly broken in spirit. Looking down at his big, ungainly feet, that did not often stand upon a carpeted floor, he seemed to feel afresh his unworthiness and said with a choking voice, 'Do you think it ud mak ony difference if I was to tak my clogs off?' He was not far from the Kingdom of God.

F.W. Macdonald, *Reminiscences of my Early Ministry*, p. 48

Sir Isaac Holden (1807–1897)

After a short interval as a Wesleyan probationer and a teacher, Holden had a highly successful career in the woollen textile business and later entered Parliament. One is left wondering whether this reported conversation had become something of a set piece when guests were present!

I remember that the last time when I was a guest of Sir Isaac Holden, in the lifetime of worthy Mrs. Holden, who died before he received the baronetcy, he spoke of the fact of his having been an accepted candidate for our ministry and having supplied circuits[27] when on the President's List of Reserve.

Mrs. Holden said, 'Perhaps it would have been better for you and you might have been a better man if you had stuck to it and been a Methodist preacher.'

Sir Isaac replied, 'No! If I had been a Wesleyan minister, I should only have been a third-rate one, and most likely have taken poor circuits. But I have made a first-rate business man.'

I thought the old lady looked proud of him, and as if she did not object to come out of that contest second best.

'A Sexagenarian' in *Methodist Recorder*, Winter Number, 1897, p. 22

William Ewart Gladstone (1809–1898)

R.W. Perks sat in the Commons as Liberal MP for Louth from 1892 to 1910.

About thirty years ago I was sitting one evening next to that wonderful man and great statesman, Mr. Gladstone. I was really not sitting next to him, for Mr. John Morley was between us, but about ten o'clock Mr. Morley had to return to the House of Commons and whispered to me, 'Take my place and talk to the old man.' I had never had any long discussion with him before, but no sooner was I seated at his side than he put up his hand to his ear, and turning to me, said, 'Mr. Perks, you are a Methodist, are you not?' I said, 'Yes, sir.' Then said he, 'Tell me how many Methodist bodies there are, and what their doctrinal differences are, and how they differ in their constitutional arrangements.' Then with his hand at his ear and his elbow on the table, he was leaning forward, waiting for my reply. 'Well, sir,' I said, ' we do not call them Bodies, we call them Churches.' 'Oh,' said the old gentleman, 'that raises a very wide question, Mr. Perks. Let us go on to the next point.' So I tried to explain to him as well as I could what were the differences between the seven Methodist Churches which then existed. The first thing I told him was that we had no difference whatever in doctrine. 'Ah!' he replied, 'I wish I could say that about my own beloved Church.' He could not say it then, nor could he say it now.

R.W. Perks, *The Aim of the Methodist Church*, vice-presidential address to the Uniting Conference, 1932

Thomas Collins (1810–1864)

Collins was a celebrated Wesleyan evangelist.

When Thomas Collins was removing from Sandhurst to Orkney, he saw his way to meet such expenses of travel as would fall upon him, but how to pay £2 10s. due to a London bookseller he could not devise. The kind-hearted wife of his superintendent, though knowing nothing of his special difficulties, offered to lend him money. This offer was, with thanks, declined. Better

---

[27] i.e., in Methodist parlance, served on a temporary basis.

beg of God than borrow of man. Besides, if he borrowed, how could he hope to repay? Thus thinking, he laid all his affairs before God.

The very next morning a gift of stationery arrived, accompanied by twenty-five shillings. The sender wrote that he had at first intended to expend the twenty-five shillings in a writing-case; but on second thoughts it occurred to him that perhaps, at such a time, cash would be more serviceable. The same day, a lady of another Church sent a request that he would call upon her. He did so, and at the farewell she slipped a sovereign into his hand and insisted upon its acceptance. Five shillings were yet wanting. Mr. Collins said nothing to anyone, but felt sure his Father would send them. He was about to mount the coach. 'Mr. Collins,' said the Rev. Moses Rayner, who was bidding him goodbye, 'it just occurs to me that upon the Narrative of William Goodsell, which we published jointly, there is a balance of ten shillings profit. Half is yours; here it is.'

Methodist Recorder, Winter Number, 1903, p. 68

Nehemiah Curnock (1810–1869)

The unpublished reminiscences of the Rev. John Thackray record events described to him by the Rev. W.O. Simpson, who had been a missionary in India and who died in 1881.

Mr. Simpson told me some stories. This is one – I forget the place & circumstances. A young minister called at a house & asked them to put him up for the night – his horse had gone lame I think. They said – very sorry, but could not. He would sit in a chair, he said – they would not hear of that. 'Well,' he said, I simply can't go on – Have you no room in which I can pass the night?' At last, very reluctantly they said there was one room but no one could sleep in it because it was haunted. He said he did not mind & so it was agreed. In due time he retired. I think there was a little moon. Naturally he did not go to sleep at once. And sure enough there glided into the room a white figure – which came right up to his bed, leaned over him & then turned down the covering & lay down by his side. An arm was stretched out & he caught sight of a ring, sparkling in the moonlight. This he quietly removed. After a while the figure rose & retired as quietly as it had come. He then went to sleep. Assembled at breakfast one asked him if he had slept well & he assured them he had. 'Did you see the ghost?' 'Yes,' he said, 'I saw the ghost,' and putting his hand to his vest pocket and producing a ring, said he, 'I took this ring from the ghost's finger.' One of the daughters looked at her hand – blushed – and hastily retired. *She* was the ghost! Her sister had been long ill in that room & she had been in the habit of going to her – sometimes remaining with her a little while. *She continued to do it in her sleep*. I don't know what followed in detail – only my 'super' told me the young man married that ghost. His name was Nehemiah Curnock. They had a son – same name. The father died in 1869. The son I knew very well. He was editor of the *Methodist Recorder* and the Standard Edition of *Wesley's Journal*.

Photocopy provided by the Rev. G. Thackray Eddy, grandson of John Thackray

William Peacefull (1810–1877)

His first appointment as a Primitive Methodist itinerant was to the Wallingford Mission in 1834, where he experienced the fierce persecution then being meted out to the preachers.

When he had been at Wallingford about three months, he said to Mr. Bishop, his superintendent, 'I shall be obliged to give up. I have but one sermon left, and I cannot go on without sermons.' Mr. Bishop replied, 'Go on, Brother Peacefull, preach that one round the station[28], and by that time God will give you another.' He was planned that night at a place where he had to preach the following Sunday. He went to the place, intending to preach his last discourse, but while giving out the hymn, two lines of it specially attracted his attention. He at once felt he could make them his text, and spoke from them that night with great freedom, reserving his sermon for the Sunday. One of his hearers told him it was the best discourse he had heard from him. From that time forward, through his whole ministry, he said he never felt the lack of a sermon...

Peacefull himself tells the following story of a haunted cottage. Today we would presumably talk of a poltergeist.

I was going to an appointment one week evening, a number of miles from where I resided. It was a village in which I had resolved to establish a society. Having walked to within about a mile from the place, I felt very weary and determined to call for a rest at the next house on the way. I accordingly turned to a cottage door, where lived a blacksmith and his wife. I asked for a drink of water, and permission to rest for a while. A clean, respectable looking woman answered the door and invited me to sit down awhile. I directly perceived that she wore a pale, saddened countenance, and I began to speak about the things of God, to which she listened silently. Meanwhile she commenced preparing tea, and invited me to stay and partake with them, as her husband would be in shortly. I readily assented to this, saying that I had to preach in the adjoining village that evening, and would return to sleep in their home. 'I am afraid you cannot,' said she, 'as we have not accommodation.' 'But,' said I, 'I have no other place, and I feel that I must sleep here tonight.' 'Well, I cannot say anything to it,' she replied, 'till my husband comes.' When he arrived she called him aside, stated the case, and received as a reply, 'Let him stay; we can manage.' During tea I spoke of my mission, and requested the man to accompany me to the village. He did so, and we had a large company, though rough and disorderly. After the service we returned. But before retiring to rest I asked for a Bible, read a portion of Scripture and prayed with them. But such a prayer! So strange and unthought of by me! I besought the Lord to deliver them from the fear of witches, ghosts and apparitions, and all such superstitious bondage. At the termination of the prayer, I felt somewhat ashamed, not knowing anything of the man and his wife. But when rising from our knees I observed that they both were bathed in tears. Nothing more was said that night, but after an early breakfast, as I was preparing to start away, she told me that they had not had such a night's rest for many months; and they felt sure that the Lord had sent me there. She further said that strange noises in the night time were continually disturbing them. Knocking and rapping were frequently heard both inside and outside the house, their impression being that the house, for some reason or other, was haunted. And so terrified were they that they could not sleep. 'I will tell you how to cure that,' said I. 'Please give me the Bible.' I turned to Num. xxiii, 23, and read: 'Surely there is no

---

28 i.e. circuit.

enchantment against Jacob, neither is there any divination against Israel: according to this time it shall be said of Jacob and of Israel, What hath God wrought.' I required them to read that passage every night, and have family prayer before retiring to rest; and I would call again when I came into the locality. I visited them about a month afterwards and received a very cordial greeting, the good wife saying, 'We have done as you told us, and have not been disturbed since.'

Isaac Dorricott, *Memorials of an Earnest Life, or Records of the Rev. William Peacefull*, 1878, pp. 15–16, 39–41

William Bond (1811–1903)

Bond was accepted for the ministry in 1834 and sent to Inverurie in the Aberdeen Circuit. Many years later, in 1897, he recounted an incident which vividly illustrates the hazards and hardships of the itinerancy in those days. The account below is a conflation of two letters he wrote to the Rev. J. Conder Nattrass.

I was glad to find... that there are so many in Aberdeen and Inverurie that still remember me... I remember with gratitude the kindness they showed me, who was then a raw young man, in the first year of his ministry, just fresh from his leading strings in far-off Lincolnshire. You refer to my deliverance from the snowstorm. I can never forget that, nor the part that good Mrs. Stephen took in it. The night before, Sunday night, she had a dream, or rather a divinely-given vision and premonition of my danger. She saw me in her vision come to her bedside and, bending over her, there fell from my fingers on her face a drop of freezing cold water, which made her shiver. She started up in her fright, woke her husband, and told him what she had seen. 'Oh!' he said, 'it's only a dream. Go to sleep again.' But in the morning, when the storm came on in all its fury, the vision she had had in the night came back to her in all its vividness. She knew I should have started on my journey back before it came on, and feared I should be lost in the storm. So she could not, and did not, rest, but went about the town, in the midst of the storm, until at last she found and got two men (for no conveyance could possibly travel in such a storm) who were willing to risk their lives and go in search of me. One of these was John Badenoch, one of our members, whom I knew well. The name of the other I don't remember...

The place from which I was returning in the snowstorm was... Newburgh, a fishing village on the coast, I think about twelve or fourteen miles from Inverurie. We had a small chapel and society there, consisting of fishermen and their families. I preached there three times on the Sunday and set out after breakfast, the morning being beautifully fine, and the country all clothed in spotless white, glistening in the cloudless sun, when suddenly a violent hailstorm came rushing along. I thought, this cannot last long, and it did not, but changed into a violent snowstorm, which raged so fiercely that it drove me from one side of the road to the other in spite of all my strength. It was after battling with this terrible storm of snow and wind for miles, and when fairly exhausted, that I met the two men who had come in search of me. Several times, in the long, exhausting struggle, I had felt an almost irresistible desire to sit down and rest. But I had the sense to know that if I did I should probably never get up again, but be frozen in the sleep of death. So I kept on my feet, struggling on till I met the two men. ... They said that when they saw me, I was reeling from one side of the road to the other, driven in my exhaustion by the violence of the wind like a helplessly drunken man. Taking hold of each of my arms, they dragged me along and through several drifts of snow up to our breasts in depth, till they landed me, more dead than alive at 'hame'. Dear Mrs. Stephen, when she met me at the door, burst into tears and then, with all a mother's love and tenderness, did everything she possibly could for my restoration.

Methodist Recorder, Winter Number, 1905, p. 89

William L. Thornton (1811–1865)

I wonder how many of my readers can recall the refined and graceful personality of the Rev. William L. Thornton. He was the President of the Bradford Conference in the year 1864, and always stands out in my recollection as the wittiest President I ever knew, notwithstanding his great dignity and grace; far more so than the celebrated Dr. Waddy, who seemed as if he could not trust himself to be witty in the chair of the Conference. There was a habit among the preachers then, which has not yet entirely died away, of remaining outside the chapel during the opening devotions, that they might exchange greetings with old friends, and drive additional arrows into the consciences of representatives. This was very grievous to the devout and godly President. At the beginning of one of the afternoon sessions he made an appeal, by no means the first, to the brethren. He said: 'If you knew what I heard them say of you outside, I think you would come in.' 'Tell us, tell us,' was the cry. 'They say, "Them's the bad lads. They weant let 'em in. They've been laking (idling, shirking duty)." And now,' he added, 'after that specimen of Northern Doric, we will hear Mr. Lomas's Attic' – and the Conference resumed business.

Frederic Greeves DD in *Methodist Recorder*, Winter Number, 1892, p. 4

Joseph Spoor (1813–1869)

Spoor made his name as an evangelist and revivalist who eventually entered the Primitive Methodist itinerancy.

Once, when planned to preach at a place where the society was almost dead, he went to the chapel and found it closed. Finding the chapel-keeper, he asked why the chapel was not opened for service.

'Because there'll be nobody there tonight.'

'Go, open the doors and light up, the place will be full,' said the minister.

Thinking that Mr. Spoor was a fool, the old fellow prepared to do as he was told. Spoor asked for the loan of a chair. Pulling off his hat, he drew over his head a close-fitting skull-cap, and throwing the chair over his shoulder, marched into the centre of the road and mounting it shouted that he was 'going to sell the devil up that night, in the Primitive Methodist Chapel'.

This he did through all the place. Needless to say, the chapel was full and a blessed revival was the result.

James Flanagan, *Scenes from my Life, both Grave and Gay*, 1907, p. 33

James Macpherson (1814–1901)

Most of the early Primitive Methodist itinerants, like the lay preachers employed by Wesley in the previous century, had few educational opportunities in their early years. Despite this, a number of them were self-educated to a level that put to shame many who had taken little advantage of their undergraduate years. James Macpherson was an example of this.

James Macpherson, by dint of incessant study, also became well acquainted with Greek and Hebrew, and had a consuming passion for helping young men in their studies. To him and his pupil James Travis we owe the Hartley College, and Mr. Macpherson became the first Principal and Tutor. An amusing story is told of how, on one occasion, he put to shame a contemptible little curate. The two were passing a Primitive Methodist chapel, the curate, either greatly daring or greatly ignorant, remarked with a sneer: 'The preachers of that chapel are an ignorant set of men; they cannot even read the Bible.' 'Well,' said Mr. Macpherson, 'I am one of their ministers. Suppose *we* read a chapter together, verse by verse? Have you got your Greek Testament with you?' 'No, sir.' 'I've got mine,' said Mr. Macpherson. 'Now let's begin.' He read the first verse, but the curate could not read the next; he did not know his Greek.

Joseph Ritson, *The Romance of Primitive Methodism*, 1909, pp. 196–97

William J. Dawson, junior (*c.*1855–post-1923)

Dawson followed his father into the ministry, but left it for Congregationalism and a literary career. He describes some of the privations and limitations of manse life in his early ministry in High Wycombe, 1880–1883.

My chief impression of the people is that they were a race apart, stubborn, boastfully provincial, but not without a certain kindliness and rough humour. They were mostly chair-makers, conducting their manufacture in flimsy buildings which burned down so frequently that the insurance companies were deeply suspicious of the honesty of their owners...

There was small respect here for ministers, especially among the ardent Radicals, who regarded ministers as objects of torture, to be bullied and humiliated on all possible occasions, lest they should think more highly of themselves than they ought to think. Nothing pleased these gentlemen so much as to inspect the furniture of the manse, with an eye for damage or misuse, and they acted as though they owned the minister as well as the furniture with which they had provided him. A notable and almost classical instance of this spirit was the earnest protest of one of these guardians of economy, against supposed luxury in the manse.

'I notice,' he said, 'that there has been two brooms bought for the preacher's house this quarter. Why two? There ain't been but one new broom bought in my house for the last ten years.'

William J. Dawson, *The Autobiography of a Mind*, 1925, pp. 107–9

William Arthur (1819–1901)

William Arthur's missionary career in India was cut short by ill health, but throughout his ministry he remained an outstanding advocate of overseas missions. On the following occasion he was due to speak at Mousehole on a Saturday evening and to preach in Penzance the following day. He was to sail from Bristol, but severe storms delayed his boat from reaching the north Cornish coast.

The boat should have reached Hayle at four or five in the morning. Saturday afternoon came and it was not signalled as anywhere within reach of the coast. Presently, about two o'clock or later, we had intelligence that the steamer had been seen from afar, having a bad time, and could not reach Hayle in time for any evening service to be conducted by a passenger, but that if she were met off St. Ives perhaps a landing might be effected about four o'clock. St. Ives, of course, is a long drive from Mousehole, and preaching after such a voyage of some five and thirty hours, Mr. Arthur being always a bad sailor, did not seem a promising outlook to those who had to meet him. We drove away, however, without any loss of time, four of us in a rather small carriage, and were just in time to send from the pier at St. Ives a message to Mr. Arthur to come at once to us and our carriage. He came, looking very feeble and worn out, but, unfortunately, did not come alone. A stout gentleman, not very clerical-looking as he stood, but yet a rector of a far-away parish, and evidently a gentleman, came with him, and desired, though he did not ask for, a seat in our carriage. Such a thing was difficult; it would add weight to our load. It would overfill the inside, for he was bulky and the carriage small; it would oblige somebody to sit with the driver. We were already sure to be too late for the service at Mousehole, and this would make us later – on a Saturday night, too, and with a large and excitable congregation waiting. Mr. Arthur, however, insisted absolutely that his fellow-passenger must go, otherwise he would be unable to get to his parish – or even to get as far on his road as Truro – that night. His family would not know whether he was safe or shipwrecked, there would be no service in his church, at Newlyn East, beyond Truro[29], on the morrow.

I was in charge, and was very much put out; I knew it would mean trouble at Mousehole; it would delay our arrival at Penzance, destroy the chance of a brief rest, or of proper refreshment, for Mr. Arthur, before attempting to preach in the village, three miles beyond Penzance, where the people would be waiting for him. However, Mr. Arthur was quietly peremptory and absolute; and with an ill grace I yielded, and we took the clergyman in, I taking the box-seat by the driver. His opportunity, it was hoped, would be gained if we let him ride a certain distance with us. The afternoon coach from Penzance to Truro was then on the road, and we should come into that same road on our way to Penzance. Only we should have to drive well; it would be a narrow chance, whether we met or missed the coach. However, when we came to the point where we were to get on to the high road to Penzance from Truro we just exactly met the coach on its way to Truro from Penzance, and so saved it; a few minutes and it would have passed beyond recall.

A few weeks later Rigg had occasion to visit Newlyn East and, meeting the local clergyman again, discovered how much he had appreciated the help given him in returning home in time to fulfil his Sunday duties.

As for Mousehole, though we hurried along, and poor Arthur had very bare refreshment, many of the congregation left the chapel before the preacher could arrive there, nearly an hour late. Many indeed came straggling back, but circumstances were untoward. It was nearly eight o'clock on a Saturday evening. The preacher, too, was, of course, utterly worn out – quite unfit

---

29 Actually, eight miles north of Truro.

to preach – and though it was a Missionary occasion, he never rose to vigour or animation. Great expectations were disappointed that evening. Some of the good people heard him at Penzance on the morrow, when he delighted his congregations. But Mousehole, a zealous and also a somewhat jealous missionary place, could not easily digest its disappointment.

James H. Rigg, *Wesleyan Methodist Reminiscences Sixty Years Ago*, 1904, pp. 58–62

George T. Perks (1819–1877)

Perks, President of the 1873 Conference and the father of a more famous son, was stationed in Bath in 1856–1859.

[My father] was an enthusiastic student of Irish history and, among other Irish celebrities, studied the life of St. Patrick. When in Bath he delivered a lecture on this Irish saint which aroused very strongly the ire of the Roman Catholic clergy of that city who, in reply, made a fierce attack on my father in the *Bath Chronicle*, a newspaper of repute then, as it is now.

Walking in the park with my father a few days after, we saw approaching us the priest who had made this journalistic onslaught. When he came near, instead of passing him by without taking any notice, my father stopped and shook hands heartily with the priest, and had a friendly talk.

When he had walked on I said, 'Father, is not that the Roman Catholic priest who attacked you in the *Bath Chronicle*?' 'Yes, my boy, that is Father so and so.' 'I wonder you speak to such a man, I replied, 'I should think you will never want to meet him again.'

Turning to me with his kindly eyes my father said: 'Bob, my lad, perhaps we shall never meet again till we meet in Heaven.' The idea of a Roman Catholic ever going to Heaven was quite a new idea to me, but this was my father's way of teaching us children, and it was my first and a lasting lesson on religious toleration.

Robert W. Perks, *Notes for an Autobiography*, 1936, p. 17

Ralph Fenwick (1819–1907)

Fenwick was a Primitive Methodist itinerant, born in Lanchester, Co. Durham. His experience illustrates what someone of humble birth might achieve despite little educational opportunity.

Most of the schooling he got was by attending the Wesleyan and Primitive Methodist Sunday Schools. Before he was eight he was compelled to sweep the waggon way and at an early age became a colliery engineman. In this capacity he developed considerable mechanical genius, an adroit use of which he once made in after years. On a visit to Stenhope, and staying with the foreman of certain quarries, the engine went wrong and the work was stopped. He inspected it and told the men he would put it right if they would promise to come to the service that night. Glad to get the work done they accepted the terms. The engine was put right, the men came to the service, Mr. Fenwick preached one of his rousing sermons, and several of them gave their hearts to God.

Primitive Methodist Magazine, 1907, p. 725

Dr. Benjamin Gregory (1820–1900)

In the course of the nineteenth century, the prayer meeting overtook the class meeting as the most popular weeknight occasion of informal devotion. Gregory recalls such a meeting in the 1820s in the North Riding of Yorkshire.

The door of the large vestry being but a few paces from our own back door, we children were allowed, on summer evenings, to attend the Prayer-meeting. This was a great treat, as both prayers and singing were of the liveliest kind; and the mode of conducting the service was utterly unconventional; and the people always made much of us for our father's sake. As the ministers preached, as a rule, six nights out of the seven, of course, they could not attend the Prayer-meeting. The leadership was arranged impromptu, by someone asking someone else to take it. The leader 'gave out' the first hymn and led the first prayer, and then 'threw the meeting open'. The free and easy, and yet patriarchal, way in which things were managed may be illustrated by the first Prayer-meeting incident I can recall. It was the custom for everyone, before lifting up his voice in prayer, to give out the verse or two which he wished to be sung. It so happened that a young man who had been up to London to learn a trade, having 'served his time' and returned home, made his way to the old familiar Prayer-meeting. Amongst other accomplishments he had acquired the Cockney dialect, perhaps with some exaggeration. He rose and gave out, with an air of 'consequence': 'A *chawge* to keep I *hev!*' Whereupon the patriarchal leader cut short his ministration, with the gruff order: '*Then sit thee doon, an' keep it.*' The time it took his Cockneyship to collapse is not worth mentioning.

Another of my earliest Prayer-meeting reminiscences is the petition of an earnest brother, who seemed to hold, in some form the doctrine of irresistible grace. He prayed: 'O Lord, bring sinners to Thy house. An' if they *we'ant* cum, tak' 'em by t'scruff o' t' neck, an' mak' 'em cum!'

Benjamin Gregory, *Autobiographical Recollections*, 1903, pp. 10–11

Gregory's days as a pupil at The Grove came to an unexpected end.

My own school-days were swiftly closing in. Then came the everlasting, hard inquiry: '*What is to be done next?*' My father's Supernumeraryship compelled the acceptance of the first feasible opening... Meanwhile the Governor began to treat me with marked consideration, repeatedly calling upon me to lead the devotions at family prayer. When I had entered on the last week of my sixth year at school, he called me into his study and informed me that the Committee had resolved, on his recommendation, and that of the masters, to ask me to remain at school as a tutor. To this I thankfully assented. A few days later the fact was announced to the rest of the boys. The immediate effect was most amusing. The arrangement was unprecedented. More than sixteen years before, Mr. Brownell, having left school at the vacation, returned as a master at its close; but all the older boys had gone, and those of whom he took immediate charge had never known him as a school-boy. It would have vastly simplified the matter in my own case had my sixteen eldest school-fellows disappeared, and [had] the seventeen youngest never known me in any other relation than that of tutor. But the change was instantaneous; one night I sprang into my crib 'Ben Gregory', and rose next morning 'Mr. Gregory'. When the school-boy George Noel Gordon Byron suddenly became Lord Byron, he asked someone to tell him how a lad looks when one fine morning he wakes up to find himself a lord! For myself, I knew not how to look, and none of my compeers could tell me.

What seemed most to disconcert my school-fellows was the change of address. James Smetham and I often laughed in later years about a little interview between himself and me which took place at this time. He came to me with all the mysterious importance of a deputation, the other lads looking on at a respectful distance, and put the following question, weighing every word with as much emphasis as it could bear, and leaving a pause between the words with a view to increased effect: 'Ben!' 'Yes, Jim.' '*Do - you- reckon - that - we - shall have* to call *you Mr* Gregory?'

'Of *course* you will, Jim; and *think on* you *do*: because, you see, I shall *be* Mr. Gregory.'

Whereat he lifted up his eyes and hands, as if the sky were in the very act of falling; and yet with an unutterably grotesque expression, and went off the very picture of 'Laughter holding both his sides'.

Benjamin Gregory, Autobiographical Recollections, 1903, pp. 177–78

As a newly appointed probationer in 1840 Gregory found himself encountering the phenomenon of Revivalism in its raw state. He was sent to give out class tickets at Guiseley.

I took the neat little packet, as if it had been my installing pastoral staff, and musingly, cheerily and merrily took on a glorious summer evening the lovely stroll to Guiseley, through Esholt Walk and Wood. The leader of the class was a patriarchal Yorkshireman; the members were, about half of them, new converts, and the rest as if they were converted anew. No lack of freshness or of individuality: 'Twas Nature all, and all delight.'

But what puzzled me, and, had the 'experiences' not been so interesting and so various, would have 'fair maddled' me, was an utterly unaccountable outcry, evidently close by, but the significance of which I could in no wise comprehend: it seemed a strange blending of 'the voice of them that shout for mastery, the voice of them that cry for being overcome, and the voice of them that sing.' Now, strangely enough, though I knew that Guiseley was in a state of Revival, it never occurred to me to connect this 'mixed and mournful sound' with that felicitous event. But, having pronounced the Benediction, given and received from the members, old and young, 'the right hand of fellowship', I turned to the leader and said: 'Well, how's your Revival getting on?' To which he answered, with a beaming face: 'Oh! brahveleh [bravely]. That din ye hear's it.' We forthwith stepped into the large schoolroom, where a great number of people knelt beside the ranged benches, and beat them furiously. The brother who had charge of the meeting walked up to me politely and, to my observation, 'I had no idea that you had such a large number of penitents,' he replied, showing the ordinary businesslike way in which he gazed upon the scene: 'Yis, I should think there's seventy agait [agoing].' I replied,: 'Dear me! in what an agony of earnestness they all seem!' He answered: 'Ay, they're wrastling like nought.' And, indeed, it was impossible not to recall our Lord's description of the effect of the Baptist's preaching and his own: 'The kingdom of heaven suffereth violence, and the violent take it by force.' One young man I can never forget. He went on wailing piteously: 'I'se willing to "liver up all".'

I listened for the advice of the prayer-leaders to the penitent, but I could hear nothing beyond the continuous heartening of them to an untiring importunity in such words as these: 'Stick tul [to]; ye'll niver hev a better chonce.' In my lonely walk back to [Woodhouse] Grove I pondered deeply the things that I had heard and seen. I could not but feel that the mode of treatment was too mechanical, and therefore far less helpful to the intelligent believing of a contrite soul... For that poor young man, for instance, who writhingly and pantingly reiterated, 'I'se willing to "liver up all"',' surely the obvious counsel was: 'Thank God! and you have nothing to do but to be 'willing to receive all God's goodness waits to give.' Are you willing for that?'... The next morning when, as usual, Mr. Morley[30] asked me how I had sped, and what I thought of the Revival, I told him freely my impressions. He replied: 'The difference between the Revivalism of my early life and that of the present time is just that. Now we have either what Dr. Bunting calls 'unholy haste' in dealing with our penitents, or else we leave them to fight their own way into 'liberty' by mere stress of feeling.'

Benjamin Gregory, *Autobiographical Recollections*, 1903, pp. 232–34

Moving to the Oxford Circuit in 1857, Gregory found Methodism 'in a truly pitiable condition', weakened by recent internal dissention and financial exigency. In his son's words, 'All the influences of an University and Cathedral town were opposed to it and were employed with contemptuous unscrupulousness.' The University was still an exclusively Anglican stronghold.

With the University the one unpardonable sin was attendance at a Nonconformist church. Dog-fighting, all sorts of loose escapades and low habits might be condoned, but the line must be drawn somewhere, and it was drawn – at the Methodist chapel. Nevertheless, 'young men', of course, in mufti, would sneak to hear the preacher of whom tidings had strangely reached them. Rarely, at first, did they venture into the body of the chapel, but they stood in the lobby, listening through the open doors. They were 'proctorised' – vainly. After a while, the scion of a noble house, who had been rescued from a fast life through hearing my father preach, defied the proctor and threatened unpleasant consequences if he were interfered with. One success emboldened others, and a fair sprinkling of graduates and undergraduates could generally be seen in the chapel when my father appeared, specially on a Sunday evening.

When my father had been rather more than a year at Oxford, an invitation, altogether unprecedented in the case of a Nonconformist minister, came to him to lunch with one of the heads of the Colleges and to address a meeting to be held in the afternoon of a branch of the Bible Society with which many University men were connected. The story of the speech he then delivered has often been told me. Beginning on the grave, argumentative line befitting an academic assembly, he rose to exposition and earnest pleading. Then, imagining erroneously, as it afterwards appeared, that the carefully prepared speech was falling flat, my father told racy anecdotes and old Methodist stories, till even the dons forgot their dignity in unrestrainable laughter and furtive wiping of the eyes. He sat down amidst tempestuous cheering. The victory was won. Henceforth gownsmen of Methodist associations dared to attend their own church openly, and some to meet in the Society class.[31]

The revival of Methodism in the villages aroused furious opposition on the part of the neighbouring gentry. Tradesmen were boycotted, tenants received notice to quit their farms,

---

[30] John Morley, Governor of Woodhouse Grove school

[31] Author's footnote: Another incident of that meeting may be mentioned. My father recited some recently published poetry by Richard Chevenix Trench. At the close of the meeting a clergyman came to him, and, shaking his hand warmly, said, to my father's intense astonishment: 'Until I heard those lines from you I had no idea I could write anything half so good.' It was the future Archbishop himself, who, visiting his brother at Islip, had been amongst the audience.

servants were dismissed. Necessarily my father was powerless to stem the torrent of persecution, though the events enabled him to lessen the pressure. The Vicar of Bladon was anxious at least to mitigate the drunkenness and immorality of the evening of the [annual] village feast. He organised an open-air meeting and asked the Methodist to join him. My father was staying at Bladon, and though not directly invited, attended and spoke at the gathering. Some sort of friendship sprang up between himself and the vicar, of which the Methodists felt the benefit. Soon an atrocious act of unfairness gave my father the opportunity he desired. The Duchess of Marlborough was in the habit of presenting gifts and prizes to the children of the National School [and] of inviting them to a treat in Blenheim Park. On the eve of the distribution and gala day she announced that only children attending the Established Church Sunday School would be eligible for the prizes, would be entitled to the presents, or would be allowed to attend the treat. The next day children who had actually won prizes went home without them, and saw them awarded to beaten competitors. My father wrote to the Duke, but no answer was vouchsafed to his letter. A threat to publish the case throughout the United Kingdom obtained more attention, but no real improvement ensued. An interview with the Duke resulted, not as was sometimes stated, in complete surrender, but in most courteous apologies; and a promise, which was kept, that all the children of the National School should stand on exactly the same footing, whatever place of worship they or their parents attended. From that time the Duke adopted a more than tolerant attitude towards Methodism, and his example was not without its influence upon other landlords.

Benjamin Gregory, *Autobiographical Recollections*, 1903, pp. 407–9

Luke H. Tyerman (1820–1889)

Tyerman was a student at Didsbury Theological College for one year early in the governorship of the Rev. John Bowers, 1843–64. At the time of the following incident, the medical effects of smoking were, of course, not known.

The Rev. Luke Tyerman, the biographer of John Wesley, was known, as a student, to be addicted to the use of 'the weed'. This sad fact came to the ears of Mr. Bowers, who was much pained on hearing of it, and decided at once to take steps to stop so pernicious a practice. Thinking that Tyerman might be in his study surreptitiously indulging himself after dinner, he marched down the corridor, calling loudly, 'Tyerman, Tyerman; is Tyerman here? I want Tyerman.' Tyerman, almost caught red-handed, instantly extinguished his pipe, locked the door, put the key in his pocket, seized his coat, hat and stick; pushed up his window, leapt out, and hastily ran round to the students' entrance door. Passing in, he walked leisurely along the corridor with his coat on his arm and his stick in his hand. There he met the Governor returning from his quest. Mr. Bowers had found the study door fastened, but was just early enough to hear an unwonted stir inside, followed by silence. 'Tyerman,' he said, 'I am glad to see that you have been out for a walk. *I feared you were in your study... smoking.*' Tyerman coloured. There was no delusion; only excellent make-believe on Mr. Bowers's side. Each understood the other perfectly. There was no need for confession or reproof. The pipe was abandoned – till later days. The Governor's tact triumphed.

Methodist Recorder, Winter Number, 1906, p. 92

Ebenezer Jenkins (1820–1905)

President of the Conference in 1880, Jenkins was a missionary in India from 1845 to 1863 and then a prominent advocate of overseas missions.

Mr. Simpson also told me of a young minister in India when he was [there]. This young man 'proposed', evidently by letter, to a young lady who lived with her aunt. In due time the young man came to meet the lady – it was where Simpson was. And the lady who came was the aunt! How they had carried on the correspondence I can't say[32] – but he was in a terrible state – and walked the garden all night. Simpson said they had much to do to get him to go on with the marriage. *He married her* & so far as I know she never knew the mistake. He returned to England. The wife died & he married again. His name, Ebenezer Jenkins.

Manuscript reminiscences of the Rev. John Thackray, via the Rev. G. Thackray Eddy

Gervase Smith (1821–1882)

Along with his former schoolfellow, Morley Punshon, Gervase Smith was one of the most eloquent orators of his time.

Perhaps his platform efforts of this period [1861] were the happiest of his life... He made large preparations, but was not hampered by them. He could rest himself and his audience for a moment as he turned aside to some playful local allusion or anecdote, and then resume his course. Not infrequently his friend Morley Punshon was on the same platform with him, and then there was a buoyancy and dash in their addresses as they exulted in their work. We recall one such occasion, Gervase Smith speaking first. The Hill Top Chapel was crowded, intelligence and culture enough present to give impulse, genial sympathy enough to supply warmth. The whole audience was carried away with enthusiasm. Morley Punshon had to follow. Quietly taking up the report from the table, he said, 'Missions have now a history and a literature of their own;' and coolly read the titles of the books, grammars and lexicons on the cover of the report. The audience settled down, adjusted themselves, whispers ran round, and at last Mr. Punshon, with a merry laugh, threw back the report on the table, saying, 'You are in a condition to be spoken to now, and were not five minutes ago. You needed a sedative. You have had enough bark[33] for the present, but if you require another tonic, you shall have it by and by.' We need not describe his glittering rhetoric. For half an hour he spoke quietly, and then using every art at his command for another half-hour, climax following climax, he wrought up the audience once more to the same enthusiastic pitch it had reached when Gervase Smith sat down.

Samuel Lees, 'Historical Sketch', in Alfred Owen Smith, ed., *Rev. Gervase Smith, DD, a Memorial Volume*, 1882, pp. xxvii-xxviii

---

[32] Thackray adds as a note to this: 'Surely the correspondence could not have been carried on long – or he would have found out his mistake. He might have sent a kindly greeting to her aunt – or his lady correspondent might have referred to 'my aunt' or 'my niece' as the case might be.

[33] The bark of the cinchona tree was used to produce quinine, which reduced fever.

George Mather (1821–1888)

George Mather [was] one of my father's colleagues at Highbury. One day he came across three ragged little urchins playing pitch and toss with a few halfpennies in front of our Highbury chapel. 'What are you doing, boys?' he stopped and said. 'I can teach you a much better game than that. Come with me and I will buy you some marbles.' So off they went to a toy shop, then back again to a game of marbles. 'Come here, boys, next Saturday and we will have another game.'

So next Saturday Mather was there down on his knees teaching these ragged little urchins how to play marbles.

'Do you know our mother?' asked one of the ragged little chaps. 'No,' said Mather, 'but I should like to know her.' So off they trudged and, turning into a small street off the Holloway Road, they came to a public house. 'This is where mother lives.' So in Mather and his young friends go. Mother, with her sleeves tucked up to her elbows, was drawing beer at the other side of the bar. 'Mother,' shouted out the lads, 'here is the gent who has been playing marbles with us.'

'I am pleased to see you, sir,' she said. 'What will you have to drink?' and she started to draw some beer.

Nine preachers out of ten, finding themselves in such a position, would probably have censured this woman. No so George Mather. 'No, thank you,' he said, 'but I wonder if you have the kettle boiling? If so, do you think you could give me a cup of tea?' 'Certainly, sir,' she said, her face beaming with pleasure, 'of course I can. It will only take a few minutes to make.'

Two men drinking beer were sitting at a table. 'May I come and sit here,' said Mather carrying his cup of tea to their table. The three little urchins clung to him all the time.

What divine power Mather had. He carried in his breast coat-pocket a list of all his converts to whom he wrote regularly.

R.W. Perks, *Notes for an Autobiography*, 1936, pp. 38–9

Luke Holt Wiseman (1822–1875)

My father always told this story with keen enjoyment. The incident occurred early in his ministry, when he was supplying in a Lincolnshire circuit. In those days the preacher would start off on Monday morning from the circuit town spending a day in each village, and returning to his home again at the end of the week.

On the occasion in question my father arrived either on the Monday or the Tuesday morning in good time at a substantial farmhouse in the village to which he was appointed. The kindly hostess welcomed him heartily, and as soon as he was seated said, 'Now, Mr. Wiseman, we're very glad to see you, and what would you like for dinner?'

'Oh, I will leave that to you,' said my father, 'I'm sure it will be very good, whatever it is.'

'But we should like to give you what you prefer, Sir.'

'No, thank you, I'll eat what is set before me.'

But the good woman would take no denial; he must choose his dinner. Walking to the window of the room my father saw some fine broad beans growing in the garden, and with a sudden inspiration said, 'Let us have beans and bacon.'

The hostess was disappointed, and thought such fare was too plain and ordinary for 'the preacher', but he insisted that she had made him choose, and he would have his choice, and accordingly the beans and bacon were served for dinner.

Next day he was met at the door by his hostess of the next village, with the exclamation, 'Oh, Mr. Wiseman, how do you do? We are glad to see you, and Mrs. ... has sent word over that you are very fond of beans and bacon, so we have got some for dinner.'

The preacher began to think it was possible to have too much even of a good thing, but got through his dinner as well as he could.

On the third day he was detained by some cause or other, and noon had passed when he arrived at the house where he was to stay. But here, also, the hostess was on the look out for him, and the first words he heard were: 'Oh, Mr. Wiseman, we were afraid you were not coming. Mrs. S... sent us word that beans and bacon was your favourite dish. We hadn't any beans in our garden, and we had some trouble getting them, and then we began to fear you would not be in time for dinner.'

By this time the very sight of beans and bacon was nauseating to my father, but he sat down to the table and did the best he could to feign an appetite. I have heard that, having his handkerchief on his knee, he kept the beans near the edge of his plate, and seizing an opportunity stealthily swept most of them into the handkerchief, which went presently into his pocket.

Visiting and conversation took the beans out of his mind for the rest of the afternoon, but his misfortunes were not over. Preaching at night in the village chapel, and growing warm in his discourse, his hand sought the accustomed pocket and the handkerchief, hurriedly snatched forth, scattered its hidden contents over the floor to the astonishment of the rustic congregation.

Probably the comment would be: 'Praicher be main fond o' beans, when he do carry 'em about in his handkercher.'

F. Luke Wiseman in *Methodist Recorder*, Winter Number, 1893 p. 71

Richard Roberts (1823–1909)

Roberts was elected President of the 1885 Conference, the first Welsh-speaking minister to hold the office.

There is an amusing story told about Richard Roberts and the Presidency of the Conference. In those days the President was not nominated, as he is today, the year before taking office; so it was not uncommon for two, three or even four expectant Presidents to go to the Conference town, uncertain which of them would be elected to the office, and each with a Presidential speech in his pocket. Richard Roberts was one of these; but he went a step further. He decided that he ought to purchase and take with him to Leeds a suitable 'Presidential Hat'. So, after conferring with his wife, being in London he went to a famous Methodist hatters in Lime Street. I think that these excellent men have since become Anglicans – why, I don't know. He asked them to supply him with a hat suitable for the President of the Wesleyan Conference. The hatters said that they had never been asked previously for such a hat, but that they thought probably an Archdeacon's hat would be the nearest thing they could suggest.

So Roberts chose the hat and took it home. Now an Archdeacon's hat has a very broad rim, held up to the top of the hat by strings on each side. Looking at himself in the glass the expectant President was not satisfied by the look of the hat. His wife suggested that they should cut the strings on both sides. This they did; but the effect was that the two broad rims flopped down on each side, completely hiding the expectant President's face. Notwithstanding these difficulties, however, he took the hat to the Conference, but three or four years had to elapse before he was elected President. Whether he wore the hat I never heard.

On a later occasion Richard Roberts gave the Conference some trouble about his dress. When stationed at Lambeth, I think it was, he appeared in the pulpit in a long black Geneva gown. The trustees complained, but he was obdurate, and a complaint was made against him at the Conference. Matters were compromised by his cutting off the lower portions of the gown and turning it into a short jacket.

R.W. Perks, *Notes for an Autobiography* , 1936, pp. 26–8

W. Morley Punshon (1824–1881)

Punshon and Mark Guy Pearse were two outstanding orators of 19th and early 20th century Methodism. Pearse recalls a sermon preached in 1865.

Yesterday I went to hear Mr Punshon. He preached a *grand* sermon, but to me 'twas like a man going along a road fill'd with costliest apples of gold, or anything you like that comes tumbling down by him, and he stoops to pick up one, when another drops; he runs to it, and then comes another; he leaves the former for that one, and is drawn off by another, till he gets to the end of the road, and, unable to go back, finds he hasn't got one of the prizes, and only remembers their beauty. I couldn't send you now a *single* idea of his sermon perfectly, yet I listen'd most attentively, and can usually carry away the greater part of a sermon that interests me.

Mrs George Unwin & John Telford, *Mark Guy Pearse: Preacher, Author, Artist*, 1930, p. 37

Punshon's first circuit appointment was to Whitehaven, where his Superintendent was the Rev. William Huddlestone, who shared the puritanical disapproval of novel-reading then widespread in evangelical circles. Huddlestone's daughter, the future romantic novelist Amelia Barr, recalled Punshon as a young man new to the ministry.

He came a great deal to our home, and used to recite for our entertainment fine examples of prose and poetry from the great writers. As long as John [her brother] was able to bear it, he frequently read aloud, and I considered him an extraordinarily clever man. And, if one looked only at his fine eyes and forehead, he was also a very handsome man. I am sure all the religious young women in Whitehaven thought so, and he was much praised and courted, the chapel being crowded whenever he preached...

I read a great deal, and kept up the practice of my music and drawing. There was a good public library, and there was my father's library, and the public one suited me best now; for I wanted Scott, Dickens and Thackeray... One day Mr. Punshon was sitting in our parlour when I came in with my hands full of books. He looked at them and asked, 'Does your father know, Amelia?' I answered, 'No, but Mother does. She says it is all right. We do not trouble Father about little things. He is not very well lately.'

'Amelia,' he continues, 'I want some books out of the library, but I do not like to go for them.'

'Novels?' I asked.

Yes,' he answered.

'I will get them for you. I am sorry for people who want novels, and do not feel able to ask for them.'

He said something about his position, and my father not liking him to go to a public library for novels, and I understood the situation.

Amelia Barr, *All the Days of my Life*, 1913, pp. 62–3

Punshon was appointed in 1858 to accompany the President to Scotland to aid the missionary cause.

His eloquent ministry and brilliant platform advocacy were intensely enjoyed by the Scottish folk. A few friends were invited to dine with him, among whom was a very shrewd Scot. Dr. Punshon's hostess invited him to take fruit pastry, which he declined. The dessert was served, and Punshon again declined to take any. The lady was surprised and said, 'Do you not take any fruit?' 'Very seldom indeed,' said Dr. Punshon.

By this time the attention of the table was drawn by the conversation – all listening with surprise.

'Won't you take an apple?'

'No, thank you; I don't eat apples!'

The shrewd Scotsman, who was deeply interested, exclaimed, 'Then ye sho'd ha' ben in Paradis' and ther' wad'na ha' ben a Fa'.'

William Allen in *Methodist Recorder*, Winter Number, 1893, p. 90

Peter Mackenzie (1824–1895)

Peter Mackenzie was one of the most colourful personalities, as well as one of the most popular preachers, of nineteenth-century Wesleyanism. His total dedication to his calling was evident from his early days as a local preacher in the Durham Circuit.

Mackenzie's contemporaries among the local preachers speak of him as having a propensity to remain to a late hour when out on the Sabbath fulfilling an appointment. He was exceedingly sociable, and the friends who entertained him delighted in his bright and genial society, and were eager to prolong his visits. On one occasion, when appointed to Coxhoe, eight miles distant [from Haswell], he agreed to meet the two brothers Phalp, who were, one at Kelloe and the other at Quarrington Hill, places from six to seven and a half miles away from Haswell in the same direction. The arrangement was that Peter was to proceed to Kelloe to supper, after which he and William would move on to Quarrington Hill for George, who was much younger and just beginning to preach. Losing all sense of time in a prayer meeting that seemed to have no end, and that was succeeded by singing and talk and cheery hospitality in the house of one of the Coxhoe friends, Mackenzie did not reach Kelloe, where his companion had waited two hours, until about ten o'clock. Turning their faces homeward, they called at Quarrington Hill and satisfied the younger brother that he was not left behind. All three then proceeded to Thornley, where it suddenly occurred to Mackenzie that someone at Kelloe had spoken of a new prayer-meeting tune, which Michael Watson rejoiced in the knowledge of. Michael Watson was another friend, musical in his tastes, who resided at Thornley, and, despite all protest, Mackenzie insisted on proceeding to his house. It was eleven o'clock when the trio arrived at the door, and all was closed for the night. In response to a thrice-repeated knock, the inquiry came, 'Who is there?' 'Glory! Hallelujah!' shouted the disturber. 'Get up, lass!' cried Watson in great glee to his wife. 'There's Peter at the door.' The door was speedily opened, coffee prepared, and the interview prolonged until the new revival tune was mastered.

Thornley was not left behind until midnight, and when they arrived back at Haswell, the caller (a man employed to waken the boys and men in the early morning) had already entered on his rounds and was breaking the stillness with his unwelcome clatter and pitiless cry of 'Get up, lad! call the lads up!' It was Mackenzie's turn to begin labour at this hour, so, without a moment's rest, after preaching probably three times and walking sixteen miles, he had to lay aside his Sunday dress, clothe himself in working garb, and proceed literally from the pulpit to the mine. The same unpalatable portion awaited his companions.

About the middle of the shift, that is, about four in the morning, the two brothers had to pass the spot where Mackenzie was employed. He was hard at work, swinging his pick with a vigour that seemed to have in it no trace of the toil of the previous day. They stood for a few moments in quiet admiration, then one of them called, 'How do you feel now, Peter? He threw down his pick and, coming towards them, said, 'Ah, lads, this won't do. We must get home sooner. She's hard. I have hardly strength to knock her down.'

Joseph Dawson, Peter Mackenzie, his life and labours, 1896, pp. 73–5

Both Thomas Burt and Peter Mackenzie began their working life in the pit.

While at Haswell, there worked in the pit beside me a young man who afterwards became famous as a Wesleyan Methodist preacher. Peter Mackenzie was, I should say, ten or twelve years my senior. He was a putter[34] at the flat where I was a trapper-boy. Well do I remember

---

[34] Another term for a 'barrowman', whose job was to remove the loose coal from the coalface to the pitshaft.

him, for he was even then stamped with a character and an individuality all his own. He was a strapping, active fellow, with great strength of will and limb, and was of Scottish accent. As yet he had not joined the Methodists; and, I believe, in after years, he was wont to describe himself as a sinner of the deepest dye before his conversion. The worst I remember of him is that he indulged in great freedom of expletives. Peter never did anything by halves. He swearing was certainly extraordinary, even among the Haswell putters, for its pith and pungency. All the putters swore, according to their respective capacities. When I first came across the phrase, 'he swore like a trooper,' I suggested to my father that 'trooper' must surely be a misprint for 'putter'. Peter Mackenzie was very like his fellow-putters, only he excelled them in impressiveness of diction. Swearing is a bad, vulgar, vicious practice, but it is not inconsistent with good and even noble qualities. Of these noble qualities Peter Mackenzie always had great store. He was truthful, honest, warm-hearted, generous, ever gentle and kindly in his ways. With the smaller boys he was a great favourite, ready always to give them a cheerful word and a helping hand. Of Peter Mackenzie I have nothing but pleasant and kindly memories.

I remember an incident connected with Mr. Mackenzie and my father which, though small in itself, did credit to both the Peters. When Peter Mackenzie commenced to hew coals he was sent for a few days to work with my father. On the pay day the whole of the money earned was paid to my father, to be divided by him. I was sent to Haswell Lane, where Peter then lived, with his share of the money. On counting it, Peter said there was a mistake: my father had sent too much. He had divided the money equally, and as he, Mackenzie, was only a learner, he should have received less than a skilled workman like my father. He commanded me, therefore, to take back part of the money, which he handed me. 'No,' said I, 'my father won't have it. I heard him say that you were stronger than he, and a good willing worker; that you had done your full share of the work, and were entitled to half the money.'

Many years elapsed before I again met Mr. Mackenzie. He had become eminent and beloved as a Methodist preacher, and I had been returned as M.P. for Morpeth. Mr. Mackenzie was to lecture on some subject – temperance, I think – in Bewick Street Chapel, Newcastle upon Tyne, and I was asked to be chairman. At the conclusion of the lecture, Mr. Mackenzie moved a vote of thanks to the chairman, remarking, after some friendly words, that we had both been pit-lads; had both become, in different spheres, public men; but, strangely enough, this was the first occasion on which we had met.

In responding to the vote of thanks, I quietly corrected the mistake, observing that he and my father had worked together at Haswell pit, and that I was a trapper-boy there when he was a putter. The scene that followed was dramatic. When I was still speaking, Mr. Mackenzie, with characteristic warm-heartedness and impulsiveness, sprang to his feet, threw his arms around me, literally hugging me to his heart, at the same time crying out: 'God bless the lad! Are you the son of Peter Burt? He was one of the best men I ever knew.'

Thomas Burt, *Pitman and Privy Councillor: an autobiography*, 1924, pp. 60–61

Mackenzie was stationed in the Monmouth Circuit from 1860 to 1862.

The first time I saw and heard Mr. Mackenzie was at our village chapel, five miles out from Monmouth and about ten miles from Coleford… When [he] came out again to preach in the same little chapel, his fame had gone abroad and the people crowded to the afternoon service so much that the building was packed from end to end. My father, in his desire to make room for others, had vacated his seat time after time, and now only the pulpit stairs seemed unoccupied. These, one after another, were filled, until, as a last resource and to make room for just one more, my father took refuge in the pulpit, little thinking of the penalty to be paid soon for such an exaltation. Mr. Mackenzie got well into his subject and made his sermon glow with life and interest as he described poor sick ones coming to an earthly physician, surrounded with bottles of medicine and ointments for all kinds of maladies. He had all these various bottles in full array on the pulpit around him. Suddenly he swept them away with both hands right and left as he introduced the Heavenly Healer, saying, 'Away with your quack nostrums! Away with them!' My father at his elbow was forgotten and he, poor dear man, was in the third heaven of delight as he drank in the blessed gospel of Jesus Christ, when all at once the preacher's powerful hand in its backward swing swept like a sledge-hammer into his face, utterly blinding him for the moment, and making the sparks fly from his eyes like fireworks, and leaving him with a never-to-be-forgotten remembrance of that immortal sermon. Mr. Mackenzie, with his usual native tenderness, turned quickly round, exclaiming sorrowfully, 'O my dear brother, I hope I have not hurt you! I am so sorry!' It was certainly most instructive to see my father's attitude of distance and caution towards the preacher for the rest of the evening.

Isaiah Gadd in Joseph Dawson, *Peter Mackenzie, his life and labours*, 1896, pp. 143–45

The following somewhat macabre incident took place during Mackenzie's ministry in the Wesley Circuit, Leeds 1877–1880 and illustrates his interest in the many facets of human nature. William Marwood was the Methodist hangman who invented the 'long drop' as a more humane method of execution.

I called to see Mr. Mackenzie shortly after a noted malefactor had been executed at Armley gaol. He said, 'Who do you think I've had here?' 'Nay,' I replied, 'how can I tell?' 'Marwood,' he whispered. 'I met him some time ago when I was out lecturing, and he promised to call and see me if he came into these parts. Yes, and he brought his bag with him, and the *rope* was in it. I got him to show it me, and I put my neck through the noose, but' - and he shook himself as he spoke - 'it felt horribly cold and slippery, and I soon had it off again.'

Rev. Samuel R. Williams, in Joseph Dawson, *Peter Mackenzie, his life and labours*, 1896, pp. 201–2

Mackenzie's memory for faces, names and other details was proverbial.

Some time during 1892 or the following year, Mr. Mackenzie preached and lectured in the Town Hall, Pateley Bridge in aid of the Mechanics' Institute. At the close of the afternoon service, I was standing in the vestibule in company with Mr. Foster, a gentleman of Middlesmoor and one of the leading Methodists there. We were watching Mr. Mackenzie as he came down the hall, shaking hands with dozens of people who crowded round him, and every now and then recognizing a friend. Mr. Foster said to one or two of us, 'I wonder if Peter will know me. About nineteen or twenty years ago, he came to lecture for us, and I met him at the station and drove him to Middlesmoor, and I don't think he has seen me since. I'll try him.'

On came Peter, still shaking hands. At last he caught sight of our friend. After a good look he said, 'I ought to know you.' Then, lifting his hand, 'Now, don't tell me. Wait a minute. You live up the dale?'

'Yes.'

'Do they call it Middlesmoor?'

'Yes.'

'You came to meet me when I was going there to preach?'

'Yes.'

'You drove an old white mare?'

'Yes.'

'You live on the top of the hill?'

'Yes.'

'Let me see – your name is Foster?'

'Yes.'

'How long is that ago?'

'About twenty years.'

'And I have not met you since?'

'No.'

> The Rev. John E. Winter, in Joseph Dawson, *Peter Mackenzie, his life and labours*, 1896, pp. 286–87

Samuel Coley (1825–1880)

Coley was theological tutor at Headingley College from 1873 to 1879.

Memories of Samuel Coley were also revived, notably the strange lapse of memory which he once recorded in the classroom as having happened to him during the delivery of a sermon at Conference time. A brother being obliged to catch a certain train in order to get home, got up and left the chapel in the middle of the discourse, and, as the tutor humorously put it, 'walked off with every thought which I had in my head. My mind,' he continued, 'was a perfect blank. I could not even remember what I had been saying.'

Then came the remarkable statement which even to this day we cannot consider without astonishment.

'Strange as the experience was I do not believe that my pulse beat one faster in the minute. *I was perfectly calm*. My mind was stayed upon God, and I believed that all would soon come right. I told the congregation of my predicament, and gave out a hymn. My mind continued a blank until the fourth verse was being sung, and then all my thoughts came back, and I went on and finished the sermon.'

Rev. W. Scott Page in *Methodist Recorder*, Winter Number, 1903, p. 100

Featherstone Kellett (1829–1906)

A few years later, in 1855, my father had an interview with a much more renowned criminal. He was travelling to Doncaster and in the carriage, going to the races, were two or three young fellows who looked like undergraduates, and a benevolent, blue-eyed, rather fat, comfortable gentleman, somewhat horsy in appearance, but pleasant and expansive in manner. Everyone took to him. The conversation got on to betting, and the gentleman told some anecdotes of his luck and ill-luck in wagers. My father was not then the man to let such an opportunity slip. He spoke strongly against all wagers.

'Look here,' said the gentleman, 'that won't do, you know. I have had bets with Lord Derby, Lord George Bentinck and Lord Hartington, all of whom I know well. You can't say that such men are all mistaken and wicked.'

My father, unmoved by this roll of noble names, held to his opinion and gave some of the ordinary arguments against betting – arguments obviously quite new to his interlocutor. Finally he observed that it often led to crime. At this the man struck his hand across his brow and said hurriedly, 'Yes, yes; there's something in that. It has cost me a lot. I must give it up.'

At this point the train entered Doncaster; the gentleman shook hands most kindly and effusively with my father and expressed a wish that they might meet again. Within a few weeks the whole country was ringing with the news of the murder of Cook by William Palmer of Rugeley, a crime which, as everyone knows, was committed to avoid paying betting debts. Soon the likenesses of the accused man were in all the papers and my father recognised, beyond a doubt, in those likenesses the portrait of his pleasant and garrulous friend of the railway train.

E.E. Kellett in *Methodist Recorder*, Winter Number, 1906, p. 67

George Warner (1829–1899)

Warner entered the Primitive Methodist ministry in 1851 and soon gained a reputation for his powerful evangelical methods, illustrated by the following incidents related by a Mr. Bird of Doncaster, to whom Warner was at that time unknown by sight.

'[On the way from Doncaster to the 1874 Conference in Hull] when we arrived at Staddlethorpe Junction we waited for the down train to take up passengers for Hull. When the train arrived and the passengers were bustling about seeking for seats, there came a gentleman who did not hurry or bustle, but moved as if he had some business to do and knew how to do it. He came up to the compartment where I was sitting and which was nearly full of corn merchants and their clerks on their way to the Hull Corn Market. A big face under a big hat was pushed through the open window. The next moment the door opened, and in came the owner of the big face and hat. He completely filled the doorway as he stood looking at the lot of us as if taking stock. He then spoke in a voice and manner that startled us. 'Gentlemen,' he said, 'I wonder whether you are all converted?' All looked up from their morning papers, and looked one at another somewhat confused, their looks seeming to ask, 'What is going to happen next?' No one answered the question for some moments. At last I ventured to say, 'I don't know, sir, but I know I am.' 'Then pray, brother,' said the strange gentleman.' This was a greater task than Mr. Bird anticipated when he answered the question as to his conversion. He had no idea who the gentleman was until the following Sunday, when he went to the Jubilee Chapel to a Love-feast, which was to be conducted by Mr. Warner. When Mr. Warner entered the rostrum, Brother Bird recognised him as the gentleman who had set him to pray at a time and in a place where he did not much enjoy it. This was by no means an uncommon incident of the kind; for Mr. Warner often contrived, when travelling in trains, to have little meetings for prayer.

Mr. Bird also gave us the following incident at the same time as he gave us the above. He was entering a train at Peterborough; in the compartment were two gentlemen. One of them remarked: 'You had better go a little lower down, and you will find two other gentlemen in a compartment who will give you a very warm reception' This excited Mr. Bird's curiosity, and he went down to see the gentlemen who would give him the 'warm reception'. When he arrived at the compartment he found George Warner and Peter Mackenzie, who were having a most glorious time together. These two brothers were likely to give anyone a 'warm reception'.'

J. Stephenson, *The Man of Faith: or the Life and Work of the Rev. G. Warner*, 1902, pp. 151–2

Towards the end of his life Warner was persuaded to visit Australia, to recuperate from the effects of overwork on his health. The following paranormal experience, which occurred while he was staying in Hobart, Tasmania, can be paralleled in the lives of a number of others.

He had some very interesting, and some rather strange, experiences in that distant part of the globe; one very remarkable. The Rev. W. Hazell[35], a superannuated minister, residing at Bath, in England, was a very warm friend of Mr. Warner's, and died while Mr. Warner was in Australia. He came down in the morning, and told the friends where he was staying that his friend, W. Hazell, was dead; and that he had seen him that night in his bedroom. In due time the intelligence of Mr. Hazell's death came to hand, when it was found that he died at the time Mr. Warner declared he saw him. Mr. Warner had no idea of Mr. Hazell's illness, nor had he been in his mind.

Ibid., pp. 263–4

Samuel Danks Waddy (1830–1902)

This was one member of the ministerial Waddy dynasty who did not go into the ministry, but had a distinguished legal career. Although he had a ready wit, as a local preacher he did not approve of levity in the pulpit.

[Like his father, Samuel Dousland Waddy] the younger Samuel conducted services with a seriousness which many mistook for undue gravity. It is all the more pity, therefore, that whenever his name was mentioned within half a century of his death, the legal profession

---

[35] William Hazell, born at Ramsbury in 1818, died on 14 November 1887.

would trot out a chestnut which they thought was funny, but which wounded him deeply. I have seen it repeated in newspapers and even in the reminiscences of a fellow barrister. The yarn was that on one occasion when he was presiding at the Courts and conducting the services at the local Wesleyan chapel, Lockwood and several other barristers turned up for a joke and sat in the front pew. They fled when Waddy announced, 'Brother Lockwood will lead us in prayer!' This would have been fully in keeping with his impetuosity and his sense of mischief, but definitely not with his sense of the dignity of worship. When my father, his nephew, asked him about it, he replied, 'No, it is not true: I would never trifle with public worship in that manner.'... But I have met persons who say that they were told it by someone present: of such stuff are rumours made! ... My father suggested once that if a rumour which spreads around the world must have an element of truth in it, it could possibly be that during the week Lockwood had said, 'I see that you are preaching on Sunday; we are coming,' though with no intention of doing so, just leg-pulling. To which the quick-witted imp replied, 'If you do, I will call on you to pray.'

J.L. Waddy, *The Waddy Family*, 1982, pp. 91–2

In the early days of the 1849 agitation, perhaps during the Sheffield Conference, when quite a youth, he accompanied a party of prominent Wesleyans on a picnic to one of the pretty spots in the Peak. At the same place there were a number of the 'Reformers'. As young Waddy looked solemnly, perhaps rather insolently, at them, one of them said, 'What is young Waddy thinking about?' To which the youth replied, with a wave of the hand towards the beautiful view and then to the 'Reformers', 'Of the lines of the poet:

Where every prospect pleases,
   And only man is vile'.

'Exquisite, Mr. Samuel, exquisite!' said the Rev. William L. Thornton, with one of his historic bows and grimaces.

C.H. Kelly, *Memories*, 1910, pp. 102–3

What a humorist and son of a humorist was S.D. Waddy! I once heard him deliver a singularly felicitous chairman's speech. The Rev. J. Ossian Davies was to lecture, and S.D. Waddy was chairman. He spoke thus: 'Ladies and gentlemen, I am given to understand that Mr. Ossian Davies is a model lecturer. I beg to announce that I am a model chairman, and I will tell you why: I never deliver a speech when presiding at a lecture. If a chairman speaks on the subject of the lecture, it is an impertinence. If he speaks on what is not the subject of the lecture, it is an irrelevancy. Ladies and Gentlemen! The lecturer!'

Dinsdale T. Young, *Stars of Retrospect*, 1920, pp. 226–7

Henry Hartley Fowler (1830–1910)

As Lord Wolverhampton, Fowler was the first Methodist to sit in the House of Lords. He was a latter-day 'Church Methodist', who built and financed Trinity Chapel, Wolverhampton and treated it as virtually a 'proprietary chapel'.

There my father insisted on a full liturgical [morning] service, very rare in those days in Methodist chapels. There he allowed no tampering with the Prayer-book, and only one very short extempore prayer in the Sunday morning service. There he supervised the hymns, and approved the tunes, though sublimely incapable of giving an opinion on the latter.

There he ruled even the atmosphere, and woe to the chapel-keeper who failed to keep the large thermometer hung in his hindmost pew up to the prescribed 60º. 'One day,' so Methodist tradition runs, 'the chapel felt like an ice-house and the thermometer when fetched registered 62º. 'Show me exactly where you placed it,' asked Mr. Fowler promptly. The man took him to the hot-water pipe, whereon in despair he had laid it. Another Sunday morning the same offending chapel-keeper fetched the bread for the Communion Service from a nearby shop. 'You bought the bread for sacramental purposes on a Sunday?' exclaimed Mr. Fowler furiously. 'Please, sir, I did not pay for it,' pleaded the culprit. 'So much the worse!' was the thunderous answer.'

Strong man though he was, he had a morbid dread of suffering and death, and greatly disliked sermons which dealt with such topics. He once wisely answered the minister thus, after such a sermon:

'I am coming to hear you on Sunday if you will not preach horrors!'

'If you knew how often we ministers address men for the last time you would not wonder that we warn them.'

'Well, I will take you on your own ground. Suppose you were seeing a dying man, and it was your last opportunity, would you preach the terrors, or the mercy and love of God?'

'The love of God, certainly!'

'Then preach *that*, it is what all men need.'

> Edith H. Fowler, *The Life of Henry Hartley Fowler, First Viscount Wolverhampton, GCSI*, 1912, pp. 535–6, 539

Perhaps one of the most amusing of his domestic characteristics was his authority; at least we, his loyal subjects, found it so. His language was always more forceful than the feeling it expressed; and he was constantly bringing to the front his verbal artillery to slay the most insignificant butterflies. Thus strangers were sometimes frightened of him; but we, who knew him, never were. His orders in the home were always stern and peremptory; but no one was more surprised than he was when they were obeyed! One morning, not long before my sister's wedding, when presents came pouring in apace, he laid down the law most emphatically that no parcels were to be opened until after breakfast; indeed, the penalty was to be almost capital if they were. For some unknown reason my sister, contrary to her custom, implicitly obeyed him, and sat down at once to breakfast, leaving all her parcels unopened; when shortly a pitiful appeal was heard from my father: 'What! am I not to be allowed to see any of your presents before I leave the table? What have I done that everything should be kept secret from me?' He always greatly enjoyed the after-telling of this story against himself.

As an instance of the disproportionate strength of his language, once – on detecting my sister in a slight exaggeration – he told her that she was 'the most inaccurate woman the Almighty had ever made'. She cheerfully replied that she was glad to be a masterpiece in any department of creation.

With servants he was just the same; and I remember my mother's maid once saying to her about a new butler: 'He is getting on much better, my lady; you see, he is learning not to take any notice of what Sir Henry says.'

On another occasion my father's indignation was aroused (and justly so) by coming into his library one night after dinner to find our old nurse (who had been with us from our babyhood) sitting in his favourite chair and reading his *Times*. After hearing him express himself with his usual volubility upon the liberty she had taken, she said: 'You are quite right, Sir Henry; I ought to have come in earlier, and then I could have finished the papers without being disturbed.'

Edith H. Fowler, *op. cit.,* p. 603

My father was a singularly guileless man. It was amazing that he could have lived so long and yet learned so little about the seamy side of life...

One day my sister and I were spectators of a very thrilling scene in Kensington Gardens. A beautifully dressed woman met a smart-looking man, and they were evidently in deep waters. The woman sat down in a chair and began to weep bitterly, while the man, with wild anguish, knelt at her feet and literally covered the hem of her dress with kisses. They were utterly oblivious to onlookers; indeed, a small butcher's boy stood close to them open-mouthed, and they took not the slightest notice of him. Once or twice the lady rose from her chair as if to walk away, and the man drew her back with passionate caresses. It was a most unusual occurrence. When we got home we recounted the incident to my father. 'Dear me! It must have been his wife,' was his exquisite comment. And he had no idea that he was being funny.

It is worthy of note that my father read a certain novel, which had obtained widespread notoriety by its suggestiveness, from beginning to end without detecting one single innuendo. He thought it a very nice story, and recommended it cheerfully to several girls.

Edith H. Fowler, *op. cit.,* p. 605

John Adams-Acton (1830–1910)

The statue of John Wesley which still dominates the forecourt of Wesley's Chapel, London was unveiled by the President of the Conference, Dr. W.F. Moulton, on 2nd March 1891, the one hundredth anniversary of Wesley's death. But the commemoration was somewhat hastily planned and the event came near to a moment of disaster. Adams-Acton's biographer drew extensively on the records of the sculptor's wife which, though sometimes suspect over details, were often revealing.

Adams-Acton was still known to many as 'the Wesleyan sculptor', somewhat incongruously, since his fame was world-wide and his portraits had included men of every nationality and of every creed. But a never-ending series of prominent Ministers had continued to come to him for their busts destined to adorn the Chapel in City Road; and when it was decided to place a statue of Wesley himself over the entrance of the Chapel, to be erected on an anniversary of the birth of the great divine, Adams-Acton was unanimously nominated as the only sculptor qualified to undertake this important work.

Nevertheless he considered that he had been unfairly treated in regard to this commission, for the time allotted for its completion was totally inadequate. One month only was allowed for him to design, elaborate and perfect a colossal figure intended to stand for all time. Yet characteristically, he determined to make a desperate attempt to achieve the impossible.

'The instant he received the commission,' his wife relates, 'he tore off his coat and began frantically manipulating lumps of clay in preparation for his task.' Subsequently he worked with feverish, tireless energy. She describes how visitors came and went, how ministers arrived to inspect or criticise the progress of his labours, but he ignored them persistently, absorbed in his craft. Then, as the date of the ceremony drew near, disquieting letters began to pour in. The bronze-founders wrote that they feared they could not get the statue cast by the required time, as they had not yet received the clay model. Wesleyan Ministers wrote desperately that all arrangements had been made for the great day, and that a Member of Parliament was coming to unveil the memorial; then more worried Ministers began to arrive at Sunnyside to discuss the situation. 'And,' she remarks, 'all seemed filled with the sentiment of the Irishman, who said, 'I don't know who is to blame, but someone ought to be killed!'

At length the day came when the plaster workers finally took possession of the soft clay statue, but even then, amidst the ensuing debris, the sculptor continued his grim struggle against time; he was blowing plaster into the cavities and corners, and shouting instructions to his men, while the onlookers stood aghast at what they believed to be the futile nature of his attempt. But when the mess had been cleared away, and the fine statue shone out in spotless whiteness, he summoned the bronze-founders and ordered them to tint it till in due course it looked like a bronze figure. Then at last, to the worried Ministers, he announced imperturbably:

'I knew that the work could not be completed in the inadequate time allotted, so I arranged a plan which I think will meet the difficulty. The plaster model now looks like a bronze. We will take it to the Chapel and erect it temporarily. The fact that it is not the finished article must be kept a dead secret. After the unveiling it must remain covered up till the real bronze is ready to replace it – otherwise some mischievous small boy will be throwing stones at it and break off a piece; after which it would be impossible ever to persuade the subscribers that they have got a real bronze, even when the real one is erected.'

The Ministers had no alternative but to agree to his suggestion, so the plaster model went down to the City Road and was erected, clothed and unveiled with great ceremony; while only one small hitch occurred. At the moment of unveiling, a fold of the hanging drapery caught on the figure, and a workman on a ladder ran up to release it, while the little high piping voice of the sculptor's boy Lionel rang out clearly – 'Is that the Member of Parliament?' There followed one awful moment when the sculptor's heart stood still as he thought, *That man will wrench the plaster arm off with his tugging!* But all went well, and when the real Member stepped forward with gracious and eulogistic phrases to announce the unveiling, the supposed bronze statue stood out fresh and beautiful before an enthusiastic crowd. In due time the real bronze was brought secretly and substituted for the plaster figure; and none save the initiated ever knew the pious fraud by which Wesley's portrait reached its destination at the appointed date.

A.M.W. Stirling, *Victorian Sidelights*, 1954, pp. 254–6)

Charles H. Kelly (1833–1911)

Kelly's daughter Blanche died in 1872 at the age of 6.

At that time I read my own Obituary. I had spoken at a missionary meeting in the Manchester District a few nights before I was summoned to return home at once, as our darling little girl was dying. Mr Clough, of Northwich, wrote to his friend, who was Superintendent of the circuit in which the first of these meetings was held, and said, 'You will be sorry to hear that Mr Kelly, who was at your meeting on Friday last, has been called home suddenly by death.'

This dear old parson, without waiting to inquire, supposing that I had been called home to heaven, furnished quite an interesting Obituary to the local paper. I was permitted to see myself as others saw me.

> Charles H. Kelly, *Memories*, 1910, p. 20

Caroline M. Wiseman (1834–1912)

The youngest daughter of the Shum family of Bath became the second wife of Luke H. Wiseman and during her long widowhood played a leading part in the development of the Ladies Auxiliary, which later became Women's Work.

'Carrie' was the youngest of their large family, the darling of their old age and the pet and plaything of the elder brothers and sisters. Her father could hardly bear her out of his sight, and in return she almost worshipped him. She was a very pretty child, high-spirited, eager and loving, all storm and sunshine, and so often in scrapes through her excitable, passionate nature, that she despaired of ever being good. But she was greatly helped by a young minister named Samuel Coley. He had a happy way of talking to children about their Heavenly Father, and to him she confided her trouble. She did so want to be good, she told him, and yet was so often naughty that she knew God must be angry with her. His answer, though a very simple illustration, came to her as a revelation and filled her with new hope.

'Suppose,' he said, 'that your father asked for a glass of water and you were in such a hurry to get it for him that you tumbled down and spilled the water and broke the glass; would he be angry with you?'

'Oh, no, no! He would know I had wanted to please him and be sorry for my disappointment. He would just pick me up and comfort me.'

Then and there she grasped the idea that she could always count on the sympathy of her Father-God, and it brought her lasting comfort. To the end of her days, when disappointed with herself and smarting under a sense of failure, she would say with a sigh of relief, 'Well, at any rate, God knows I *wanted* to please Him.' But the sense of sin never left her, and her favourite description of heaven was:

> There we shall see his face,
>   And *never, never* sin.

Whenever she quoted it, her face shone...

When still a young woman living at home, she worked as a volunteer in a ragged school.

Out of her Ragged School experiences grew her rescue work, begun at such an early age that it is a wonder she won her parents' consent; especially as the girls of her time were not supposed to know that any need for it existed. Perhaps a perilous adventure of her own had something to do with this early start. It happened in Paris when she was on her way to Germany to join the two friends who had preceded her there. The lady who should have met her and helped her to change stations failed to appear, and as she stood on the platform wondering what to do, a woman came up, who spoke very kindly and offered to befriend her. Nothing doubting, she gladly accepted her escort, and they were just leaving the station when an unknown lady noticed the beautiful English girl and saw that her companion was a woman of bad character. She at once stopped them and took charge of the girl herself, so saving her from an unspeakable fate. In telling this story in after years, Mrs. Wiseman said, 'I was a rescue case, if ever there was one.'...

I once told her about an old church I had just seen which had a leper squint, through which in bygone days lepers used to watch the communion service. I remarked how sad it would be to join in it, under the very eyes of these outcasts – 'Ah, but I shouldn't be there,' she said in a flash, '*I should be outside with the lepers.*'...

The mere thought of a little child suffering would fill her eyes with tears, and I well remember the accent of distress with which she told me of a letter just received from India on the eve of a dreadful famine. It described the children coming to school too faint with hunger to attend to their lessons. She seemed to *see* them sitting limp and wasted before their pitying teacher, and she made me see them too. Something must be done, but what? That night, like Hezekiah, she 'spread the letter before the Lord', and as she prayed an inward voice said to her, 'Get up and write.' Her writing things had all been put away for the night, but rising from her knees she got them out again and then stood wondering what she had to do next. Then in a flash all became clear. She would write a letter to the *Methodist Recorder.* It was near Christmas and she would tell of a Christmas stocking hung up at the Mission House, not for toys and sweets such as happy English children were looking for, but for money to buy food for famine-stricken children in India. That letter went by the midnight post, and when we were next at the Mission House she hung a big grey stocking in the packing-room and awaited results. Money came pouring in, in hundreds of small sums with lovely letters from little children and poor folk, some of them hardly able to write, and in the end the Famine Fund realised over £1800.

Her success in getting money for the work was due partly to a magnetic personality, but still more to prayer offered with a faith strengthened by much experience... Once she undertook to collect £1000 for a special purpose before the end of the year; and when the last day came, she was still £20 short. As the evening drew to a close someone said to her, 'You surely don't expect that money now?' 'Yes I do – *and there it is*,' she added, as the postman's knock was heard; nor was she disappointed, for one of the letters he brought contained a cheque for £20...

Mrs. Wiseman was a wonderful help in times of illness, for she was a born nurse, knowing exactly what to say and do in a sick-room, and though living in a constant rush would enter it as calmly and quietly as if she had nothing to think about but the patient... On one occasion she had promised a little grandson whom she dearly loved to be with him during an operation. When the time came, the doctors begged her to leave, reminding her that when he was under the anaesthetic he could not know whether she was there or not. 'I promised him,' was her only answer, and nothing could make her stir from his side. The experience taxed her endurance to the utmost and she came straight from it to her Thursday afternoon class looking as white as a sheet and much shaken. 'But,' she said, 'I would not have broken my promise to that child for worlds. His first words on coming round were, 'Are you there, grannie?' and I should never have forgiven myself if I had not been there to answer him.'

Anna M. Hellier, Just Nothing: memories of Caroline M. Wiseman and her work, 1925, pp. 8–9, 16–17, 18, 24–26, 34–35

Thomas Burt (1837–1922)

Burt rose from being a pitboy in a Durham coalmine to become an MP and a Privy Councillor. In his autobiography he remembered the occasion on which he made his debut as a reciter during a Sunday School anniversary at South Hetton.

Though I continued to take part in the Sunday-schools, as pupil or teacher, till my early manhood, this was my first and last performance of the kind. Not that I failed. On the contrary, it is said that I did my little part very creditably. Certainly I gave great satisfaction to my admiring parents. There had been some slight controversy, not unfriendly, between the Sunday-school superintendent and my father as to the selection of the piece. The former had chosen some jingling rhyme of a goody-goody kind, poor and empty enough, I dare say, but not on that account unattractive to the juvenile taste. I rather liked it. My father's view was different. 'That won't do,' he said emphatically. 'I'll get him a short piece out of the Bible.' The chapter selected by my father was the 35th of Isaiah, beginning: 'The wilderness and the solitary place shall be glad for them: and the desert shall rejoice and blossom as the rose.' The superintendent objected – not perhaps unreasonably – that there were too many 'hard words' for a child of my age and training. 'I'll drill him,' said my father. 'Let him have something that is worth saying.' When I now read that fine prose poem, with its beauty and majesty, with its rhythm, its music, and its melody, I see that my father, who had never been at college and only a few weeks at school, must have known a good thing when he saw it. Apart from any religious lesson the chapter may contain, I feel grateful to him for having thus early placed before me such a model of strong, lofty, melodious prose. If I did but scant justice to the piece, and if I have not taken full advantage of the object-lesson, the fault was not my father's, but my own.

Thomas Burt, *Pitman and Privy Councillor: an autobiography*, 1924, p. 44

I enjoyed, and no doubt profited by, my attendance at Sunday-school... At the head of the Sunday-school were the superintendents, who did duty on alternate Sundays. The names of these gentlemen were Thomas Robinson and Henry Nicholson. Two men more entirely dissimilar I never knew. Thomas was a gentle, reserved, mild-mannered man, who ruled the school, not ineffectually, in his firm, undemonstrative way. He was a universal favourite. 'Harry' was more boisterous and severe. He was a native of Tyneside, and had the Northumberland burr in full flavour. In his youth he had been a rather wild, out-of-the-way character, addicted to drinking, gambling, and other vices. Methodism caught hold of him, and he was now quite a reformed character. To his work in the chapel and Sunday-school he was devotedly attached. He was a rough, unpolished gem – a kind-hearted, witty, impulsive man, whom it was not possible to keep within strictly conventional lines. Harry was precentor in the chapel choir as well as superintendent of the Sunday-school. Funnier precentor choir never had! When he failed to pitch the tune properly – and that often happened – he would look calmly up to the preacher and call out: 'Let's hev hor ower agyen, hinney!' When the verse was read out again, the second attempt was usually, though not always, more successful.

Harry on one occasion, to which I was an ear-witness, came near to getting into disgrace by an inopportune witticism. A very popular local preacher, Turnbull by name, was appointed to preach at South Hetton. Great were the expectations, Harry especially having looked forward with eagerness to the happy day. Mr. Turnbull, through illness or other cause, was unable to fulfil his engagement. As a substitute he sent a young man named Beaney. Harry's expressive face showed that his mood was not angelic. Everything went wrong with the service. The tunes could not be started at the proper pitch. In angry, peremptory tones Harry called for the lines of the hymn to be given out again. The preliminaries were got through with difficulty. Then came the sermon, which was a greater trial still. The preacher was young, unpractised in speech; he was addressing an unsympathetic, a disappointed audience, many of whom had expected, and all of whom , no doubt, wished to hear somebody else. In the concluding prayer the preacher was unfortunate enough to quote the passage of scripture which runs somewhat thus: 'If I go away, I will come again,' when Harry's overburdened soul found utterance by calling out in clear, strong tones, audible to the whole congregation: 'Wey, lad, thoo dissent need to mind.'

> Thomas Burt, *op. cit.*, pp. 87–8

Alice Macdonald (1837–1910)

The oldest of the five daughters of the Rev. and Mrs. George Browne Macdonald married the artist John Lockwood Kipling and became the mother of Rudyard Kipling. Like her sisters, she was highly gifted, had a ready wit and reacted against her Methodist background.

To her sisters she represented everything that was daring and unexpected, and they were never tired of discussing her exploits, her poems, her songs that she set to music, and her mild love affairs that seemed so wild... One outrage that she perpetrated must have awed any superstitious child within hearing, when, in helping to pack for another move, Alice came upon an envelope, yellow with age, on which was written in faded script: 'A lock of Mr. Wesley's hair'. She took the precious relic out of the envelope and with the words 'See! A hair of the dog that bit us!' threw it on the fire.

> A.W. Baldwin, *The Macdonald Sisters*, 1960, p. 32

The house in Lahore, to which the Kiplings moved in 1875, did not endear itself to Alice, even after improvements had been made.

Even after everything was redone to her satisfaction, and at her wittiest, Alice never forgot this beginning. A visitor looking around commented, 'I say, Mrs. Kipling, your house is simply A.1.' 'Ah,' replied Alice, 'you should have seen it B.4.'

> Judith Flanders, *A Circle of Sisters*, 2001, p. 147

John Wilson (1837–1915)

John Wilson was one of those who rose from humble beginnings to prominence in political and trade unionist circles. In his early manhood, he spent three years seeking to improve his prospects in America, but then returned to his native Durham.

When we were leaving Irwin Station for home there was living near to us at Larrimer's Station, a man (Mr. Hepple) who had left Haswell before we did. He asked me if I would bring home a family Bible for his father. I gladly accepted the commission. When I arrived I handed over the book, thinking that would be an end to the transaction. In that I am glad I was mistaken. It was, so far as I am concerned, one of the most profitable pieces of work I ever took in hand.

'Willie' Hepple was a saintly, well-meaning man. The bringing and handing over the Bible made us acquainted, and he availed himself of every opportunity to call and see me. He had a twofold purpose in view: he loved to talk about his son, and he had a very great desire to give me good counsel and induce me to lead a better life. By-and-by the conversation had effect and I began to reason with myself and question whether I was not wasting my life, and whether it were not possible for me to make a better use of my time and powers.

As I have indicated there were two things of which I was enamoured; very few more so. I mention them to show how they were shaken off. The gambling went first, and in this way I say no more than that it was with me an infatuation...

There was yet the other force from which I had to break. It held me fast for some time longer, but the freedom from it came in the following manner. I have said that old Mr. Hepple used to call as he was passing our house. On his way to Sunday School one Sunday morning, in the early part of February 1868, he came with an old friend, Mr. T. Dagg. They both came in. I had taken too much the night before, and was sitting holding my head, and trying to coax an appetite, but everything (presented to me by a wife too kind for me under those circumstances) was nauseous. In his cheery voice my old adviser cried out, 'What's the matter this morning?' 'Oh,' she said, 'he was drunk last night and cannot take his breakfast.' As if moved by inspiration, the old man said (inconsequently, no doubt), 'Be a Sunday School teacher.' My answer was readily given, 'Yes, I will.' Without another word they turned and went out as quickly as they could and did not give me time to recall my words. After they had left I said, 'Do you see what I have done? I have promised them to be a teacher in the Sunday School, and I don't like to break my word. I never thought what I was saying at the time.'

It was their monthly teachers' meeting, and when that part of the business was reached Mr. Hepple proposed, and his friend Mr. Dagg seconded, that I should be accepted as a teacher. There was general surprise. 'Which Wilson is it?' The answer was, 'He lives in the Long Row.' 'What! Jack Wilson! Why, he never comes to chapel.' 'Never mind,' said the confident old man. 'Take his name, give him a month's trial, and we are sure he'll be here, now he has promised.' All beside them doubted, and thought it was a mere matter of form, and agreed to the proposal as it would please the old men, but the end of the month would show how far wrong they were, as I was sure to go wrong before the time of probation was up...

The old men called on their way home and told me what they had done and pledged in my name, and I assured them (after thinking carefully over the question) that I would keep my word and be at school when the month was up. Whatever might be their fear when they came, they had none when they went away. At the end of the probation I was ready for them when they called. As we went up to the chapel, one on either side of me, they were as proud as if they had found a diamond of the first water, and with tears in their kind eyes and joy in their hearts they presented me to the school... I never lost my great regard for the two Christians, for such they were in the truest sense of the term, and I have today the highest respect for their memory. It would be a blessing if there were more like them... To me and mine they were God-sent on that Sunday morning, and by their trust they called forth the best that was in me. If they had stopped to lecture me on the evils of drink and my bad conduct, they might have created a different feeling. Instead of that, having got my word they accepted it in good faith and threw themselves on my manhood, and their faith had its reward.

> John Wilson, *Memories of a Labour Leader: the autobiography of John Wilson, JP, MP*, 1910, pp. 201–5

William L. Watkinson (1838–1924)

President of the Wesleyan Conference in 1897, W.L. Watkinson's tall, lanky, almost emaciated figure earned him the description of 'the giraffe of Methodism'. He was widely known for his ready wit.

Both lanky and gawky, he suggests in some ways the figure of Abraham Lincoln; his sprawling legs make the story easily believable that once having to borrow a pair of pyjamas, and asked how they served, he replied, 'Very well as far as they went.'

> Robert Ferguson, *Some Reminiscences and Studies*, 1961, p. 5

Once in his prime, when he deputised at short notice for Dr. Parkes Cadman at a Tuesday lunchtime service in the Manchester Central Hall, he excused himself by saying dryly, 'I ought not to be here. If you take a good look at me, I think you will agree that nature never intended me to fill a gap.'...

A master of repartee, he was brilliant in debate... Once when Sir Robert Perks was telling Conference about the evil days of his youth, he complained they were so bad that he was actually thrashed for telling the truth. 'Yes, and they cured you,' Watkinson was heard to murmur as he sat with the Legal Hundred...

This distinguished man once went to stay with two ladies who had provided him with hospitality before. On his arrival they told him tearfully that their dear little dog, Fido, had passed away, and they would not be comforted until he had written something suitable in their autograph album. Reaching for his pen, he scribbled, to their obvious satisfaction, 'Fido, thy barque is on the other shore.' A newly-rich landowner one day pointed out to him the avenue of trees he had designed as an approach to his recently-bought mansion. 'Them's beech trees,' he exclaimed proudly. 'They'll never be much in my time, but they'll come in for my posteriors.' 'In that case,' drawled his tall listener, 'wouldn't birches have been more appropriate?'

> John F.C. Dakin

Thomas Bowman Stephenson (1839–1912)

Stephenson was to become well known in the Wesleyan connexion as founder of both the National Children's Home and the Wesley Deaconess Order. He began preaching while still a pupil at Wesley College, Sheffield and heard a call to the ministry soon after leaving school.

I had been preaching for several weeks, with apparent appreciation by the congregations, and with a growing sense of the holiness of the work, which is a supreme equipment of the preacher. We Methodists are accustomed to look for signs and wonders in the name of Jesus, indeed we doubt whether any man can be sure of his own vocation for the ministry unless, in the minor office of local preacher, he had commended himself to the people and had received the heavenly stamp upon his work. One week I had been greatly troubled because I could not trace any direct spiritual good to anybody as the result of my preaching; and on my knees I had pleaded with God that if he wished me to give myself to the work of soul-saving He would be pleased to give me some sign of His goodwill and favour. I was to preach in a Tyneside village on the following Sunday night. I went, and from the first moment the service seemed to be baptized with a heavenly glow. The majority of the congregation were intelligent working men. They entered fully into sympathy with the preacher; many wept; some uttered prayerful ejaculations. That same night twelve of those fine Tynesiders chose Christ as their Saviour and Leader. I felt that this was a sign and a call which I must not neglect. It decided my career. Fifty years afterwards, being in that neighbourhood, one of those men, now grey-headed and bent with years, took my hand and thanked me for the word spoken that night so long ago.

> Quoted in William Bradfield, *The Life of the Reverend Thomas Bowman Stephenson*, 1913, pp. 30–31

Stephenson's gift of relating to children became proverbial.

One of the Sisters tells how she took a little girl who had just been received to have her first interview with 'the Doctor'. He always kept biscuits and sweets for the newcomers, and usually succeeded in making friends with them immediately; but for once (and it was the only time Sister remembered) here was a newcomer who would not go to him. She had been cruelly beaten with a belt and was absolutely terrified of men. 'Never mind, Sister,' he said, 'she will be all right in a day or two.' But the one interview had really been sufficient, for as the poor little ill-used child was being taken away she enquired, 'Be any more gentlemen like that? I likes that sort'; and when she next saw him, she went to him with perfect confidence.

Another says: 'Very often in the evening the organ of the little chapel would be heard, and Doctor would be found playing with a little waif or homesick orphan sitting on the organ stool near him, while he played the sorrow or rebellion out of its young heart. It was his custom, after the music, to tell the child its first Bible story, and many a time he has seen the tears flow as the child has for the first time in life heard the wonderful news of the love of Jesus. Then Doctor and the bairn would be seen coming down from the chapel hand in hand, both very happy, and he would take the newcomer to his or house and Sister.'

[A committee meeting] was held in Dr. Stephenson's room at the Children's Home, and strict orders had been sent out that there was to be no noise in the playground, and no visitors could be seen, nor must the Committee be interrupted by anybody. But a little girl, who had been accustomed to report her proceedings to the Doctor from time to time, in order to get a kiss, and had just been absent from the Home for a day, felt it necessary to tell him of her return; so she fearlessly knocked at the forbidden door, and when some grave Committeeman opened it, marched past him, straight up to Dr. Stephenson with a bright smile, saying 'I have just come to tell you I have come back, Doc.,' and held up her face to be kissed. The kiss was given, and the happy child walked serenely out of the room, leaving the Committee to go on with their work in an atmosphere freshened by a breath as from heaven itself.

William Bradfield, *op. cit.*, pp. 158–9, 170–1

Stephenson's musical gifts were many and various and extended well beyond playing the organ.

On one occasion, in 1878, he was accompanying his children's choir on a small harmonium at an annual meeting in Exeter Hall. The instrument presently collapsed under his vigorous playing. 'Now you go on singing,' said he, quite oblivious to the opinion of the great congregation as he plumped onto his knees, repaired the collapsed bowels of the instrument, and was soon up again conducting. His amiability and all-round efficiency on that occasion so impressed one lady in the audience that she at once gave herself to the Home as a voluntary worker and served it with generosity and devotion for more than a quarter of a century afterwards.

William Bradfield, *op cit.,* p. 192

Elizabeth C. Walters (1840–1902)

Elizabeth Rought, the daughter of a Baptist minister, married the Rev. W.D. Walters in 1862. They had sixteen children. Both her husband and her son, the Rev. C. Ensor Walters, were closely involved in the work of the London Mission. She died in tragic circumstances on October 8th, 1902.

One morning friends who thought of my mother as still living and still enjoying the best gifts of life, read the following brief announcement in various newspapers: 'The wife of the Rev. W.D. Walters, of the London Mission, living at Highgate, was leaving the Woolwich Arsenal railway station yesterday, when she saw a little boy, aged four years, in danger of being run over. She ran across the road to save him, but was herself knocked down by a brewer's van. The wheels passed over her chest and on being picked up she was found to be dead. The child was unhurt.'

E.W. Walters, *The Energy of Love, a memoir of the Rev. W.D. Walters*, 1914, p. 96, supplemented by notes from David Ensor

Charles H. Gough (1841–1926)

Gough was accepted for the ministry in 1863 and sent immediately to his first appointment at Ramsey in the St. Ives and Huntingdon Circuit.

I well remember the first Sunday School teachers' meeting I attended at Ramsey. On inquiring how it was that there was no Sunday School in connection with one or two of the smaller country chapels, I was told that the clergymen of the parishes in which they were situated would not allow the children to attend the Day School unless they went to the Church of England Sunday School. I was very indignant at such bigotry and said I would write to the clergymen, and if they interfered with our Sunday Schools, which I resolved we would start, I would report the matter to the Board of Education, which I did in due course.

'But we cannot afford it, sir,' said a poor, ill-paid country labourer.

'What do you mean?'

'Well, sir, it's like this,' said the good man, very humbly and respectfully; 'we are all poor people and unless we send our children to the Church School the parson refuses to give us any of the parish doles of money and blankets, and other things, and we cannot afford to lose them.'

I replied, 'These schools shall be established, and I will make myself responsible to give the full value of any gifts which may be withheld from anybody because they send their children to the Methodist Sunday School.'

It was well for me that I was never called upon to fulfil my promise, for my circuit allowance was under £60 per annum. This was in the early sixties of the last century, before the establishment of School Boards, and the adoption of the Conscience Clause in the so-called National Schools...

During the year we were honoured with a visit from the Rev. John Rattenbury to Ramsey to preach the anniversary sermons... I was introduced to the great man, who treated me very kindly and gave me some very wise and fatherly advice to the following effect: 'See that you always have good thick soles on your shoes and carry a stout umbrella, and when you stay at a large house, and they want to put you in the best bedroom, which is reserved for visitors, and is, therefore, very liable to be damp, you say, 'If you please, may I sleep in the servant's bed, and let the servant sleep in the best room.'

Methodist Recorder, Winter Number, 1907, pp. 77–8

Frederic W. Macdonald (1842–1928)

Macdonald's first experience of circuit work was in the Potteries.

Soon after coming into the district I was invited to preach [Sunday] School sermons in a colliery village some few miles away... The services were in the afternoon and evening, and the chapel was crowded in every part. A wooden stage of seats rising one above another had been erected round the pulpit, which was thus rendered inaccessible by the ordinary means of approach. When the time came to begin the service a small ladder was brought and passed along over the people's heads till a footing could be found for it, the other end resting upon the pulpit's edge. Amid the breathless attention of the congregation I ascended the ladder and dropped safely into the interior of the pulpit. The ladder was then removed, and my retreat effectually cut off. I was like Robinson Crusoe in his tree-fortress, save that he pulled up his ladder after him, while mine was borne away by others.

At the close of the afternoon service I was carried off to have tea at the house of a hospitable collier, who had invited a few friends to meet me. The kitchen in which we took our tea was warm and cosy, and the provision was abundant. But conversation was the difficulty. My host was painfully shy, made no remarks, and generally replied to mine in monosyllables. His friends were equally silent, so it fell upon me to keep the conversation in some sense alive... In an interval of silence that I began to find embarrassing, by way of saying something, I remarked, 'A very large congregation this afternoon.' To which my host slowly replied, 'Yes, it doesn't matter who preaches the School sermons.'

Some months later I preached again in the same chapel. It was not School sermons this time – no crowd, no need for a ladder to give access to the pulpit, and a collection of the smallest. Once more I found myself the guest of my taciturn friend, and, for want of anything better to say, I ventured the remark, 'Not a very large congregation today.' 'Well, you see,' said he, *'they've heard you before.'*

Frederic W. Macdonald, *Reminiscences of my Early Ministry*, pp. 23–5

Mark Guy Pearse (1842–1930)

Pearse was one of the most popular preachers and authors of his time and served as Hugh Price Hughes' colleague in the early days of the West London Mission.

His first sermon was thrust upon him. He had no choice in the matter. He has told the story himself. The superintendent minister was ill, and he volunteered to ride down to the village eight or ten miles away with a message that there would be no service.

'But what are the people going to do?' asked the steward when he got there – a saintly old shoemaker sitting amongst the odds and ends of his work.

'Well, I suppose they can have a prayer-meeting.'

'No, no,' said he; 'you're here, and you will have to preach to them.'

'Nonsense,' said I, 'I can't preach.'

'He took a Bible and held it out to me.

'Here,' he said, 'go out into the orchard and look for a text.' I took the Bible and went.

'Now, strangely enough, that morning in my reading I had come on a passage of which I had said, 'I think I could make a sermon from those words if I were a preacher' – *'Be strong, all ye people of the land, and work, for I am with you, saith the Lord of Hosts.'*

'As I prayed and meditated my sermon came, and I went and preached it. And as I rode home in the summer evening I felt the die was cast, the Rubicon was crossed. Some day I knew I must be a preacher.'

Mrs George Unwin & John Telford, *Mark Guy Pearse: Preacher, Author, Artist*, 1930, pp. 91–92

It was during one of his visits [to Southport] that I first made the acquaintance of Mark Guy Pearse. He was then in his prime, and immensely popular throughout the country as a preacher and lecturer. A Cornishman himself, he knew the Cornish people inside out and could tell

Cornish stories by the hour, tell them in the vernacular, and with that curious lilt and intonation which are specialities of the Delectable Dutchy.

During a visit to the far west of Canada, 'Mark Guy' visited a mining camp to which a number of Cornish miners had emigrated, and in the largest hall in the place gave his lecture on 'The Old Folks at Home'. The Cornish people., of course, were delighted. It was like being at home again to hear stories of the old county told in the quaint vernacular, and with faultless intonation.

At the close of the lecture a Cornishman came up to him with shining face and misty eyes, and shook him heartily by the hand.

'Lor, Maaster Pearse,' he said, 'it's like being down to home again to hear 'ee spaik, and I've been wondering all the while how you do it. You bain't livin' in Cornwall be 'ee when you be home?'

'Oh, no, I live in London.'

'Well, now, there 'tes. An' yet you do remember everything 'zactly like they used to was. All they curious words, and all they funny little turns. Lor, how I ded laugh. I caan't think how tes you ain't forgotten 'em oall. Why, Maaster Pearse, I hadn't been out in this country six months before I's forgot every bit of my Cornish.'

    Silas Hocking, *My Book of Memory*, 1923, pp. 118–19

One other story I must tell which Pearse does not tell himself. Perhaps it is not true, so I give it for what it is worth.

The story goes that he was preaching and lecturing in a small town in Cornwall. At the afternoon service the chapel was packed out, crowds of people who had come from a considerable distance being unable to gain admission.

Between the afternoon's sermon and the evening lecture a public tea was provided in the schoolroom. Mr Pearse, however, had his tea quietly by himself in the minister's vestry.

Scarcely had he finished his tea when two of the stewards entered.

'Mr Pearse,' said the spokesman of the pair. 'We be come to lay before 'ee a plan for raisin' heaps more money.'

'Yes?' Mr Pearse questioned.

'Well you knaw that, though they was settin' sideways in chapel this afternoon, haaf of the people couldn't get in, and they be terrible disappointed. Lots of 'em caan't stay to the lecture tonight, and crowds more waan't be able to get inside, an' some of 'em 'ave been talkin' to we about it.'

'Well?'

'Well, it's just this way, Mr Pearse. Oall these people be terrible anxious to see 'ee, and Brother Buddle and me 'ave been puttin' our 'eads together, and us 'ave 'it upon a plan that'll plaise everybody and raise a lot of money to boot.'

'And what is your plan, David?'

'Well, it's just this, Mr Pearse. You just set 'ere in your chair in the vestry. You don't need to do nothin' but just look plaised. And us'll just let the people in ten or twelve at a time to look at 'ee, an' charge 'em sixpence each. Don't 'ee see?'

Needless to say, much to the steward's disappointment, the plan was not carried out.

Silas Hocking, *op. cit.*, pp. 120–21

No appreciation of the great days of the West London Mission would be adequate without reference to [Hugh Price] Hughes's brilliant colleague, Mark Guy Pearse. He was, in many ways, one of the most remarkable personalities of his period. He was distinguished in many fields: as preacher, lecturer, artist and writer... As a preacher and lecturer he was known in every corner of the land. At his best, and in his own line, he had no rival.

His special work in the Mission was the Sunday morning service. There he built up one of the largest morning congregations in London. His crowds came from the ends of the earth. In his moods of banter, which were frequent, Hughes would tell Pearse that he duty was to coddle the saints in the morning, whilst he himself caught the sinners in the evening. To which Pearse would reply that his congregation got sermons in the morning, and Hughes's crowd got 'a few remarks' in the evening! How they loved to chaff one another. Each was the perfect foil of the other.

W.H. Lax, *Lax - His Book*, 1937, p. 167

John Smith Simon (1843–1933)

Simon devoted his retirement years in Southport to a monumental five-volume biography of John Wesley, but the final volume was left to be completed by his son-in-law, A.W. Harrison.

The eighteenth century at last became more real than the twentieth... He lived with Wesley, slept with him and almost literally died with him. But he began his darling theme too late. Four volumes he accomplished, but the fifth he never finished. He would try and try again to get up to the death of his hero, but the old loyal heart fainted, and the old hands faltered and crossed out and recrossed out, and he could not come at it. He never had the heart to inter even Charles Wesley. The attempt to do so cost him dear.

To those who dismantled that quiet study at the end, it seemed like the place of the communion of saints, and it was not without its own stigmata... The camps which marked the pilgrimage were little bits of paper found all about the books, with jottings upon them of how long it had taken to write the chapters. He must have known it was hopeless when the separate entry of months added painfully up to six for Chapter xxii. But like [Scott's] Polar party he was not going to let anyone know that he knew he was beaten. Under a load of ninety years, and afflicted as Browning's Grammarian, he toiled on and dropped in his tracks.

It was only on the day before his death that he suggested the possibility that he might not finish his book. He was conducting a family meal through its slow meandering with his habitual old-time courtesy, when he asked quite suddenly if his son-in-law, A.W. Harrison, would finish *John*

Wesley for him. 'I shall never do it – I have every confidence in him,' he said. Then clearly and generously he discussed details whilst those with him felt they looked on things apocalyptic. They were dimly conscious of the lengthening shadows creeping up to surround their Venerable Bede. 'There is yet one sentence unwritten, dear master.' 'Write it quickly.' 'It's finished now.' 'You speak truth, all is finished now.' That evening at the family altar he rejoiced in prayer and praise... The rest of the evening he spent quietly in his study and went to bed at his usual hour, heavy with sleep. The Methodist was the Methodist to the end. All was in perfect order – shoes ready, watch wound up against the coming of the morning. But he never woke again. He had no tryst remaining to be kept with John Wesley, and so he slipped quietly away.

G Elsie Harrison, *Methodist Good Companions*, 1935, pp. 151–54

Sir Thomas Barlow (1845–1945)

A member of the staunch Wesleyan family of Edgworth, Lancashire, Barlow had a distinguished medical career, culminating in his being President of the Royal College of Physicians. In his private practice he counted Archbishop Davidson and members of the royal family among his patients, but 'carried his many high honours with a beautiful modesty, and was one of the most friendly of men'.

Some years ago he was knocked down in a street accident in London, taken to hospital and placed in a public ward. When later the authorities discovered who he was they wanted to remove him to a private ward. But he refused this and said, 'I have spent much of my life in hospital wards, and now I will be a patient in one.'

W. Bardsley Brash, obituary in *Methodist Recorder*, 25 January 1945

Sir William Hartley (1846–1922)

Primitive Methodism's principle benefactor was more than scrupulously fair to those fruit growers who supplied his jam factories.

His usual principle was to determine the price himself after the fruit had been delivered. One grower who felt that this was 'not business' insisted on the price being fixed beforehand. Mr. Hartley acquiesced; but the price was much less than he would actually have given had the matter been left to his discretion. I remember how more than thirty years ago a friend of my own was talking to a Herefordshire fruit grower who supplied M. Hartley with strawberries. Quite unaware that my friend knew something of Mr. Hartley in another connection, he told him that he had such confidence in him that he left the fixing of the price entirely to him and found it altogether satisfactory. Another friend tells me that on one occasion Mr. Hartley had engaged to purchase blackcurrants at a fixed price. It turned out that there was a great scarcity that season, but this man fortunately had a very good crop. Mr. Hartley paid him the market price, which was far higher than that which had been agreed upon.

A much more remarkable example has been communicated to me by the Rev. J.T. Barkby [Hartley's son-in-law]. He was dining one night at the National Liberal Club with a number of friends. Sir Henry Holloway said to him: 'I heard a lovely story about your father-in-law a little while ago. I was up in Scotland and was in the company of a cultured gentleman who was a fruit farmer. I asked him what he did with his fruit and he said, 'I send all of it to Sir William Hartley, and I shall not send any to anyone else.' 'That is a great thing to say,' I replied. 'Yes, and I mean it,' the farmer said, 'and if you had experienced at the hand of another the kindness that Sir William has shown me, you would say the same. Last season was a bad season. I had arranged with Sir William about the price as usual and had sent on my stuff to him. Unfortunately the farms produced much less than was expected. There was a shortage of fruit and the price went up, so that I was losing heavily. Without my saying a word to Sir William, I one day received a letter from him in which he said, 'I am sure you must be losing money on the fruit you are sending to me; tell me frankly the position.' I wrote and acknowledged the receipt of his letter, saying how good he was to me and at the same time laying before him the facts of the situation. He replied, saying how sorry he was for me, and quite spontaneously sent on a cheque for a large sum of money to help cover my deficiency. Do you wonder that I say what I do in relation to sending to Sir William?' Mr. Barkby tells me that he believes the cheque sent by Sir William was for some thousands of pounds. He wrote to Sir William, thinking that the story would cheer him in his illness, but the letter reached his house on the morning of the day on which he had passed away.

Arthur S. Peake, *The Life of Sir William Hartley*, 1926, pp. 61–2

He had by nature a fundamental integrity of character which furnished the sound basis for the finer graces and qualities of his personality. A friend of mine was once in a grocer's shop and heard a customer expressing himself scornfully about the Nonconformist conscience. 'What is this 'Nonconformist conscience,' I should like to know?' he said. The grocer promptly reached down a pot of Hartley's jam and, placing it with some emphasis on the counter, said, 'That's the Nonconformist conscience!'

Arthur S. Peake, *op. cit.*, p. 218

In 1909 Hartley was unanimously elected President of the Primitive Methodist Conference, although he was neither a local preacher nor free to travel round the connexion in his presidential year. The Rev. John Welford was appointed Vice-President to act in a supporting role.

His conduct in the Presidential Chair was marked by great dignity, combined with a tendency to curb prolixity and accelerate business. He had little patience with overmuch talk in business meetings. I remember a humorous comment he made in one Conference when a question involving about £20 was being debated: 'I could make the money in the time you are talking about it.'

Arthur S. Peake, *op. cit.*, p. 97

He was not talkative about his religious experiences, but no one who knew him intimately could doubt that his reticence veiled an intense spiritual life... A touching story, communicated to me by the Rev. George Trusler, exhibits his devoutness in a less familiar light. It should be said that Mr. Hartley was in the habit of visiting the Primitive Methodist places of worship in towns or villages where he was staying or through which he was passing, in order that he might acquaint himself with the condition of the structure and its adequacy for the neighbourhood in which it was situated. When Mr. Trusler was a minister at Ryde, in the Isle of Wight, more than thirty years ago, Mr. Hartley visited the island, and in addition to seeing the minister went to the Primitive Methodist chapel. The chapel-keeper was an elderly woman and was at her work when he entered the building. She told how a gentleman had come in and asked many questions about the work carried on and the minister, and continued, 'He took hold of my hand before leaving and said, "Let us pray", and he stood and prayed for you and for us all.' She added: 'I've shown lots of you ministers the chapel, but none of you ever prayed with me as he did.' It was a great joy to her when she learned who the visitor was.

Arthur S. Peake, *op. cit.*, pp. 220–1

Sir William P. Hartley was interested in my work for the lay preachers. He provided prizes for the students of a School for Lay Preachers which I organised at Surrey Chapel in 1902. Later, when I proposed that he should pay half the cost of £5 worth of books if lay preachers would pay the other half, he jumped at the opportunity. 'How much will it cost me?' he asked. 'I hope it will cost you £1,000,' I said, 'but I fear it will not.' He hoped it would cost more... The response surprised us all. The £1,000 mark was soon passed. Sir William seemed to think there was a sort of bet between him and myself. A card would come most days, 'Figure today, £2,000' and it mounted till it reached £7,000. I am sure that he got more satisfaction over being called on to pay £3,500 than if he had made £50,000 extra profit in his business.

Harry Jeffs, *Press, Preachers and Politicians. Reminiscences: 1874–1932*, 1933, pp. 146–7

William Theophilus Davison (1846–1935)

A son of the manse, Davison had a distinguished academic career at Kingswood School which ended in a fall from grace.

In those days, in addition to the Headmaster, whose duties were confined to scholastic discipline, there was a Governor who had charge of the domestic and religious side of school life. Unfortunately the Conference sometimes appointed for this purpose elderly ministers who had deserved well of the Connexion and who were glad to have a less arduous post than a circuit superintendency before retirement. At this time the Governor happened to be an old man, who was an invalid and quite unsuitable for boys.[36] Davison in after years referred to him as a 'vinegar cask'. Now on the last night of the school year it was the custom for some of the 'Levites' to climb up to the tower. This was at all times strictly out of bounds. Davison and his friend Mowat on this occasion followed the tradition, and they needed and took lights with them. The Governor seeing the lights in the tower came up after them to discover what they were about. The boys heard his steps, but not recognising him in the dark turned a hose on the intruder. The result may be imagined. Disobedience was bad, but the insult to humiliated majesty was far worse. The boys were to regard themselves as expelled. Early the next morning Mr. Shum received a letter informing him that he must fetch his grandson immediately as he was leaving the school in disgrace. And that was the day on which the head boy was to have left his school in triumph, carrying away a load of prizes!

Twenty-eight years afterwards a little boy staying at Bath on a visit was being conducted round Kingswood school with his elder brother by an assistant master. In the Library he was shown a row of well-bound books. 'These,' said his guide, 'were won by one of the most brilliant boys

---

[36] Francis A. West, Governor at Kingswood 1860-1867, died in 1869.

that ever passed through Kingswood. But on the last night before he should have left with flying colours, he thought that he could do just what he liked, and break the rules of the school. So these books were withheld from him.' Davison was never known to refer to this bitter experience even to his closest friends. But many years later a nephew who lived for a while under his roof got into slight trouble, together with half the class, with an assistant master whose great learning was not matched by common sense. The boy confessed the scrape to his uncle, fully expecting a sharp reprimand. To his surprise Dr. Davison showed the warmest sympathy, only adding with unusual vehemence: 'No man without a sense of humour has any right to be a schoolmaster.' After thirty-five years the wound had not completely healed!

W.F. Howard, memoir in W.T. Davison, *Mystics and Poets*, 1936, pp. 13–15

Hugh Price Hughes (1847–1902)

Appointed to his first Superintendency in 1881, Hughes found the Oxford Circuit in a moribund state. With the support of James Nix, a leading local preacher, and his brother Josiah, he introduced several new forms of missionary outreach, including annual 'Open-Air Days' in nearby villages.

It was felt that we ought to do in Oxford what we had done in the villages; and I vividly recollect the astonishment with which my eminently respectable congregation in New Inn Hall Street heard me announce that on the following Sunday there would be no service in the church except a very brief one in the morning, as the services were to be held in a beautifully shady field near Magdalen College. I proceeded with the utmost calmness to announce further that, after the brief service in the morning, I should be accompanied by my two circuit stewards, who were to walk on my right and on my left, and that we should be followed by the entire choir. I may say that I did not consult any of those distinguished persons, because they might, perhaps, have hesitated if I had given them the opportunity of doing so. But after that public announcement they could scarcely be conspicuous by their absence.

So, on a lovely Sunday morning in June, I marched from New Inn Hall Street, with my circuit stewards right and left of me, and a great retinue of well-dressed ladies and gentlemen, who formed our admirable choir, followed, leading the singing most beautifully. Behind them came the whole of our New Inn Hall Street congregation, who had never confessed Christ in that public way before. A great multitude of people collected out of curiosity, so that on that day I marched past Balliol College, over the very spot on which the martyred bishops were burnt – the spot now marked by a cross – accompanied by at least two thousand people, and by all my church officers. In fact, everyone I knew was in the procession, except one of my own little daughters, who was too bashful to perform in that way in public, even in the society of her father. With much self-consciousness, she walked alone on the pavement, and tried – in vain – to look as though she had no connection with the processionists...

Chairs and benches were provided in the beautiful field for those who could not stand; and in the city of Oxford, as in the villages, the Open-Air Day proved a great blessing, not only to multitudes who under ordinary circumstances would not hear the Gospel at all, but to our own people, who needed to be shaken up from their false respectability and to be lifted out of the rut into which we are only too apt to sink.

Hugh Price Hughes, in *Methodist Recorder*, Winter Number, 1898, p. 19

Methodism was held in very low esteem at Oxford in the 1880s.

At a meeting where the Rev. Mark Pattison, Rector of Lincoln College, was in the chair, my father referred to the fact that no adequate memorial of John Wesley existed in a university of whose sons he was one of the greatest.

The rector stirred and audibly corrected, 'Not one of the *greatest.*'

Hearing which the speaker replied, 'I repeat what I said, sir; one of the *greatest.* Indeed,' he continued, 'nothing has caused me greater astonishment since I came to Oxford, than the ignorance of the University with regard to the world-wide work and influence of Wesley. The founder of a Church which numbers twenty-five millions...'

'No, no, Mr. Hughes,' interrupted the rector; 'twenty-five thousand, you mean, not twenty-five millions.'

Amid breathless silence the speaker dived into his coat pocket and produced a pocket-book, from which he proceeded to verify his statement. A correspondence ensued, in which the rector and the superintendent had a long discussion upon Wesley's claim to greatness. If a man with so world-wide an influence, and so palpable an effect on history, was not great, was the substance of his argument, who then was?

Dorothea Price Hughes, *The Life of Hugh Price Hughes*, 1904, pp. 161–2

Early in his ministry, 'Lax of Poplar' found himself a junior colleague of Hugh Price Hughes in the West London Mission.

Hughes was constantly challenging convention. He put every custom or habit into the crucible of his reason. He accepted nothing on the mere authority of tradition. Forty years ago a religious service was expected to last an hour and a half. He believed that an hour was long enough, especially in Mission services... He would ask me sometimes how long I had preached on the previous Sunday evening. (I suspect he had heard of my long-winded tendencies!) If I told him half an hour, he would reply that I ought to have had a tooth extracted for every minute that I preached beyond twenty! I fear that I should soon have had complete dentures of the artificial variety had that dictum been strictly kept.

But I saw another side of that remarkable man. I lived in or near Taviton Street during my term in the Mission. Frequently we walked together to meetings or services. He was always anxious about his preparation in anticipation of preaching. Perhaps he had been worried by matters of routine or organisation, or problems of policy. In all these things he found refuge in prayer. Often, he would take my arm, suggesting that we should not take up the interval of walking to the Hall in talk about trivial things, but in prayer. In turn, therefore, as we walked along Oxford Street, eyes open, we held a prayer-meeting, speaking in low tones as though we were in an orthodox building. It was certainly novel in method, but it was also a real preparation of heart.

W.H. Lax, *Lax – His Book*, 1937, pp. 168–9

Hughes' daughter records how, one evening during the first year of the West London Mission, her father came home to supper looking deeply agitated and told the following story.

I have had the most painful experience – most painful. It is so distressing indeed that I scarcely know how to relate it. I passed a public-house quite close here on my way back from Tottenham Court Road, and I saw that a commotion was going on, so I stopped to observe it. A hansom cab-driver had just come out – half-drunk evidently – and had managed to mount on his box. His wife, a slight, fragile creature, with one baby in her arms and another, half-unclothed, clinging to her skirt, was standing below. [Here the speaker paused and then resumed.] She wanted the man to give her money, and he would not, and at last it fell to quarrelling – and there she was shouting up at him – oh, it was most painful – till quite a crowd collected. Of course she spoke very improperly, poor thing, and there was the ragged child clinging to her skirt all the time. This went on for some minutes till the man drove away. I felt someone should go and speak to her, yet for some reason I could not. I shrank from it. So I turned on my heel and got as far as Gower Place, when I felt so ashamed of my cowardice that I had to turn back. I wasn't long in overtaking her, for that had taken place which I knew would happen. [Here the speaker threw up his hands.] No sooner was the public-house out of sight than she had burst into sobs, and the wretched little children were sobbing too. Then I went up to her very quietly and said, 'Excuse me, but can I assist you in any way?' 'Thank you, sir,' she said, and looked up at me. She was Irish, as I had noticed from the first. And then she began sobbing even more bitterly, but I spoke to her very quietly. 'If you will give me your address I know a lady – a Sister – who will call upon you immediately and will endeavour to be of some assistance to you,' and she gave it to me. So I thought of Sister So-and-so – she is Irish, and was a Roman Catholic in her youth. She will know how to deal with the case.'[37]

Dorothea Price Hughes, *op. cit.,* pp. 214–15

One of his colleagues told me that he asked Price Hughes how it was that the Mission's lay evangelist got so many conversions, while they seemed so rare under the preaching of Price Hughes and himself. 'The explanation,' said Price Hughes, 'is that the man has been down there himself with them. He sees what he was himself in those people and he speaks to himself in them. You and I have never been down with them and we do not know how to approach them.'

Harry Jeffs, *Press, Preachers and Politicians. Reminiscences: 1874–1932*, 1933, p. 131

In 1901 the strain of his work at the West London Mission led to a period of enforced rest. The following year found him and his wife recuperating in south Devon.

What delightful rambles we had on those lovely Devonshire moors! It was our custom to start early in the morning, taking our lunch with us, or else getting it at some hospitable farmhouse. On one occasion an amusing incident occurred. Our hostess at the farmhouse where we stopped was not altogether pleased to see us (I think it was her washing day) and she was a bit tart in her manner. She ordered my husband to help her in the preparation of our repast in a truly Martha-like manner and he meekly obeyed. Suddenly one of our party spied hanging on the wall a photograph of the Rev. Mark Guy Pearse, whose name was honoured and revered throughout the length and breadth of Devonshire and Cornwall. 'Oh,' said she, 'you have a photograph of the Rev. Mark Guy Pearse, but you ought also to have one of his colleague, the

---

[37] It was to meet such circumstances as these in Victorian London that Katherine Price Hughes had begun to recruit her 'Sisters of the People'.

Rev. Hugh Price Hughes.' She replied, 'Yes, I do so want to see him, I have read a lot about him, and when he comes down here, as they say he is going to do soon, I shall go to hear him wherever it is.' 'Well,' she said, 'you need not go far to see and hear him, as at this moment he is watching the eggs boiling in the saucepan in your back kitchen.' The good woman collapsed gasping on the nearest chair, exclaiming: 'Well, I never! To think of sending him out there into the back kitchen.'

Katherine Price Hughes, *The Story of my Life*, 1945, pp. 95–6

Josiah Nix (1847–*c*.1932)

While Hugh Price Hughes was Superintendent of the Oxford Circuit from 1881 to 1884, the circuit experienced a remarkable spiritual revival. One convert was Josiah Nix, who became an outstanding evangelist.

I have often told the story of Josiah Nix. When I went to Oxford he was a lazy and self-indulgent Christian, with plenty of shrewdness and talk. Having nothing better to do he spent a great deal of time in criticising the ministers and explaining their intellectual deficiencies, but one Sunday morning it pleased God to open my friend's eyes to the folly and wickedness of a life of Christian idleness. I was preaching from the vision of God to young Isaiah, and like that noble youth Josiah Nix said in his pew, 'Here am I, send me.' After giving himself up to Christian service he was willing to do anything or go anywhere – except, by the way, to preach or to sign the pledge. I told him that it was nonsense for a Radical politician like himself to say that he could not preach. If he could pitch into his political opponents, much more could he pitch into the devil. He has a story about me to the effect that I gave him an appointment, that he came to me on the Saturday to explain he could not take it, that I thereupon basely increased my pace, being young, thin and athletic; and as he was somewhat stout at the time, he could not keep up with me, and that I left him panting in the rear with no alternative except to take his appointment. He adds that in a parting shot, as I disappeared in the distance, I exhorted him to 'give the devil a dig in the fifth rib'. At that first service Mr. Nix broke down. That is to say, he forgot the oration he was going to deliver – which was a great mercy – for at least two unconverted men broke down with him, and so God placed his seal upon a ministry which has been so much blessed since.

There was even a greater difficulty about Mr. Nix's beer, for although he never got drunk, he really liked malt liquor, and also had an idea that there was something mean and miserly in total abstinence, something inconsistent with genial hospitality. It so happened, however, that he was the secretary of the Mission Band which I have already described. We had a large number of converts at the close of the Mission in Oxford City itself. There were at least 200 young people converted. Following my usual plan, I invited them to tea on the Monday night after the Mission closed. I invariably on such occasions invite the converts to sign the pledge and to join the Church on the spot. I remember going to Mr. Nix and saying that I had promised him that I would not worry him about teetotalism, but that I was in a little difficulty, as it was my custom to invite the new converts to sign the pledge, but how could I do that in the presence of my secretary and right-hand man, when everyone there would know that he himself had not signed? However, I felt so much sympathy with him in that position that I would undertake to abstain from asking any of them on that occasion to sign the pledge, if he would take the responsibility of my silence and would justify it to Christ on the Day of Judgment. I left him; but before the meeting was held in the evening Mr. Nix came to me and said that he could not assume the responsibility of preventing me from making the appeal, and therefore he himself would sign the pledge and set an example to the rest! The effect of his example was enormous, and more than 200 persons followed it. From that time forward Temperance work went hand in hand with evangelistic work, to the immense advantage of all concerned.

Hugh Price Hughes, *The Revival of Oxford Methodism*, 1903, pp. 44–6

Sir Robert Perks (1849–1944)

Perks, the son of the Rev. George T. Perks, had a highly successful secular career and was a leading Wesleyan layman in the early years of the 20th century.

The whole future character of a child may depend on its nurse. A little incident occurred when my father was stationed as a minister in Bath. Our nurse belonged to a sect then known as Ranters.[38] She was a fanatical teetotaller and felt it her duty to teach me some of the rhymes in her hymn-book. Among others, one ran as follows:

Water, pure water, bright water for me,
Wine for the drivelling debauchee.

A few Sundays after I had learned those lines a benevolent-looking old Methodist Preacher came to supply for my father at the Walcot Street Methodist Chapel. He dined with us, and after dinner my mother asked him if he would like a glass of port wine. He said he would. Total abstinence was not so common then as it is today among the Methodist Preachers.[39]

As he was drinking his wine I turned to him and said, 'Sir, are you a drivelling debauchee?' 'Robert,' said my mother looking in horror at me, 'whatever do you mean?' I then repeated the lines which nurse had taught me. The old preacher laughed most heartily: but my mother looked very grave. I am not sure, in spite of Harry Lauder, whether Scotch people have a very keen sense of humour.

R.W. Perks, *Notes for an Autobiography*, 1936, pp. 9–10

Perks was a pupil at Kingswood School from 1858 to 1865, while it was still exclusively for the education of ministers' sons.

I am afraid I cannot say much for the religious atmosphere of Kingswood in my days. Now and then, during my seven years, messages were sent periodically to the Conference that 'a gracious revival had taken place at Kingswood'.

But the 'outbreak', as it was called, of a revival at Kingswood has left an unpleasant memory. The process was as follows: that a 'Revival would break out on Monday fortnight.' On the given day all sports were suspended. No cricket, no football, no fives were allowed. The ordinary classes were suspended. The day was set apart for prayer and the singing of hymns. The boys

---

[38] i.e. the Primitive Methodists.

[39] Perks means 'among the Wesleyans', who were very slow to take up the temperance cause.

were collected in numbers of thirty or forty into separate class-rooms. In each of these rooms, each under the supervision of a master, the lads were ordered to kneel down and 'plead for mercy' in silent prayer. A master walked round inquiring if this lad, or the next, or that other one, had 'found peace'. If not, the poor lad was kept for an interminable time on his knees. As soon as a lad had 'found peace', or thought he had, he was allowed to get up from his knees and go out into the playground. All lessons were suspended for this awful day. The lads were, however, allowed to walk about in twos or threes, supposed to be discussing with one another the state of their souls. Is it surprising that such an experience gave me, as it did many another lad, a queer feeling about 'revivals'? Nor is it surprising that our thoughts instead of turning to God and Heaven were fastened on the cricket ground.

R.W. Perks, *op. cit.*, pp. 20–1

In 1864 the Rev. George T. Perks moved with his family into Wesley's house, 47 City Road.

My small bedroom was at the back of the house and was John Wesley's 'praying room'. The maidservant nearly terrified me out of my senses by telling me that the ghost of Wesley at times came back there to pray. The old chapel keeper, Willmott, asserted most positively that he had seen John Wesley's figure walk across the chapel yard...

As a lad I saw from the windows of Wesley's House in 1864 one of the most wonderful sights London has ever witnessed. It was the entry into London of Garibaldi, the famous Italian Liberator.[40]

To welcome Garibaldi my father and I had made a banner and, in big red letters on a white ground, we printed the words, 'John Wesley welcomes Garibaldi.' We hung it in front of our house. When Garibaldi's carriage, drawn by two white horses, came opposite, the General saw our banner, and at once stopped his carriage and, standing up, took off his grey slouch hat with its black feather and made a low bow to our banner amid the loud huzzas of thousands of people...

To me, one of the saddest memories of City Road was the death of my dog. I determined he should be buried in hallowed ground. So at daybreak I rose early and dug a grave as near as I could get to John Wesley's. Two of my sisters followed my dog to the grave, but my eldest sister refused. She did not think that dogs had souls, but I stoutly asserted that this was contrary to Wesley's teaching. My father, when appealed to, said that it was a point he had never heard discussed at the College he attended; but he felt sure that if dogs ever got to heaven my dog *ought* to be there.

R.W. Perks, *op. cit.*, pp. 23–4, 30

---

[40] Two others with a Methodist connection witnessed Garibaldi's visit to London. Edward Jones (later Burne-Jones) and his wife Georgina, daughter of the Rev. George Browne Macdonald, watched from their lodgings at 62 Great Russell Street as Garibaldi, 'followed and surrounded by a great cheering crowd that surged through the gates and up to the [British Museum]. There he stopped before entering, and as he turned on the top step and stood bareheaded for a moment, his red-shirted figure showed clear above the dark mass of the people.' (Georgiana Burne-Jones, *Memorials of Edward Burne-Jones* (1904) I p.276)

In his early married life, Perks lived at Widmore, near Bromley, where he started a Sunday School, which soon had nearly 200 pupils. The following incident reminds us of the far-from-satisfactory relations in those days between 'Church' and 'Chapel'.

There was then no public elementary school in the village. Children coming to our Wesleyan Sunday School had for the most part to be educated in the National Church of England Day School, which was under the control of the Vicar of Bickley.

One of the troubles we had was with the 'Church Ladies' who, stylishly dressed, used to station themselves outside our chapel gates, trying to induce the children not to come into our Sunday School. I frequently had to go out and order these ladies away.

Shortly afterwards things came to a climax. At the School Sports of the National village school the first prize for the long foot race was won by a Methodist boy who attended our Sunday School. When, however, he went forward to receive his prize he was told that, as he attended the Wesleyan, and not the Church of England, Sunday School, he could not have the prize.

As soon as I heard of this I wrote to the Vicar, Mr. Weldon, asking him for some explanation. I pointed out to him that more than half of the Widmore children who were scholar at the National Church Day School were Methodists; that the Sports were the Day School and not the Sunday School sports; that we did not think it just or reasonable that the boy who had won the race should be disqualified simply because he went with his parents to the Wesleyan chapel and was a scholar in the Wesleyan Sunday School; and I requested that the boy should receive his prize. I also said that if this was refused I would at my own expense build a Wesleyan Day School in Widmore and take away the whole of the Methodist children. The Rev. Mr. Weldon, the Vicar of Bickley, who was a broad-minded man, came to see me. He apologised for the 'Church Ladies', who, he said, gave him much trouble. He said he had looked into this case and he had arranged that the boy should have his prize and it would be sent to his house.

'I am sorry, Mr. Weldon,' I said, 'that this has happened, but I regret I cannot agree to your suggestion. The boy has been publicly deprived of his prize and he must now publicly receive it.' This was done, and so the episode was closed. We saw no more of the 'Church Ladies'.

R.W. Perks, *op. cit.*, pp. 39–40

Edward Smith (1849–1902)

Smith had a short but memorable ministry at the St. John's Square mission, Clerkenwell, between 1886 and 1889. He avoided publicity through the popular press. His account of those years leaves one with the feeling that he was not altogether pleasant to know.

I remember that, in the early days of the work, there came to me after service one Sunday morning a seedy-looking mortal, who informed me, with an important air, that he was a 'reporter'. 'I am come to report for the ...' (naming a local publication), 'and there are some things about the service and in the sermon that I don't care for and cannot agree with, and I shall say so.' 'All right, sir, ' said I; ''tis with me as it was with the eels.' 'Eels, sir!' replied the man, who looked all the time as though he would gladly give a laudatory account, if I would but tip him with a new suit of clothes. 'Eels, sir!' said he, 'what of them?' 'Well, after the cook had skinned them, some one protested against the cruelty of the process. 'Ah, poor things!' said she;

'but it's nothing when they get used to it.' And, sir, your criticism will be nothing to me. I am used to that sort of thing.' Needless to say, he did not report anything flattering either of the preacher or of the service.

Edward Smith, *Three Years in Central London*, 1889, pp. 40–1

Thomas Jackson (1850–1932)

The future superintendent of the Whitechapel mission had made his mark as a mischief-loving boy in Belper. He and his closest friends had some contact with local Primitive Methodism.

When winter came the boys found shelter from the bleak weather in the 'Ranters' chapel, where, though tolerated, they were never welcome visitors. Well known as disturbers of the peace, they were always escorted by a seat-steward to a triangular pew at the very top of the gallery. He, good man, tried to give adequate oversight to the group of young scamps, but whenever, in the ardour of his devotions, he ceased to watch, pea-shooters were produced, and the missiles found a mark in the singers' pew, or even in the pulpit. Ignominious ejection followed.

During a period of prolonged drought, the 'Ranters', undisturbed by any doubt regarding the intervention of the Deity in weather conditions, decided to pray for rain. Meetings were held in a little thatched cottage with only a ground floor. The occupant was an elderly woman who never failed to 'engage'. Her prayers invariably ended with the high-pitched petition: 'Lord, pour out Thy blessing upon us. Let it come in bucketfuls.' Tom Jackson, who believed then, and believes still, that prayer is a co-operative concern, decided to lend a hand. One night three boys took pre-arranged stations. One crouched under the window, listening; another stood by with a bucket of water; and Tom Jackson was on the ridge of the roof near the chimney. Loud and earnest were the voices within the cottage. When the boy near the window whispered, 'She's started,' the second boy handed up the pail, and with the final petition, 'Send it down in bucketfuls,' Tom emptied the bucket of water down the chimney, and more soot than blessing fell upon the worshippers.

William Potter, *Thomas Jackson of Whitechapel*, 1929, pp. 7–9

Accepted for the Primitive Methodist ministry in 1876, Jackson was thrown in at the deep end by being appointed to the East End and expected to launch a mission there. He was scarcely exaggerating when he later wrote:

'Being pitchforked into the superintendency, the arduous duties of a new station, the demands of probationary studies, the erection of two new school chapels during probation, and details associated with the social ministries to the needy, rendered the demands upon health and strength at times very exacting.'

I entered upon my new duties on October 13th [1876]. The first Sunday I preached in London I preached at West Street[41] in the morning and had three persons as congregation. In the evening I preached at Squirries Street when, during the earlier part of the service, I had only the chapel-keeper as my congregation. In the afternoon I visited the notorious Mile End Waste, and was shocked by the profanity and Sabbath desecration that I witnessed. I took my stand amidst the hubbub and alone commenced to sing a hymn, and then exhorted the unsaved to turn from their sins and serve God. The experience of that first Sunday greatly distressed me; but it so profoundly stirred my soul that I resolved with the help of God, I would devote myself unreservedly to the work of serving and saving the poor in the East End. A mission in notorious, defiled and squalid Whitechapel from that day was the goal of my missionary ambition...

The second Sunday in London was spent at Walthamstowe, where my congregation numbered three persons in the morning and five in the evening. For a time my wife and I had to act as chapel-keepers. I resolved to devote my attention to the poorest districts, and systematically visited from room to room and house to house. The sights of suffering and privation I met with powerfully affected me. My rule was to pray with every person or family I visited whenever possible. But to pray with starving persons and not to do something to relieve their suffering I felt to be impossible. As we had no funds, and my salary was only one pound per week, my wife and I resolved to consecrate to our mission-work the few hundred pounds we had saved and the proceeds of the sale of our Sheffield house and furniture. On Lord Mayor's Day, November 9th, 1876, we held our first gathering of destitute men and women from the slums. A meat-tea was provided, followed by an evangelistic service. During the subsequent winter months when distress was acute, fifty families were provided with a breakfast each Sunday morning in our schoolroom, the proceedings being closed with a short gospel address and prayer... The idea of appealing to the public for funds to carry on this benevolent ministry did not occur to me until all our private means had been expended and we had experienced considerable domestic impoverishment.

Quoted in H.B. Kendall, *History of the Primitive Methodist Church*, 1905, II, pp. 507–8

At West Street Thomas Jackson grappled with the first of his many financial schemes. The sum involved was eleven pounds, the cost of a new harmonium. He set about making the acquaintance of possible helpers, and visited first of all a man who plied the humble but lucrative trade of Cats' Meat Merchant. 'I don't know you,' said the vender of feline provender, 'but you seem a decent chap and trying to do good. I'll give you half a quid.'

A greengrocer was the next victim. 'Go to the devil, you and your harmonium,' said he. 'Well, you are likely to supply his address,' was the retort. 'I think that's worth a bob,' replied the greengrocer, and forthwith the coin changed hands.

A tailor's workshop was next visited.

'Give us that song you sang at the corner of West Street,' pleaded the master tailor.

'Which song?'

---

[41] Not the former Wesleyan chapel in the West End, but what had been a beer house in the Bethnal Green Mission.

'That one about Zion's hill. Mates, listen to this gent sing a solo.'

The collection taken after the performance realised five shillings.

A retailer of sheep's heads and feet had no money to spare, but offered 'a head and a few trotters'.

'Will you keep them for me until next week?'

The tradesman agreed. Next week there was a well-patronised fourpenny supper at which fingers were more freely used than knives and forks. By such means the money was raised and the harmonium paid for on delivery.

William Potter, *Thomas Jackson of Whitechapel*, 1929, pp. 23–4

In 1883 Jackson launched a mission in Lower Clapton. Here, as in the East End generally at the height of Victorian England, desperate poverty was in evidence everywhere.

On a bitterly cold morning that winter, Thomas Jackson visited an elementary school in the district.

'It is heart-breaking work, this, Mr. Jackson,' said the headmaster. 'Some of the children fainted this morning through hunger, and many of them have had no breakfast.'

'How many do you think have come without breakfast this morning?'

'At least three hundred.'

'Send that number to my schoolroom tomorrow morning, and they shall have breakfast.'

What an undertaking! Three hundred guests to be provided for in the morning. There was a schoolroom, and there were tables, and facilities for boiling water; but no crockery, no food, no money, and less than twenty-four hours' notice. But there was a young man of ardent enthusiasm and inflexible purpose, burning to do his Master's work and not to be turned aside. The caretaker knew that 'it could never be done', until he was assured that it was going to be done. Then his doubtful attitude became one of eager helpfulness. Willing helpers came as they always do when the leader is there. The tradesmen refused to give credit, but what did that matter? The missionary had a presentation gold watch and chain, which could be changed into bread and jam and cocoa and mugs for the time being. Three hundred pinched children had breakfast that morning and went to school happier than they had been for many a day. After this, through many winters, breakfasts were provided for hungry children on each school morning.

A clothes store was also established for the children. As they came in for breakfast, Thomas Jackson would stand at the door, keenly watching for those with insufficient clothing or worn-out shoes. He would wrap a warm garment round a shivering child, and none was allowed to depart inadequately clad. The need of the clothes and boot store met the workers at every turn. A boy, having finished his breakfast, asked if he might leave before the others. When asked why he wanted to leave early, he said, 'My young brother is waiting at home for my boots, so that he can come for his breakfast.'

William Potter, *Thomas Jackson of Whitechapel*, 1929, pp. 43–4, 46

Jesse Boot (1850–1931)

The chain of chemists that became a familiar feature on every High Street was founded on popular advertising and a flair for undercutting rivals that characterised its founder. (For an interesting parallel, see John Mackintosh, below.)

Boot's great problem in planning to break into the patent medicine trade in a big way was shortage of capital... The principal source of capital was necessarily the small sums that [he] and his mother scraped together from their trading profit.

To win the turnover he needed, Boot had to advertise; after laying his plans for months he launched a major advertising campaign in one of the Nottingham newspapers, the Liberal *Nottingham Daily Express*, in February 1877... Boot took the biggest advertising space in the *Express* and under the headline 'PATENT MEDICINES RETAIL AT WHOLESALE PRICES' offered 128 separate proprietaries at cut prices, arranged alphabetically from Allen's Hair Restorer (3s. 6d. for 6s. bottle) to Woodhouse's Rheumatic Elixir (2s. 6d. for 2s. 9d. bottle). The list included 'Boots Patent Lobelia Pills for asthma, indigestion and spasms (one of his father's remedies), 'Boots Celebrated Bronchial Lozenges', 'Boots No Name Ointment', and 'Boots Aromatic Composition powder'. The truth of Boot's discount claims was borne out in numerous advertisements for proprietary medicines in the adjacent columns.

The advertising campaign enjoyed immediate success. As Boot recalled: 'When his scheme had been in operation for a month or so he found he was doing nearer £40 than £20 a week, and his business increased very rapidly.' The advertisement was continued three or four times a week until the beginning of April when Boot, acquiring more confidence daily, became more bold. M. & J. Boot now appeared as 'The People's Stores' and answered some attacks on their integrity with the heading 'FREE TRADE AND NO MONOPOLY'.

Boot's reputation among the working classes spread rapidly and in May he was taking £100 a week and opened his first bank account. Country people who flocked into Nottingham on Saturdays formed queues outside the Goosegate shop to seize upon new bargains. He advertised that 'LARGE SALES, ever increasing, have enabled us to make STILL FURTHER REDUCTIONS IN OUR PRICES' and added eight glowing testimonies to 'Boots Patent Lobelia Pills' which he epitomised as 'Health for a Shilling', a fairly obvious cut-price rejoinder to Beecham's well-known slogan, 'Worth a Guinea a Box'.

Stanley Chapman, *Jesse Boot of Boots the Chemists*, 1974, pp. 39–40

Frank Ballard (1851–1931)

Another man who made a great impression on me was Dr. Frank Ballard. Dr. Ballard was a man with qualities that were strikingly diverse; he was a man of profound learning and marvellous memory. I think he preferred to address meetings of men only; if they were inclined to be aggressive and unlikely to share his views, so much the better.

Bradford was a town which was becoming famous for its 'independent thinkers', and the working-classes, as they were called and proudly called themselves, were reading and studying, and inclined to be pugnacious, for religion was suspect.

One Sunday afternoon meeting for men attracted a large crowd to Carlisle Road. I have forgotten the subject of Dr. Ballard's address, but I shall never forget the 'Question Time' that followed it. The address had been forceful; but it had not convinced everybody.

A man rose to his feet.

'Ruskin says somewhere...' he began, and was promptly pulled up.

'*Where* does he say it?'

The man was able, after a pause, to reply correctly, and was allowed to continue. He quoted accurately a passage from the book and was about to comment on it, when he was again stopped.

'Carry on with your quotation,' said Dr. Ballard.

'How do you mean – "Carry on"?'

'Continue the quotation to its end. It doesn't finish where you ended.'

'It's all I remember,' the man answered.

'Then I'll finish it for you,' said the Doctor. Without a pause he did so; and the addition made all the difference to the speaker's argument.

A little later another man got up.

'It says somewhere in t'Bible...'

'And in what part of the Bible?' inquired the Doctor.

'I couldn't tell you, but I know it's there,' said the other.

'Carry on!' said the Doctor, and the quotation was rendered correctly.

'You are quite right; it *is* there. It is in the ... chapter of Isaiah and the ... verse,' said the Doctor.

I forget the chapter and verse that were quoted, but I checked them at the time, and they were correct. It was not only the strangers in the company who marvelled.

William Riley, *Sunset Reflections*, 1957, pp. 78–9

James Flanagan (1851–1918)

Flanagan worked as a lay missioner in Nottingham before entering the Primitive Methodist ministry.

It is now [1907] about twenty years since I resolved to make an attack on the crowds which attended a fair held near the city of Nottingham. When I arrived on the ground, the carnival was in full swing. Clowns, Pantaloons, Columbines, Man-Monkeys, old Bruisers, with all the other conglomerate of non-descriptive items which make up a country fair, were there. The row was fearful. Each show was trying to outdo the others in loudness of din. It was no mean task to face this Babylon of noise and pleasure. Borrowing a chair from a cottage, I fixed it at the entrance of the fair, that I might catch the people who were going to it. Mounting the chair I commenced to sing. The crowds of folk passing along appeared heedless. Some jeered, others laughed, while a number flung jokes as they swept on their way to the shows. But not a soul lingered to hear my message. In the midst of my singing I saw a man reeling along the road drunk. Steadying himself, he tried to fix his unsteady gaze upon me. Then he made a rush. Seizing me by the legs he shouted:

'Come' – hic – 'come' – hic – 'down, or I'll knock you down.'

Seeing my opportunity, I commenced to wrestle with the fellow, knowing that, he being drunk and I sober, I had the advantage. After a few minutes' struggling, in which I pretended to have the worst, I allowed him to pull me down from the chair. As soon as he released me, I leapt upon the chair again. This game continued for several minutes, I going up and down like a Jack-in-the-Box. The struggle drew the crowd. Hundreds came round from the neighbouring shows to see the parson get a drubbing. Just at the height of the fun, when I felt that I had had enough, a policeman pushed his way through the crowd and touching my opponent on the shoulder said:

'Here, come on. I've been watching you. Now off you go, or I'll run you in.' The fellow sheered off with a sheepish look, leaving me with an audience of over five hundred people whom I held for forty-five minutes by a straight and happy talk on sobriety and religion.

Flanagan's first circuit as a minister was Southwark.

The humour of the London street children is proverbial. They can sum up your character as by instinct and give you a name which will cling to you for years. I had taken a deep interest in the most neglected of them and consequently I was known to many of them in the slums. One day I turned the corner of a slum street rather suddenly and saw just ahead of me half a dozen ragged Irish youngsters sitting on and around a battered doorstep. Their conversation was such, no doubt, that they did not wish me to hear. Soon as they saw me, one in a loud whisper said:

'Whist! Whist! Mike, shut up, see, here comes 'Father Flanagan.'

Passing an old house one day in a side street, some two or three youngsters were pressing their faces against the panes, when one of them catching sight of me shouted, 'Hi! mother, hi! Look! Look! Here comes the father of us all'. I admired the boy's meaning, but decidedly objected to his bold statement.

One day a friend of mine, a minister, came to give the gutter youngsters a [magic] lantern service. The place was crowded, the order perfect. Ignorant of what the silence meant, he thought he was making a profound impression. To clench the nail he commenced at the close to tell them of a good little boy who always said his prayers and went to school. One day this boy died, but just before he passed away to heaven he sang a sweet and holy hymn. 'Now,' he said, amid the most perfect stillness, 'I wonder if there is a boy here who can sing the hymn which this good boy sang before he entered heaven.' Up went the dirty hand of a ragged youngster in the front. 'Oh,' said the minister, 'I am delighted to see that there is one boy who thinks he knows it. Now, my boy, stand up and sing the hymn which you think this good boy sang before the angels bore him away.' Judge of the man's surprise and horror when the young scoundrel, clearing his throat, struck up with 'Ta Ra Ra Boom De Ay'.

James Flanagan, *Scenes from my Life, both Grave and Gay*, 1907, pp. 34–5, 154–5

Katherine Price Hughes (1853–1948)

As the daughter of the Rev. Alfred Barrett, Governor of Richmond College, Hugh Price Hughes' wife was brought up in a 'well-to-do middle-class' family and accustomed to moving in intellectual circles. Her first encounter with a congregation of 'small shopkeepers, artisans and the highly respectable poor' in Brighton forced her to recognise that she was 'a contemptible little snob'.

We employed a working man, a cabinetmaker, to make a chest for us to house the various presents of silver which we had received as wedding gifts. I interviewed him with dignity and proper aloofness (as I, poor, silly little fool, thought), and then I was dumbfounded when the man, a kind, gentle, humble soul, asked me most respectfully if I would accept the silver chest as a little present to me and my husband on our marriage. My silly class pride was shattered, and I felt utterly humble in the presence of that kind, simple man. Indeed, he and I changed places at that moment. I felt that I was the inferior and he above me in simple kindness and goodness. I possess the chest that he made for us to this day. It is the memento of the destruction of my youthful snobbery. After that, I was not slow in making many friends among the members of our chapel at Warwick Gardens, and such kind, true friends they were. I found amongst them real saints and such true nobility of character. I also began to visit the very poor and got a little insight into the sufferings of their lives. No Old Age Pension for them, and for the aged, only one long bitter struggle to keep out of that horror, 'the Workhouse'.

Katherine Price Hughes, *The Story of my Life*, 1945, pp. 51–2

Moving from Brighton to Tottenham (then still a quiet village), she found that she still had much to learn about housekeeping responsibilities and those of a minister's wife.

The first nerve-wracking occasion that I had to encounter was the sewing meeting, held monthly by the ladies of the congregation. It was the custom to hold it at the houses of those ladies who were willing and able to receive the members; and, of course, I, as the minister's wife, was expected to lead off and do my share in giving the first entertainment when the sewing meeting opened for the winter. My old school friend, Alice Gardner, came to give me moral support on this momentous occasion. The ladies turned up in crowds, or so it seemed to my agitated mind, all agog to see the minister and his young wife and the house in which they lived. My heart sank, and I wondered how on earth I was going to deal with such a crowd in our small rooms. However, by carrying in most of the chairs we possessed, we found seats for the ladies and the sewing went on as usual while Alice Gardner read aloud to them. At five o'clock tea had to be served, and, as we had no room or table large enough, the tea had to be handed round, while I served it from the corner of a table in our sitting-room. I breathed a little more easily as all seemed to be going well and the ladies chatted and enjoyed themselves, when, suddenly, crash – down went my tall, silver cream jug, discharging all its precious contents into the lap of my best black silk frock, put on specially for the occasion. Oh, the awful ignominy and confusion of that moment! I longed for the earth to open and swallow me up. I felt that all the eyes of the assembled company were upon me as I mopped up the mess, with the aid of a maid, as best I could, and with a strong effort of self-control went on with my job. Then, suddenly, yells from our little nursery above sounded through the house. My friend Alice rushed up and returned to inform me that the baby, who was just beginning to toddle about, had fallen and cut her head. I felt that my doom was sealed. I flew out and found the baby's golden locks all stained with blood. However, the hurt was very slight and the baby soon comforted, and I returned to my company below feeling that I did not care in the least what might happen next. To my great relief, my husband had arrived on the scene, and was entertaining the ladies in his own inimitable way and I felt a load lifted from me.

Katherine Price Hughes, *op. cit.,* pp. 54–5

It was always a joy to attend a committee of the West London Mission with Mrs. Price Hughes in the chair. She quietly senses the capacity of each member, and no point escapes her. I once remarked, 'But surely that woman is a hopeless case!' I felt I had received a deserved rebuke when Mrs. Hughes replied, 'We are here to deal with what are called 'hopeless' cases.' About two years ago in gratitude to her, I gladly furnished a room at the Katherine Price Hughes Hostel for these 'hopeless' cases, where many women get a new start in life. She told me a story showing that in social and religious as well as in journalistic and political work the art of establishing contact, of which I have already given instances, is all important. One of the sisters of the Kingsway Mission called one day at the house of a woman who lived in the slums, and who was regarded by everyone as most difficult. The door was banged in her face. This happened several times. One day the sister knocked at the door with a bunch of snowdrops in her hand and said to the woman, 'I thought you might like these.' She immediately replied, 'Come in,' and exclaimed, 'Snowdrops! Snowdrops! Now you've broken me down. I used to be good,' she said, 'and every spring morning my mother used to put snowdrops on the kitchen table in the little cottage where we lived in Bedfordshire.' This incident removed all the past hostility. The woman began to attend the Mission and it finally led to her conversion.

Agnes E. Slack, *People I Have Met and Places I Have Seen*, 1941, pp. 104–5

John Scott Lidgett (1854–1953)

Lidgett has sometimes been called the greatest Methodist since John Wesley. His first circuit appointment, in 1876, was to Tunstall.

Shortly after my arrival in Tunstall, the President of the Wesleyan Conference, the Rev Alexander McAulay, a notable evangelist, who had made a great mark in the East End of London, signalised his year of office by arranging, indeed almost decreeing, that an evangelical mission should be conducted throughout the country, and should be carried out by a regular exchange of ministers throughout each District, each minister being called upon to give a week's mission in a neighbouring Circuit to his own... The arrangement of a week of special services in Tunstall gave a great opportunity to the more emotional and demonstrative section, who welcomed the opportunity of promoting and taking an active part in a revival. The institution of the 'Inquiry Room' had been recently introduced into this country by Moody and Sankey, and it was arranged that at Tunstall my three colleagues and I should take turns in helping the Missioner by taking charge of the after-meeting, held in the halfmoon-shaped vestry behind the large Wesley Chapel... On the Monday night of the mission I returned from a village service to find the excited and noisy evangelists in control of the after-meeting, the Superintendent Minister looking on in helpless inaction. The following night I was to be in charge, and I determined that there should be no recurrence of this excitement and disorder. So when the after-meeting was about to begin, I took up my stand in the vestry, and as each noisy person came in conducting young people who had been impressed by the service, I placed him and them at vacant places in the room, with strict instructions to each helper that he was to give *whispered* advice, so that those for whom he was concerned might understand the seriousness and full meaning of what they were about. Whenever noisy ejaculations began to break out, I either gave out a hymn, or called upon the interrupter to offer *extempore* prayer. Thus for two hours the meeting proceeded in as orderly a way as in any regular Church service. Needless to say, some of these 'Sons of Thunder' looked askance upon me when I met them in the street on the following day.

J Scott Lidgett, *My Guided Life, 1936,* pp. 82–84

The large Sunday School of Wesley Chapel [Tunstall] held an anniversary meeting in the spring of each year, and on one occasion I took part as a speaker. The proceedings were appallingly solemn, consisting for the most part of earnest but dull and misplaced addresses and of pious recitations given by a selected number of the scholars. The meeting was held on the middle floor of the large three-decker day school, the beams of which were supported by some half-dozen slender iron columns on each side of the hall. By the time the interval was reached in the middle of the meeting, my endurance of its gloomy solemnity was exhausted, so I rose and requested the chairman that I might be allowed to offer a prize, a proposal to which he graciously consented. I at once called upon the boys to take their stations at these iron pillars and to await my signal to swarm up them! There was an immediate rush in obedience to my order. I called, 'Once, twice, three times – off!' and up went the boys who had succeeded in finding a place. I gave a prize to the boy who had won the race. Needless to say, the chairman and the audience were astonished at this incursion into the proceedings, but they bore it with true forbearance.

J Scott Lidgett, *op. cit.,* pp. 84–85

St George's House was part of Lidgett's Bermondsey Settlement.

In connection with St George's House I may mention an amusing incident which took place in the autumn of 1905. I was invited to open a social institute, which was being established by a Wesleyan minister in Leicester. He had taken a house adjoining his church for the use of the young people of his congregation. On the appointed day he met me at the railway station, and then informed me that his project had encountered the strong opposition of the more old-fashioned members of the Church. I enquired whether they would be present at the meeting, and when he assured me that they would, I promised that I would find some way of dealing with the difficulty. The opportunity soon came. The chairman introduced me to the large congregation in a laudatory speech, in which he referred to my services on the London County Council, of which I had just been made an Alderman, to my impending presidency of the National Free Church Council, and, if I remember right, to my theological writings. On rising to speak, I thanked him for what he had said about me, but went on to say, 'I don't know what bearing all these matters have upon the present occasion, but I will tell you what *is* of importance to it. I am the proprietor of a Thurston's billiard table, and am known to His Majesty's Excise as a licensed retailer of tobacco and snuff.' Having flung this bomb into the camp of the enemy, I took it as my text and discoursed upon the religious, as well as social, value of the work in which they and I were engaged. This incident shows what those of us were 'up against' who, in those days, taught, and especially who acted upon, the teaching that the spiritual must needs seek and find fulfilment in the social.

J Scott Lidgett, *op. cit.*, pp. 125–6

Lidgett belonged to a generation which practised austerity in ministerial dress and deportment. He never himself abandoned this and, though far too great a man to attach undue importance to so secondary a matter, the following incident would suggest that he looked askance at the laxity of some of his younger brethren. He was passing one of the young ministers when he heard himself addressed: 'Good morning, Doctor.'

'Who are you?' he inquired.

'I am so-and-so, a minister in your District.'

Lidgett glanced at the young man, lightly garbed and with soft collar and coloured tie, and replied, 'Oh, are you? Then all I can say is you are suffering from ecclesiastical nudity. Good morning.'

Eric W. Baker in *John Scott Lidgett, a symposium*, 1957, p. 32

One of the wisest things Henry Carter did was to create the Temperance Council of the Christian Churches with its four Presidents, the Archbishop of Canterbury, a Free Church leader, the Roman Catholic Cardinal and the Salvation Army General. He had now devised a five-year plan to carry national temperance reform beyond the provisions of the 1921 Licensing Act. It was for the Temperance Council to lead this effort and an invitation meeting was arranged in the Egyptian Hall of the Mansion House to expound and press for local option, which was the spearhead of the campaign. By some ingenuity, a group of representatives of the licensed trade secured seats in the hall. The Archbishop of Canterbury, Dr. Randall Davidson, presided, and opened with an admirable speech in unqualified support of the policy. He then called upon the next President, the Roman Catholic Archbishop of Westminster, Cardinal Bourne. His alleged support of the proposal was so hedged about with qualifications and limitations that it lost all value and played right into the hands of the brewers. The temperature of the meeting fell to zero, and under these conditions Dr. Scott Lidgett, the Free Church President, was called upon. With graceful courtesy, he complimented the Cardinal upon his address and proceeded to interpret and embellish what had been said. In the skilful hands of Dr. Lidgett the audience could not fail to realise that the Cardinal had done a great service to the campaign. I have never heard anything more masterly, and it must have been impromptu. The meeting was saved and the forthright words of the General of the Salvation Army, the fourth President, formed a fitting climax to the statesmanship of Dr. Lidgett.

Another story about Dr. Scott Lidgett is worth telling. He had been brought specially to a meeting of the Temperance Council of the Christian Churches in the anticipation that he would resolve a situation of rather acute tension. Henry Carter explained the position with meticulous care. Gifted speaker as he was, he could be boring when he over-explained a complicated matter. This was such an occasion, and immediately he had finished Dr. Lidgett was called upon to speak. Instead of healing the rupture, he said all the wrong things and left the issue worse instead of better – to the complete dismay of those who had arranged his presence. A few days later I met him in one of the corridors of the Central Hall at Westminster. He looked at me rather quizzically and said, 'I'm afraid I did not help things very much the other afternoon.' 'Help!' I said. 'Why you put both feet into the trouble and stirred it up.' 'Well, I'll tell you a secret,' he replied, but you must not pass it on. Henry Carter sent me to sleep and I did not wake up until I heard my name called and had to get up to speak.' The interesting thing is that no one had guessed that as a possible explanation.

E. Benson Perkins, *So Appointed: an autobiography*, 1964, pp. 48–50

Creative work was his recreation. His holidays were found mostly in change of work. I recollect running across Dr. Dinsdale Young in the train, and, to my utter amazement, saw he was reading one of Edgar Wallace's books. 'I'm astonished, Doctor, I exclaimed. 'I thought I'd find you reading John Trapp, the prince of commentators, as I heard you once describe him.' Dr. Young replied, with a twinkle in his eye,: 'Ah, yes, but the bow must be unbent sometimes.' But when I saw Lidgett in the dining-car of the Atlantic Coast express, with the meal and all its distractions proceeding, lo and behold, he was reading a ponderous theological tome. 'I should find it difficult to read that at any time, most of all under these conditions,' I said, not daring to remark that the doctor was enjoying a cigar also. 'Then,' was the reply, 'you have not practised full mental control.' I sorrowfully agreed.

Eric S. Waterhouse in *John Scott Lidgett, a symposium*, 1957, p. 178

The World Methodist Conference of 1951 met in Oxford. A highlight of the programme was a service in the University Church of St. Mary the Virgin, where John Wesley had preached on several occasions. Despite his age (he was then 97) and increasing infirmity, Lidgett was the appointed preacher. The following account of the occasion is based on the evidence of several eye-witnesses.

Because of his frailty, medical help was in attendance and he was seated in a chair near the lectern, from where he could preach without having to climb the pulpit steps. Well before the Nicene Creed was recited, he struggled slowly and painfully to his feet to be ready for it.

His sermon was on 'The Modernity of John and Charles Wesley' and was delivered without the aid of the microphone, which had broken down. At the end of his forty-minute address he collapsed and had to be carried into the vestry. Rex Kissack, then the minister of Wesley Memorial Church, wrote: 'I have a fleeting vision of the other scarlet robed and hooded figures catching him and bearing him out. I confess it seemed like a painting of the 'Deposition from the Cross'. The general impression was that this must be the end, and how utterly fitting for the greatest Methodist of his age.'

Arthur Hill, the Methodist surgeon from Ipswich, was on hand to give him an injection and he began to recover. According to Paul Sangster, 'one hooded vulture's eye opened, looked at the syringe in the surgeon's hand and his voice croaked softly, 'That gave you a nasty shock, didn't it?' Rupert Davies recalled that 'he was already becoming conscious as he was lowered onto a stretcher and remarked: '*facilis descensus*'. He did not add, as Vergil did in his *Aeneid*, '*Averno*' ('to the lower regions' – i.e. Hell).'

Kissack said that Gordon Rupp, who was mainly responsible for the invitation to preach, 'told me how he reassured the reviving hero in the vestry ... 'Dr. Lidgett, you were terrific!' To which the answer came: 'Terrific? What do you mean? That I struck the congregation with fear?!' When Raymond Stringer, who was covering the event for the *Methodist Recorder*, came out from the vestry, Dr. Sangster (who had a keen eye for a good news story) said, 'Don't you wish he'd died, Mr. Stringer?'

The next morning, Rev. Dr. Harold Roberts reported to the conference that he had since visited Dr. Lidgett, who was resting comfortably in hospital. When he told him of the Americans' concern that his magnificent lecture had had such a distressing effect, Dr. Lidgett replied, 'I always say preaching is of no avail if it doesn't take something out of you.'

My father [W.E. Sangster] delighted in the story of how he met Scott Lidgett on the day F.D. Roosevelt died. 'Doctor,' said my father. 'This is sad news.' 'Terrible,' said the old man, 'I haven't had such a shock since the day Lincoln was assassinated.'...

The story that involved both patriarchs [Luke Wiseman and Scott Lidgett] was especially dear to my father. I strongly suspect that it is apocryphal, but that seems a carping reason for omitting it. Both were at luncheon. Scott Lidgett, then more than ninety, was always interested in social welfare and became concerned over the great trouble the young waitress was taking. He asked kindly, 'What time do you finish work, my dear?' She withered him. 'Too late for you, old cock.'

Paul Sangster, *Doctor Sangster*, 1962

Lidgett died at the age of 98, having been in the ministry for 73 years.

The well-known story of the artist is typical. When he had completed his portrait of Lidgett at the age of seventy-five, the artist, a much younger man, said to him: 'Doctor, I should like to paint you when you reach your hundredth birthday.' Lidgett, looking him up and down, replied: 'Well, I don't see why you shouldn't; you look quite strong and healthy.'

Eric W. Baker in *John Scott Lidgett, a symposium*, 1957, p. 36

Joseph Rank (1854–1943)

A self-made millionaire, Rank gave much financial support to the 'Forward Movement', especially by funding the building of Central Halls. His parents had been Wesleyans, but his lavish generosity in later years to Methodism might well have been directed elsewhere, but for the following occurrence.

In the first years of their married life Joseph Rank and his wife began to attend the services at the parish church. Since leaving the Beverley Road Sunday school, he had rarely gone to church at all, but his new responsibilities, doubtless reinforced by the Victorian convention, led him to take a more serious view. There came a Sunday, however, when the vicar preached a sermon strongly emphasizing predestination. Joseph Rank waylaid him afterwards, to say, 'Mr. Davis, I'd like to be sure I understood your argument. You say that God determines, before a child is born, whether he shall be saved or damned?' The vicar agreed. 'Then, if I had two sons,' said his questioner, 'no matter what their abilities might be, according to your belief one might be predestined for Heaven and the other predestined for Hell? If I believed *that*, I'd never be responsible for bringing another child into the world.'

When he reached home, he told his wife what had happened. 'I've done with that church,' he said. 'I can't believe that stuff!' They at once decided to try somewhere else. Alfred Gelder invited them to share his pew one Sunday in Kingston Wesleyan Chapel. They went, and that morning the preacher was the Rev. Simpson Johnson, one of the ablest Methodist ministers of his generation, then in the full power of his early promise. Joseph Rank was much impressed and presently decided to rent a pew.

In church life as well as business life he would often do the unexpected thing... One evening in Hull an old pensioner reached the room on the ground floor of the premises in which Mr. Rank's class usually met, but was bitterly disappointed to find it closed for decoration. A notice directed members to meet upstairs. The old man could not climb the stairs, and, almost in tears, turned away to go home again. Before he had gone far, however, he met Mr. Rank, who stopped and asked him why he was looking so miserable and why he wasn't heading for class. The old man disconsolately told him what had happened. 'Why, is that all!' cried the leader. We'll soon put that right. You come along with me.' When they reached the foot of the stairs he suddenly stooped and said: 'Now, get on my back. I'll carry you up – I've carried many a sack of flour heavier than you!' - and in that unconventional fashion they mounted the stairs to class.

In any discussion, whether in a business council or a church group, he would say bluntly what he thought, with a Yorkshire disregard for minor courtesies, and even his fellow Yorkshiremen did not always relish his treatment of them. At Queen's Road Church [Hull] one evening he attended a meeting of the leaders after a long and trying day of unusually exacting business, and, in an irritable mood, began to criticise in very strong terms a member of the meeting who was not in the room. [The Rev.] George Marris was presiding and, taking the first opportunity, quietly said, 'If I were you, Mr. Rank, I shouldn't go any farther along that line.' The miller was furious. 'Are you telling me to sit down?' he demanded. 'Well, yes, Mr. Rank, if you put it that way,' the minister replied, calmly, 'I should advise you to sit down.' He at once sat down, but as soon as the Benediction had been pronounced, instead of chatting for a few minutes and saying good night, as he usually did, he went out in a rage.

When the minister reached home, he said to his wife, 'Mary, I think you had better begin packing. I have upset Mr. Rank, and I feel we shall have to leave Hull at Conference.'

The next morning, while the minister and his wife were at breakfast – in gloomy mood, for neither of them wanted to uproot themselves as yet from a city they both liked and from a ministry which he regarded as full of possibilities for good service – they heard the front-door bell ring, and the maid announced that Mr. Rank had called. In the drawing-room the minister found Joseph Rank pacing up and down in much agitation of mind, looking pale and haggard. Turning as the door opened, he said at once in his forthright way, 'Mr. Marris, I've come to ask your forgiveness. You were right and I was wrong. I haven't been able to sleep all night. I oughtn't to have said what I did.'

At once, gripping his hand, the minister responded: 'That's all right, Mr. Rank; there's no need to ask my forgiveness. I only tried to save you from yourself; but let me say this: I was faced with a temptation last night – the temptation to say to myself, "I know what I ought to do; indeed, what I should do at once if anybody else was talking like that. But Mr. Rank is Mr. Rank – and he's a rich man, and powerful; I'd better let him go on."'

Joseph Rank respected his minister all the more for that. As for George Marris, he often declared that Joseph Rank was the most generous and deeply spiritual layman with whom he had been associated throughout his ministry.

Rank was a staunch Sabbatarian, refusing to allow his mills to operate on Sundays.

The uncompromising nature of his conviction on this matter was shown when a breakdown at one of his large mills in the north reduced output by more than half for at least three weeks; indeed, at one time it looked as if the stoppage would go on for much longer. The commercial manager was at his wits' end to know how to deal with the mounting total of orders that could not be supplied. In order to make up some of the leeway, he decided to run the part of the mill that was still in action right through the weekend.

Joseph Rank knew nothing of this until, at the close of the following week, the manufacture sheet revealed what had been done. Immediately, he left home and travelled north through the night, and on the following morning was down at the mills soon after eight o'clock. He wasted no words. He asked the manager: 'Did you run the mills through last Sunday?'

'Yes, sir,' he replied, and began to explain; but he was cut short.

'Why didn't you telephone London and ask permission to do it?'

'Well, sir, I knew that if I did I should only get a refusal; and we were in such an awful mess that I felt we had to pull the ox out of the pit even though it was the Sabbath Day.'

That touch of humour allayed the Governor's wrath a little, and his eyes began to twinkle.

'That's all very well,' he said, 'but I don't like it. I don't like it. You know the rule. My mills are never run on Sunday. Now, don't you ever do it again.'

Nothing more was said. He knew when to leave well alone.

Not that he was always like that. On another occasion quantities of flour had been missing from the mill over a long period. Joseph Rank hated any sort of waste, but this was worse – it was evident that extensive pilfering was going on, and he made up his mind to stop it. When every other plan had failed, the police were called in, and one morning a detective went to Rank and told him the culprit had been discovered. 'Who is it?' he asked. The name given was that of a foreman who had been with the firm from the early days – a man he had liked and trusted. After expressing pained surprise, he said, 'Well, I'll deal with him. I don't want to bring any charge against him.'

'I'm afraid it's too late, sir. He's admitted his guilt, and we've arrested him. We shall have to charge him – and he'll certainly go down the line.'

Greatly troubled and perplexed, that evening Joseph Rank walked alone to the street of workmen's dwellings where he knew the man lived. As he came to the house, he noted the tidy curtains and the clean, whitened window-sills and step; it looked, as he had expected, thoroughly respectable. He knocked on the door, and as soon as the wife saw him she burst into tears.

'Now, it's no use crying,' he said in kindly tones. 'Will you let me come in?'

She admitted him, and in the quiet little parlour he said, 'Your man's done wrong. I'm afraid he'll have to go to prison – probably, they say, for six months. Now, tell me – what made him do it?'

It was a pitiful story to which he listened – of domestic trouble and debt; and when she had finished he exclaimed: 'But why ever didn't he come to me? Surely he knew I would have helped him?'

That was always his point of view. He regarded himself as the father, so to speak, of a big business family, and perhaps did not sufficiently understand the spirit of independence in his men – though, of course, there must have been other, and less honourable, motives in this man's case.

'Well, now,' he went on, 'there's no need for you to worry. While he's serving his sentence your money will come to you just as it always has done; and when he comes out, send him round to see me.'

The man served his sentence, and then called at the office. Joseph Rank told him exactly what he thought of him, read him a lecture on the sin of dishonesty, and then said: 'Well, that's that. You've had your lesson. You'll understand that I can't take you on again. But – now, listen. In … Street there's quite a good little provision business. It's for sale. I want you to buy it. Oh, I'll find the money – and put you in to run it. So, go along and get it.' He did, and the business thrived.

> R.G. Burnett, *Through the Mill*, 1945, pp. 36–7, 77–8, 139–41

Joseph Rank had a problem with anything other than the simplest forms of Methodism. The Rev. C. Leonard Tudor (later General Secretary of the Methodist Home Mission Department) was a young minister in Northampton at Park Avenue church and wrote to Joseph asking for money to help with the building. The letter came back saying that if the building had a spire he would not contribute to it. Tudor replied, 'It has a spire and you can keep your money!' To which Joseph replied, 'Good for you, here's a cheque.' Joseph liked domes, wasn't keen on spires, but admired confidence above both.

> Michael Wakelin, *J. Arthur Rank: the Man behind the Gong*, 1996, p. 30

If the Methodist Conference was held in Hull or Manchester or Liverpool, or any other city where he had an office, he would combine attendance at it with business engagements. On a day when Conference assembled at the Central Hall in Manchester he went first to Rank's office, and after seeing to the necessary business asked the young man with whom he had been talking how far it was to the hall. Knowing his chief's peculiarities, he did not offer to drive him over in his car, but asked, 'Well, sir, will you walk or catch a tram?'

'How much time would a tram save?'

'Very little, sir; you could probably walk just as quickly.'

'Then I'll walk. D'you think you could spare time to show me the way?'

After giving the question ostentatious consideration, he replied, 'Well, yes, sir, I think I could just manage that.'

The 'Governor' was pleased at that, and they set out at a brisk pace. In one of the side streets a young woman overtook, and passed, them. Joseph Rank stopped in vexation. 'When I was younger,' he exclaimed bitterly, 'I'd let nobody pass me! Now even women can pass me in the street. I must be getting old!'

He was nearly eighty!

Rank's giving was as discriminating as it was generous.

Among his chief concerns in dispensing money was his anxiety to stimulate and not discourage local giving. He knew that a church, like any other organisation, is valued in proportion to the sacrifice its members are willing to make for its upkeep. Hence, whenever he responded to an invitation to support a building or extension scheme he would do so in the form of a challenge, promising to provide a definite percentage of the sum raised by the people themselves. This was not always understood, and once it led to an amusing situation in which he turned the tables on a business friend. Hearing that Joseph Rank had agreed to double the collection at a certain mission anniversary, he thought he would make the miller pay more than he intended; so he persuaded several of his well-to-do business friends to go with him to the meeting and each put £50 into the collection; but to his surprise, Joseph Rank, instead of showing dismay, was delighted – had not his offer been intended to stimulate local effort?

Another story told about him in this connection concerns a bazaar at a Methodist mission. At one of the stalls he inquired the price of a shawl. The stallholder, seeing a chance not to be missed, at once said, £5 to you, Mr. Rank.' 'Oh,' he said with a smile, 'but Mrs. Rank really has more shawls than she knows what to do with. I'll give you £2 for it.' For some time they haggled and eventually he bought it for £3. The lady, herself no inexpert bargainer, may have thought him mean; if so, she was astonished when later it was announced that he had doubled the total proceeds.

Rank's decision to build the Clarence Mills in Hull, complete with the latest machinery, was the first step in the growth of what became a multi-million-pound flour-milling business.

Joseph Rank's last visit to Hull was overshadowed by tragedy. Those who stood beside him as he gazed upon the ruin of the mills he had built in his prime were deeply aware of it. So, no doubt, was he. But he gave no sign. He was always at his best when facing difficulty.

The Clarence Mills, his first great achievement and the symbol of his life's work, had been destroyed by German bombs. True, the high stacks and the lofty outer walls still stood beside the murky river, but they were no more than a gaunt and broken shell. Where the heavy rollers had ground the grain, where the mighty engines had throbbed night and day, all was silent as a tomb. Some men would have looked upon it as a tomb, the final grave of valiant and high-hearted enterprise.

As Joseph Rank looked at those blackened walls, a man far in the eighth decade of his life, only a few months from its end, his mind must have returned to the days when he first planned these mills. It was his boldest venture. It marked his emergence from the mass of men. It laid the foundations of his fortune, and of many another's. All that he became, all he was able to do for his countrymen, was there in embryo. The mill became a landmark. It may be said to have done much to establish the commercial prosperity of Hull. It was the apple of his eye. Now – only desolation remained.

Yet of the little group about him in the yard he asked only one question, in his blunt, Yorkshire way: 'Did you get the horses out?'

Yes – they had got the horses out. Every one of them. That satisfied him. He had always loved horses and could not bear to think of any of them suffering. As for the mills, turning back to the car, he exclaimed: 'What's done can't be undone. It's no good thinking of the past. It's the future that matters. A few bombs can't destroy our work. After the war we shall build new and better mills.'

And he drove away without a backward glance.

R.G. Burnett, *Through the Mill,* 1945, pp. 8, 193, 203–4

Sir John Bamford-Slack (1857–1909)

Solicitor, Liberal MP and local preacher. Through his friendship with Hugh Price Hughes, he became closely involved in the work of the West London Mission, including its open-air witness.

He was a great believer in the local preacher's 'oldest work' – organised open-air preaching – and was sometimes to be seen speaking on a Sunday afternoon in Hyde Park. These efforts tried him much more than many a service, because of 'the enormous feeling of responsibility'. One Sunday morning he had promised to speak with Sir Percy Bunting at an open-air service on Kingsland Green – a happy hunting-ground for the blatant unbelievers of London. He was greatly troubled as to the line of argument and subject matter he should take. He spoke to Mr. Price Hughes about it. 'There is no difficulty,' said Mr. Hughes. 'Tell them the account of your own conversion, that is the best sermon and the most unanswerable argument you can give.' So the practised speaker and debater told the simple story of his conversion, and few listened unmoved. He used to say that the inquiry-room at St. James's Hall furnished him with his best arguments for the power of saving grace, and the most potent inducement to sinners to decide for Christ.

Arthur and Ensor Walters, *Sir John Bamford-Slack*, 1910, pp. 42–3

Frederick Luke Wiseman (1858–1944)

Wiseman was the second President of the newly united Methodist Church, in 1933. Harold Murray illustrated his versatility.

What was the greatest thing I ever saw the Rev. F. Luke Wiseman do? Preach a dramatic sermon in that stentorian voice of his? Sway Conference by a statesmanlike speech?

No, I saw him kneel down in the market place on a bitterly cold day – there was snow on the ground – and point converts to Christ...

It seems almost incredible, but Mr. Wiseman was told by his parents that at the early age of three he was found sitting up in bed (when he was supposed to be asleep), singing 'O happy day that fixed my choice'!...

When F.L.W. was a young student at Didsbury College, he was sent to a slum area in Salford, and on arrival after a long walk round he was expected to speak in the open-air. He said to the old man who met him, 'Where is the congregation?' 'Ee, lad,' said the good old Lancashireman, looking round an empty and desolate street lined with dilapidated houses, 'your congregation's theer, all right. It's t'other side o' t' keyhole.' Mr. Wiseman never forgot it, and has quoted the saying hundreds of times in his appeals for open-air evangelism. 'Behind the window curtains' would probably be more accurate, but it would mean the same thing.

> Harold Murray, *Press, Pulpit and Pew*, 1934, pp. 52–3

Douglas Cock recalled Wiseman as a very old man, during the years when his son was editor of the Methodist Recorder.

I lived then in digs, next door to Dr. Wiseman's house in Wandsworth Common. It was bombed during the second world war and it was later reliably reported that he was dug out of the rubble, although the additional detail that when his rescuers reached him he was singing 'O for a thousand tongues to sing my great Redeemer's praise' is generally thought to be apocryphal.

In those pre-war years, Dr. Wiseman occasionally wrote 'leaders' [for the *Recorder*] and I would collect these from his house. They were handed to me by his housekeeper, and I never saw him. One Sunday, my landlady – a faithful and pious Baptist – went to a neighbouring Methodist Church to hear Dr. Wiseman preach for the first time. She came back clearly unenthusiastic. When I pressed her, she said she had lived next door to Dr. Wiseman for several years, had caught glimpses of him in his garden, and he had never once spoken to her. His text that morning had been 'Who is my neighbour?' I think an innate reticence sometimes gave him the unfair reputation of autocracy. Like his two sons, he was a great lover of people.

> Douglas Cock, *Every Other Inch a Methodist*, p. 19

Samuel Chadwick (1860–1932)

This story was told about Chadwick's mother, who as a matter of principle had never been inside a theatre.

Her husband said he thought a certain play, perhaps it was 'The Sign of the Cross' or something like that, was good and might be seen without harm, so she allowed herself to be taken for the very first time into a theatre. When she took her seat, she immediately bowed her head in prayer.

'Come, come,' said her husband, nudging her, 'people don't pray here.'

'*Don't* they?' said the good soul, 'then it's no place for *me*. I shall not stay.' And out she went.

> Harold Murray, *Press, Pulpit and Pew*, 1934, p. 40

His humble origins in Burnley taught Chadwick some important truths about Christian discipleship. He was converted at the age of 10 at a Sunday School Anniversary service.

The preacher was the Rev. Samuel Coley, Professor of Theology at Headingley College. The boyhood mind was arrested ... by a story which the preacher told about Newton, who had said if he were a shoeblack he would be the best shiner of boots in his village. When the preacher talked about shining boots the boy sat up. Here is his story:

'I hated to clean boots, especially father's Wellingtons. The Anniversary Sunday was a wet day, boot-cleaning the next morning was at its worst. I began with the Wellingtons, on the principle that the irksome part of the task is best tackled at once. I got through and put them down with a sense of relief. Then, as I looked at them, the preacher's words about shining boots as if Jesus Christ were going to wear them challenged me. I had no idea about being a lily among thorns, but I wondered if those Wellingtons would look well on the feet of Jesus Christ. For answer I took up the boots and began again. It was a simple thing to do, but I believe, in the light of after years, that it was the most important thing I ever did in my life. It was the adoption of a fixed principle from which I have never gone back. I got into the habit of doing the simplest duties as unto, and for, Jesus Christ... I always believe that Anniversary Day was the day of my conversion. I went to no enquiry-room. I joined no Society Class. I was only a lad, but I knew Jesus. Taking up the boot a second time to do it for Jesus was the confession of my choice. It registered my decision.'

> Norman G. Dunning, *Samuel Chadwick,* 1933, pp. 30–1

Before his acceptance as a ministerial candidate, Chadwick's service as a lay agent at Stacksteads near Bacup foreshadowed some aspects of his evangelical ministry. The following incident occurred during a week of intensive prayer meetings in the church he was serving.

One night there came to the meeting the most notorious drunkard in the town. His name was Robert Hamer, but everybody knew him as 'Bury Bob', and he himself had forgotten his proper name. He had been guilty of every brutal crime in the calendar except murder, and the exception was of grace. He had fought a fierce bull-dog with his hands tied behind his back, worried rats with his teeth, eaten glass, swallowed knives, smashed furniture, wrecked public house bars, mauled policemen, and fought all comers. He was a terror. His presence in a religious meeting was a sensation. When he walked to the table and asked for a pledge card the excitement was overwhelming. There was a stillness like the silence in heaven, as he took the pen and made a cross opposite his name. The following Sunday he was gloriously saved. Next morning he was first at the quarry, and very quietly he told every man as he came what had happened. Then hell was let loose. Men who a week before dare hardly have looked at him sneered and taunted, tempted and teased the great giant. He bore it meekly until Friday. Then as they were moving a huge piece of rock it caught his finger, and before he knew it he swore a great oath. Then they laughed with a great laughter and asked what had happened to his religion. They released his finger and offered to bind it up. To their surprise he dropped on his knees, clasped his hands, and while the blood dripped off his elbow he cried to God in a great agony of soul. When peace came he rose quietly, and every man of them was standing with his cap in his hand. Next Sunday morning the town turned out to see Bob go to chapel. One would have though the Mayor and Corporation were going... The revival went on for months, and hundreds of the very worst people were gloriously saved.

Norman G. Dunning, *Samuel Chadwick, op. cit.*, pp. 44–5

Chadwick's second circuit, in 1887, was Clydebank, Glasgow.

There was a new building at Clydebank, and the first Sunday in September was practically the opening Sunday. A few people had worshipped in a wooden shed, but when the young minister arrived, both Church and congregation had to be gathered. There was no reception. the first people saw of him was at a street corner on Saturday night preaching the Gospel. Nobody knew him. He found a place which he thought was ideal for an open-air meeting. There was a row of houses opposite. He went to the end cottage and knocked at the door. It was opened by a big, bulky, strong-looking woman, with her sleeves rolled up above her elbows. Mr. Chadwick asked her if she would let him have a chair for an hour. 'No!' she said, banging the door in his face. The young man was not dismayed. His first impulse was to ask at the cottage next door, but thinking that he might get the same reply, he ventured to knock at the same door again. The same woman answered. The second time he asked for the chair. 'I told you once,' she said, 'you won't get it,' and again the door was closed. He knocked a third time. The woman opened the door in a rage. 'I want to give you a shilling for the loan of a chair,' said Mr. Chadwick. The woman was hesitant for a minute, then she replied, 'Why didn't you tell me that at first?' She brought the chair and he put his hand in his pocket and gave her the shilling, saying, 'I'll give you another, if you will come and hold it for me while I stand on it.' The big woman walked across the square with the frail-looking little minister. He put the chair where he wanted it, stood on it, and told her to put her hand on the back of it. Then he turned round and gazed at her. What a scene for the middle of a Scottish town on a Saturday night! A young man standing on a chair, gazing down at a big, masculine-looking woman! Some people were passing, and they stayed to see what it was all about. The man on the chair uttered not a word. More people came and stood. Presently there was a crowd around. 'What is it for, Guv'nor?' shouted somebody. Mr. Chadwick did not answer. 'He's selling pills,' replied another. Still Mr. Chadwick did not speak. The crowd began to get excited. At the end of twenty minutes the woman had had enough, and bolted. Mr. Chadwick preached to his first audience at Clydebank. Within a few days the whole town was talking about him. His church was soon full. He had to begin at the beginning. His own converts became the church officers, and three of his keenest workers he got from behind the publican's counter.

Norman G. Dunning, *op. cit.*, pp. 64–6

The Conference of 1890, at which Chadwick was ordained, took the unprecedented step of appointing him Superintendent of the Leeds Mission. One of his strongest supporters in the Mission was a bow-legged cobbler named Tommy Dougill.

With his pony-cart he spent his Mondays collecting shoes to be repaired, and at the end of the week returned them to their owners... Tommy had not been converted long before he began to preach. He became quite a character in the neighbourhood. He called at a house one day to collect a pair of shoes which required some attention, and the lady, who knew his story, introduced him to the curate, who was paying a pastoral visit. The curate was amazed at the information that this illiterate cobbler was a preacher, and especially when Tommy proceeded to give him an outline of the sermon he had preached in a village chapel a week before. His subject was 'Three Fools'. 'The first fool was the man who said in his heart, 'There is no God.' He was a fool in the realm of his thinking. The second fool was the fool who said to his soul, 'Eat, drink, and be merry.' He was a fool in the realm of his living. The third fool was a fool for Christ's sake.' The curate was impressed. 'Why do you not join the real Church?' he said. 'Well,' replied Tommy, 'I have three reasons for being a Methodist. First, I was converted in a Methodist chapel, and I reckon it's good enough reason for belonging to a family that you are born in it. Second, Methodist religion suits the likes o' me. You see, in your Church you do so much getting down on your knees and up again, and my strong point isn't in my legs. Third, the Methodist Church gives me some work to do and I like it.' 'Oh,' said the curate, 'we will find you plenty of work to do in the Anglican Church, Mr. Dougill.' 'No, you wouldn't,' replied Tommy; 'not the work I should want to do. You wouldn't let me preach in your Church, would you? You wouldn't even let my minister preach there, and he can lick all on you.'

Norman G. Dunning, *op. cit.*, pp. 71–3

In 1913 Chadwick succeeded Thomas Cook as Principal of Cliff College. The Whit Monday Anniversary was a highlight of the college year, both spiritually and financially.

On one occasion the Chairman for the Anniversary meeting came for the weekend. At the close of the morning service on the Sunday they were walking together in the grounds. 'I have been blessed this morning,' said the Chairman, 'and I want to give you a cheque for a hundred pounds.' The Principal stopped to receive it, then lifting his eyes to heaven he said, 'Lord, bless him again tonight.' The Lord answered the prayer, and the Chairman increased his donation to two hundred and fifty pounds.

Norman G. Dunning, *op. cit.*, p. 199

Dr. Chadwick was one of the most gloriously natural saints I ever knew. A short time before his death he took me on one side and told me he was really a bit worried because of certain criticisms that had come from 'narrow people'. Many who did not know him would have said he was pretty dogmatic and old-fashioned. He could surprise you.

At a Mission Anniversary I heard him say, "A lady said to me the other day, 'Isn't it dreadful that the girls of today should wear their skirts so short?'" At that point in his address some women began to applaud loudly. They didn't expect what followed.

'What do you think I replied?' continued Dr. Chadwick. I said, 'Eh, but *aren't their legs bonny?*'

After saying things like that he would express the hope that they wouldn't be reported. 'They slip out,' he told me, 'just when I don't intend them to...' He would suddenly, in his later years, bring out a joke that to some would spoil a great sermon, but which, whether it was a good illustration or not, he couldn't have kept back anyhow.

The best example I can remember was a great evangelical sermon in which he made us roar with laughter over the story of the Lancashire men who argued over a piece of music. One said, 'I tell ye it's a refrain from Waggoner.' The other, having been up to a board displayed on the bandstand, said, 'Lad, ye're wrong. It's refrain fra' spittin'.' But what the story was supposed to illustrate in the sermon no one could say.

Harold Murray, *Press, Pulpit and Pew*, 1934, p. 43

In 1918 Chadwick was elected President of the Conference.

Perhaps no appointment which he took that year thrilled his soul more than his return to Wesley Church, Burnley [his birthplace], as President of the Conference. A great reception was given in his honour. The folk who knew him as a mill-lad turned up in their scores. Methodist dignitaries in the neighbourhood made eulogistic speeches. Burnley was hailing one of its greatest sons that day. Mr. Chadwick often told, in later years, of the wonderful addresses to which he listened that afternoon. He had no idea that these important people of the Methodist Circuits of Burnley thought that there were such possibilities in him, for one after another said that from his early days as a preacher they knew he was destined for the highest office the Church could bestow. 'And then,' Mr. Chadwick would add, with a twinkle in his eye, 'we went downstairs to tea, and one after another of these same folk came up to me and said, 'Aye, Sam lad, who'd ha' thought it?'

Norman G. Dunning, *Samuel Chadwick,* 1933, pp. 186–7

Henry J. Pickett (1860–1931)

Dr Wilbert F. Howard used to tell the following story about the former Principal of Hartley Primitive Methodist Theological College.

Once at an acrimonious meeting, Pickett was told by his people, 'Remember you are our servant.' 'Yes,' he retorted, 'I am your servant, but you are not my masters.'

Gordon S. Wakefield, *Robert Newton Flew 1886–1962*, 1971, p. 172

Rodney ('Gipsy') Smith (1860–1947)

Gipsy Smith's mother died while he was still a boy and one day he startled himself by declaring, 'By the grace of God, I will be a Christian and I will meet my mother in heaven!'

A few days afterwards I wandered one evening into a little Primitive Methodist chapel in Fitzroy Street, Cambridge, where I heard a sermon by the Rev. George Warner. Oddly enough, I cannot remember a word of what Mr Warner said, but I made up my mind in that service that if there was a chance I would publicly give myself to Christ. After the sermon a prayer meeting was held, and Mr Warner invited all those who desired to give themselves to the Lord to come forward and kneel at the Communion rail. I was the first to go forward. I do not know whether anybody else was there or not. I think not. While I prayed the congregation sang --

> I can but perish if I go,
>   I am resolved to try,
> For if I stay away, I know
>   I must for ever die.

And --

> I do believe, I will believe
>   That Jesus died for me,
> That on the cross He shed his blood
>   From sin to set me free.

Soon there was a dear old man beside me, an old man with great flowing locks, who put his arm round me and began to pray with me and for me. I did not know his name. I do not know it even now... So there and then I placed myself by simple trust and committal to Jesus Christ. I knew He died for me; I knew He was able to save me, and I just believed Him to be as good as His word. And thus the light broke and assurance came. I knew that if I was not what I ought to be, I never should be again what I had been...

Next morning I had, of course, as usual to go out and sell my goods. My first desire was to see again the little place where I had kneeled the night before ere I commenced my work for the day. There I stood for some minutes gazing at the little chapel, almost worshipping the place. As I stood, I heard a shuffling of feet, and turning round I saw the dear old man who had knelt by my side. I said to myself, 'Now that I have my goods – clothes-pegs and tinware – with me, he will see that I am a gipsy, and will not take any notice of me. He will not speak to the gipsy boy. Nobody cares for me but my father.' But I was quite wrong. Seeing me, he remembered me at once, and came over to speak to me, though he walked with great difficulty and with the aid of two sticks. Taking my hands in his, he seemed to look right down into my innermost soul. Then he said to me, 'The Lord keep you, my boy.' I wanted to thank him, but the words would not come. There was a lump in my throat, and my thoughts were deep beyond the power of utterance... The dear old man passed on, and I watched him turn the corner out of sight for ever. I never saw him again. But when I reach the glory land, I will find out that dear old man, and while angels shout and applaud, and the multitudes who have been brought to Christ through the gipsy boy sing for joy, I will thank that grand old saint for his shake of the hand and for his 'God bless you!' For he made me feel that somebody outside the tent really cared for a gipsy boy's soul. His kindness did me more good than a thousand sermons would have done just then. It was an inspiration that has never left me, and has done more for me than I can describe.

Gipsy Smith: *His Life and Work by himself*, 1902, pp. 70–74

My first books were the Bible, an English Dictionary, and Professor Eadie's Biblical Dictionary... These three mighty volumes – for they were mighty to me – I used to carry about under my arm. My sisters and brothers laughed at me, but I did not mind. 'I am going to read them some day,' I said, 'and to preach too.' I lost no opportunity of self-improvement and was always asking questions. I still believe in continually asking questions. If I came across anything I did not understand, I asked what it meant – I did not mind. If I heard a new word I used to flee to my dictionary. I always kept it beside me when I read or tried to read. Then I began to practise preaching. One Sunday I entered a turnip-field and preached most eloquently to the turnips. I had a very large and most attentive congregation. Not one of them made an attempt to move away.

Ibid., pp. 76–77

I was still far from perfection in this art [of reading]. I certainly could not read a chapter from Scripture right through. What was I to do with the big words? First of all, I thought I would ask a good brother to read the lessons for me. 'No,' I said, 'that would never do. I think that the people would prefer me to read them myself.' Then I thought I should get over the difficulty by spelling out to them any word that was too difficult for me. But I felt this would be like an open surrender. The plan I adopted was this – I went on reading slowly and carefully until I saw a long word coming into sight. Then I stopped and made some comments; after the comments I began to read again, but took care to begin on the other side of the long word.

Ibid., p. 96

Much of Gipsy Smith's effectiveness as an evangelist lay in his patent sincerity, often expressed in homely illustrations from his own experience. His father had been a stern parent, yet a loving one too.

It was his custom when he came home to embrace us one by one and speak words of tenderness to us. On this occasion, as on others, we all made our way for the baby [Tilly]. It was my turn next... But Tilly stayed such a long time in my father's arms that I became very impatient. 'Look here,' I said, 'it is my turn now; you come out!' 'All right,' said Tilly quite cheerfully, 'you get me out of my father's arms if you can.' I knew that I could not do that; so I said, 'Never mind, there is room for me too, and I am coming in,' and in I went. There is room, too, in our heavenly Father's arms for all. He pours out his love over his children with more fulness and tenderness than ever earthly father did; and remember, no one can take us from our Father's arms.

Ibid, p. 61

During my first pre-war visit to Cliff, I had met Gipsy Smith. In private conversation , I found him gentle, friendly and benign. His style of preaching and oratory would not, I fancy, now attract the vast crowds it did in his hey-day.

In those early, more expansive days – even before my time with the *Methodist Recorder* – circulation manager Reuben Rees had accompanied Gipsy on his tours. Harold Murray (a first-rate journalist of the old school) would report the meetings at great length. Mr. Rees told me that once, when Gipsy Smith was in full spate in a packed Methodist church, he and HM (as Mr. Murray invariably signed his colourful reports) were in an adjoining schoolroom. Gipsy was telling his life story, with liberal helpings of pathos and humour. The two men could not hear what Gipsy was saying, but could hear the congregation's reactions. 'In two and a half minutes,' said Murray, who had heard it all many times before, 'you will hear a loud laugh.' A slightly sceptical Reuben Rees looked closely at his watch. In precisely two and a half minutes, a loud laugh was heard reverberating through the church. Whatever one may feel or think about such oft-repeated precision and timing, this was clearly the performance of a consummate artist.

Douglas J. Cock, *Every Other Inch a Methodist*, 1987, p. 109

Dinsdale T. Young (1861–1938)

Dinsdale Young was not only one of the best-known preachers of his time, but also a prolific writer. His autobiography, however, yields few memorable anecdotes about himself.

I was promoted to the dignity of a reviewer of books in the pages of the *Methodist Times* in its primal years, and I accomplished a somewhat extensive service in that line of business. I received my dismissal in a very kindly fashion, and Hugh Price Hughes explained that my reviews were usually too favourable!! I paid this, and very resignedly paid, the price of being too gentle in the use of the reviewer's wand.

Dinsdale T. Young, *Stars of Retrospect*, 1920, p. 159

Peter Lee (1864–1935)

From the humblest of beginnings, Peter Lee rose to become an outstanding mining trade unionist and a respected public figure in the North East.

The people of Wheatley Hill, generally, were so satisfied with Peter's activities on the Parish Council that in 1907 they elected him to the Rural District Council of Easington. And there was great need of his virile presence there, too.

There were only two water taps in Wheatley Hill, which is a very large colliery. Peter soon saw to it that every house had a tap of its own, and water. There was no sewerage system – just open channels. One night a woman lay dying and Peter Lee was sent for to pray with her. He did, and when he came out of the house he had to step over the open channel with its smell. 'There is need of something more than praying here, I think,' he said. That ended the system and gave Wheatley Hill a proper sewerage system.

Jack Lawson, *Peter Lee*, 1949, p. 81

Though largely self-educated, Peter Lee became an avid reader and among his interests was the literary associations of places he visited.

As a delegate to a conference in Birmingham he went to visit the country of George Eliot. That done, he made his way to Stratford-on-Avon. Passing through the streets, people on every hand stared or turned to look at him. A friend jokingly told him that people thought the great playwright had come back to life, a point which was further emphasised when he was in the old church.

The verger was showing him Shakespeare's bust and telling him the story of that famous work. As he did so he looked at Peter, then at the bust. His tale rather wandered and did not run as easily as usual, for he seemed overcome by his visitor. Hesitating once, he looked at the bust of Shakespeare, then at Peter, and finally said: 'You know, sir, you are wonderfully like him.' And he was. Years after, the delegates to Miners' Conferences who knew him well playfully called him 'Old Shakespeare'.

Jack Lawson, *op. cit.*, p. 112

Peter Lee was a conspicuous figure at the annual Big Meeting of the Durham miners. One year it was invaded by a group of khaki-clad intruders intent on disrupting the event.

After the ordinary meeting Peter Lee and others were to address a Labour meeting, where the work of the County Council would be dealt with. He, with others, moved towards the platform, only to find it already occupied by the men in uniform. Peter at once proceeded to mount the steps leading to the platform, but his way was barred. Little the lads who had taken on this job knew about either the man they were dealing with or that crowd. They were obviously strangers, under orders from somewhere and someone who knew as much about the Durham crowd as they knew about the South Sea Islanders. Peter Lee began to fight his way up. He was then getting on towards seventy years of age, but he was soon fighting up the steps with men hanging on to him.

Friends shouted to him to let the police do their proper work of clearing the platform of the unauthorised persons. That was not his way of doing things. With eyes flashing he turned and raked his friends with words of scorn. Would they yield to a crowd of nobodies like this? Would they stand having the Durham Miners' Meeting taken possession of by a crowd of low-down nobodies? No waiting for police to do what he thought he ought to do himself. So he turned again, and fought, with men clinging to him. He was now joined by a friend. They won to the platform but were pinned by two separate groups of the strangers, who evidently had friends in the crowd. Peter addressed the crowd while he was assailed from before and behind. But those who started the thing had lots to learn. Men from the crowd, putters and hewers of the heftiest type, swarmed onto the platform, and the little mysterious army disappeared as suddenly as it had appeared. This thing was an offence to old-established custom. Huge as the crowds had ever been, good conduct was the very soul of the gala... No one in that crowd wanted trouble, but when the old rules were broken by men who evidently knew nothing about them, there was no doubt about action. The sight of Peter Lee fighting like a tiger was as a spark to powder. The crowd held fast, but the necessary number were detached for action, and peace reigned as suddenly as the storm had come... One thing it proved. The benign, patriarchal Peter was still his two-fisted self.

Jack Lawson, *op. cit.*, pp. 170–71

George Jackson (1864–1945)

While umpiring a school cricket match, Jackson received a summons from the Superintendent of the Redruth Circuit which changed the direction of his life.

Ushered into the preacher's study at the time appointed, he was dumbfounded by the request made to him, which was that he should preach at two village chapels next day. It was in vain that he pleaded that he had never preached in his life, and indeed had never thought of preaching. The old minister was in difficulties. A number of his lay preachers, using a weapon with which we are very familiar today, had gone on strike, and refused to take their appointments because of what they considered unjust treatment of one of their number.

Finding himself unable to withstand the old man's pleadings, George at length yielded and promised to do his best. On the way home he bought a twopenny exercise book and set to work to make his first sermon. All night he toiled at it, and then paced his room while he committed it to memory. Next day he set off on foot to a distant village chapel, and had to explain to the stewards why he had come.

He announced the first hymn and read the first verse. Nothing happened. Organist and choir had also gone on strike – so he raised the tune and practically sang a solo. The remainder of the hymns he read through. The service over, he made his way to a farmhouse where the preacher was expected for dinner, and where he received a warm welcome. His host, however, told him he would be well advised not to go to the second chapel, as the stewards there were entirely in sympathy with the lay preachers and would not allow him to enter the pulpit, basing their action on the ground that he was not an 'accredited substitute'. He took the good farmer's advice, having had enough of adventure for one day, and decided that discretion was the better part of valour.

Annie Jackson, *George Jackson: A Commemorative Volume*, 1949, pp. 5–6

Jackson succeeded John S. Simon as tutor in Homiletics and Pastoral Theology at Didsbury College in 1913, but only after his appointment had been challenged in Conference by a fundamentalist faction.

In all the Methodist Colleges there had been a rule forbidding students to smoke while in residence. This rule was modified by the Conference of 1913, the ban in future being lifted at 9 p.m. A non-smoker himself, he nevertheless rejoiced that he had not to administer such a rule... His predecessor, Dr. Simon, to whom a pipe seemed indispensable, had felt he could not forbid the men to smoke and at the same time indulge himself. He therefore gave up smoking for the twelve years during which he was he was Governor at Didsbury, but resumed the practice as soon as he retired – a triumph of self-discipline. Once when some students were browsing in my husband's study, he was asked how, on a Methodist minister's stipend, he had been able to accumulate such a library. Spreading his arms in the direction of his loved companions, he replied: 'These, gentlemen, are my smokes.' But his own abstinence created no intolerance of those who indulged. Indeed in Canada, where at the time of our stay it was unthinkable that a Methodist minister should smoke, I remember him saying: 'If anything would persuade me to change my custom in this respect, it would be this law, unwritten perhaps, but none the less understood, which robs a minister of the freedom which every layman enjoys.'

Annie Jackson, *op. cit.*, pp. 39–40

Arthur Samuel Peake (1865–1929)

Peake was the son and nephew of Primitive Methodist ministers. His outstanding career as a biblical scholar began at Oxford. 1890 was a memorable year for him, in which he was appointed lecturer at Mansfield College and elected to a Merton College fellowship. He also won the Ellerton Essay Prize for an essay on Montanism.

He was a tremendous worker, and whatever he did was thoroughly well done. He loved discussion and was most tenacious in argument. In his judgment of people he was balanced and always gave credit for excellencies which some of us in our partisanship were apt to overlook. His memory was phenomenal and he seemed to forget nothing, however trivial, and it appeared no trouble to him to recollect anything he had read. Once when we were discussing some matter, he recited Browning's *Johannes Agricola in Meditation* as being upon the point. I asked him if it had taken him long to commit this to memory, and he replied, 'When I first read it some years ago, I was struck by it and read it again carefully. I have not seen it since.'...

He was a local preacher in those early days and took frequent appointments in our two Oxford churches. His statement that generally he had not the faintest idea of the subject for his sermon until the service was proceeding and that usually he fixed on a topic during the reading of the Lesson used to fill me with undiluted wonder. Such a habit would have been fatal to most men. The quality of his sermon matter was always excellent, for he spoke out of a well-stored and well-ordered mind, but, as might have been expected, it was difficult afterwards to remember in detail what he had said. He was fluent and never at a loss for a word.

In his post-graduate career at the University, he took the Denyer and Johnson Theological Scholarship and the Ellerton Theological Essay Prize. With regard to the latter I have an interesting recollection. He had spoken much about it to me and stated that he had chosen 'Montanism' as his subject. The time for sending in the essay drew near and he had not written a line. Then one day he set to work. He wrote all that day and through the night, with very short intervals for refreshment, and all the day following. During the afternoon of the second day I called at his rooms. He seemed very tired and nodded to me, but it was evident that it was not a convenient time for a visitor, and I left at once. Some time during that night the essay was finished. He chose as his *nom de plume* 'Quench not the Spirit', which he considered appropriate to the subject, as indeed it was. When the result was announced, 'Quench not the Spirit' was declared to have won the prize.

J. Harryman Taylor, in *The Holborn Review*, January 1930, pp. 25–6

The following reminiscences came from one of Peake's closest friends at Oxford, the Rev. E.R. Buckley, later rector of Colchester.

To be badly off, unfashionably dressed, a nonconformist and a teetotaller were serious drawbacks in such a college as St. John's in those days. [But] his wit, his unfailing good temper, his courtesy and personal charm, made him one of the most popular men in college...

The quickness and aptness of his repartee were astonishing, and his most crushing retorts were always made in a gentle voice and with a winning smile.

Member: Sir, can we have a photograph of the Society?

Peake: Sir, I am afraid you will only succeed in obtaining a negative.

On another occasion at the St. Hilary Essay Society a man called Gresham had read two papers: one on 'Christian Socialism', another on 'Christian Secularism'. We were discussing subjects for the ensuing term. 'Mr. Gresham no doubt,' said Peake, 'will give us a paper on Christian Atheism'...

It was in my company, and I think at my instigation, that he paid his first visit to the theatre. J.L. Toole was touring in a play called 'The Don'. Miss Eva Moore was playing the leading lady (Dora), and at the end of the play after Toole had come before the curtain and made a speech there were loud calls for Dora. I can still vividly recall Peake standing beside me on a bench in the pit, rather flushed, very excited, and shouting 'Dora' at the top of his voice. Many years after (about 1920) when I was passing through Manchester and spent an afternoon with him, I asked him whether he still went to the theatre. 'No,' he said, 'I have had to sacrifice it to the Higher Criticism.' He explained that as some more conservative members of his connexion looked rather askance at him for championing Old Testament Criticism, he did not wish to give them a handle to say that this Higher Criticism leads to play-going and suchlike evil ways.'

Quoted in Leslie S. Peake, *Arthur Samuel Peake: a memoir*, 1930, pp. 94–7

The Rev. E.R. Buckley recalled Peake's passion for 'penny dreadfuls': 'At the time he was working very hard for the Denyer and Johnson Scholarship he read one every night. I remember going with him to a dirty little stationer in St. Clements to buy them. He would buy half a dozen at a time – usually Red Indian or pirate stories.' Samuel Horton recorded a similar recollection.

Peake had a gracious sense of humour which carried him over many a difficulty and cast a genial ray across his almost too intensive intellectualism. He loved to tell a story against himself... [One] was that when asking for some shilling shockers by their names at a railway bookstall, the young lady attendant advised him 'to read something that would do his soul good.'

His students not only admired him, they loved him. He won their admiration by his great intellectual gifts, and their love by the radiant charm of his personality. He was very thorough in his methods and had a quiet, but effective, way of rebuking lack of interest and slipshod methods. Once, when he had slightly exceeded the usual time for a lecture, the students began exhibiting signs of restlessness and impatience. This evoked from him a quiet: 'Wait a little longer, gentlemen, I have a few pearls to scatter yet.' Needless to say, they listened till he had finished. On another occasion, when giving a lecture, he, as was his usual custom, stopped to write a Greek word on the blackboard. 'You need not trouble to do that, Doctor. We understand the Greek,' said one of the students. 'I wish I did,' was the devastating retort.

'Dr. Peake,' said a disturbed lay preacher, after listening to him one Sunday morning, 'you say there were two Isaiahs. I say there weren't.' 'Well, that settles it, doesn't it?' replied Peake with a disarming smile.

Samuel Horton, *Dr. A.S. Peake: Reminiscences of this beloved professor*, 1937, pp. 5–7

William Riley (1866–1961)

Son of a Bradford businessman, William Riley began his working life in the family firm, but unexpectedly changed course in middle life and made his name as an author with the publication of his first book, Windyridge. His autobiography recalls some of the Methodist personalities of his early years, including William Willis Wood, father of his closest school friend.

I liked Mr. Wood because he always had a smile and a friendly word for me. He was the prosperous owner of a worsted mill in the neighbourhood, so that his position was much superior to my father's; but as he too was a Methodist local preacher the two men had common interests; and he was the chief or one of the chief supporters of the Bradford Moor Old Sunday School, which my father had attended in his early days.

Affable, without being condescending, even to the poorest, 'Willis', as everybody called him, was one of our notabilities. As a local preacher he was not taken very seriously and in this capacity was on a lower level than my father. It used to be said of him, perhaps humorously, that a great many texts lent their aid to a very few sermons.

He was public-spirited and, when he entered the Town Council, he found his niche and soon made his mark. He became one of the town's most notable officials and was on three occasions Mayor or Lord Mayor. His popularity with all classes of the community was well-deserved for 'he carried no side'. He never tried to conceal the fact that his eminence gave him great satisfaction, and everybody knew it.

Confirmation of this came to me at the time of his death, many years later. There was a civic funeral, and I went down from my place of business to the Town Hall Square to see what went on. A large crowd had gathered; when the long procession of police, mounted and on foot, of fire brigade, of Lord Mayor, Aldermen and Councillors in their robes, of mourners in coaches and private carriages following the flower-bedecked hearse, had gone by, a woman at my elbow remarked in a low voice that was charged with emotion: 'Eh, Willis, lad, if thou can only look down and see this, will'nt thou be a proud man!'

It was an apt remark.

The following incident relates to the Carlisle Road Methodist Church in Manningham, Bradford, where his family belonged.

My mind lingers on those days. We had a fine choir and first-rate organists; the quip that when the devil gets into a church it is by way of the choir was not applicable in our case. Many members of our choir were amongst our most devoted church workers, and there was a fine spirit of loyalty to each other. I remember only one disquieting incident, and the humour of it saved the situation. There came a time when the harmonies of the choir were constantly spoiled by the harsh notes of an elderly lady who in her day had done excellent service. Everybody liked her and admired her loyalty; but everybody – more especially the young folk in the choir and the choir-master – fervently wished the good lady would realise that her days of service in this direction were over.

At length she did, and stated that she thought it was time she 'dropped out'. The others concealed their satisfaction and spoke sympathetically of the help she had given in former days. All of them subscribed to a presentation and stayed behind after a morning service to make it.

This touched the dear soul's heart and she broke down and sobbed: 'I didn't know you thought so much of me. After this I *can't* leave you!' And she didn't!

William Riley, *Sunset Reflections*, 1957, pp. 31–2, 67

William H. Lax (1868–1937)

Though he will always be associated with Poplar, Lax grew up in a Lancashire colliery village.

I once witnessed a strange occurrence in one of our prayer meetings. The hero of the incident was William Parr, a man of striking appearance, with a large, bald head. He was, moreover, a man mighty in prayer. It was the custom in our little chapel for the prayer leaders to go to the front pew, near to the communion rail, as soon as the prayer meeting commenced. Upon this band of faithful stalwarts the preacher could always depend when he required anyone to engage in prayer.

On this occasion he called upon 'Brother William Parr' to offer prayer. This Parr did with remarkable effect. It was not unusual for him to become so lost in the fervour and ecstasy of prayer as to leave his pew while still on his knees, and crawl, as he prayed, the length of the aisle and back. On this particular evening he had reached the end of the aisle, and had turned back, still moving upon his knees, wildly gesticulating all the time. Suddenly there was a profound silence. What could have happened? We looked over the pew tops to discover the reason for this extraordinary state of affairs. Brother Parr was groping on the floor. Soon the bald head reappeared, and a glad cry went up, 'Bless the Lord! They're not broken!' And he resumed his progress and his prayer.

In his agitation he had dropped his spectacles. Happily they were not broken.

W.H. Lax, *Lax – His Book*, 1937, pp. 52–3

Some of my early adventures in preaching fill me with dismay even now. When I preached my trial sermon for the Local Preachers' Plan, I was accompanied by an elderly and much respected local preacher named C.G. Cook. I had to preach at a village called Standish. My hearer and critic had to report the results of my effort to the Local Preachers' Meeting.

I had spent much time in preparing my discourse, and had carefully committed it to memory. Alas, for my poor effort! I broke down hopelessly. Again and again I tried to pick up the tangled threads of my theme, but it was no use! I brought my untimely homily to a close in ten minutes! Covered with confusion and shame, I descended the pulpit steps and poured out my apologies to those whom I met in the vestry. I scarcely dared look them in the face.

'Never mind,' said Mr. Cook, with a smile, 'you did better than I did when I preached my trial sermon. I only managed to go on for *eight* minutes! You've beaten me by two minutes!'

I have always regarded this rejoinder as a perfect example of tact and wisdom and grace. I blessed him then, and now, half a century afterwards, although he is in heaven, I repeat my benedictions.

I had not finished with this lamentable failure, however. My Uncle Richard heard my report with consternation, and duly admonished me. 'Never break down, lad; keep on talking – talk nonsense, if need be – but *never break down*!'

W.H. Lax, *op. cit.*, pp. 109–10

At one of our open-air meetings, a voluble woman began to heckle the speakers. As often as she was beaten in argument, she turned to the abuse of Poplar. It was a rotten place! She wouldn't stop another day in it!

'What's the matter with it, missis?' a man inquired.

'It's all wrong,' she replied. 'It's cold and damp, and it's full of Methodists!'

'Well then, missis, 'said one supporter, go to 'ell! It'll just suit yer! It's warm and dry, and there ain't no Methodists there!'

W.H. Lax, *op. cit.*, p. 181

It is an interesting fact that our Mission church [in Poplar] was the first to be used as a means of propaganda for the cause of Votes for Women...The scene took place at one of the anniversary meetings of the Mission. Mr. Sidney Buxton, who was at the time a member of the Liberal Government then in power, was advertised to preside over the meeting. There was a crowded audience. The programme proceeded as arranged, and the Chairman had commenced his speech, when, at a concerted signal, thirty or forty women rose to their feet and began to shout, 'Votes for Women!' More than that, they chained themselves to the pews, for the architecture, being Gothic, lent itself to that manoeuvre.

The stewards were nonplussed. They could not eject those who were chained to the pews, for the keys had been thrown among the congregation, and in the confusion could not be found. Meanwhile the astonished audience gazed upon a spectacle that was entirely novel – brawling on a widespread scale in a place of worship. From the point of view of tactics, the women had completely outwitted the men, who could do nothing but look on. Pandemonium reigned. There was a steady, monotonous drone of 'Votes for Women! Votes for Women!' In vain the Chairman appealed to them to remember the sacred character of the building. This was met by the retort that 'Votes for Women' was a sacred cause. Then questions began to be put to the Chairman. Would he bring the subject before his colleagues in the Cabinet? At first he stubbornly refused to be coerced. At length, however, they brought him to his senses and he promised.

In the end locksmiths were brought in to let loose the chained women. They had won the day, but they had spoiled the meeting. And, incidentally, they gave the historic touch to an ordinary anniversary meeting.

W.H. Lax, *op. cit.*, pp. 195–6

John H. Ritson (1868–1953)

Ritson's first circuit appointment was to Weaste in the Eccles Circuit. Here he formed a class meeting for men who were not church members.

One member, typical of the North Country, was rough and uncouth in appearance and manner, but had a heart of gold. He worked in a mill, at which a post better than his became vacant. He applied for it and was appointed. Then he found that a workmate, who had never been too friendly, had also applied and been turned down. As my friend thought of this man's wife and children, he was sore troubled and arranged that his own increase in wages should be divided equally between the two of them. I once called to see him in his home as he returned from the mill in the early evening. It was the washing-day, and the good wife had not quite finished. There are advantages in calling on a washing-day. The housewife talks because you have come at such an awkward time and does not want you to stop long, and, as cleanliness is next to godliness, it is easy to say the right word and be gone. It was the husband I wanted to see, and, like a wise man, he remarked, 'We'll leave t'missis to 'er washin'. Let's go out.' We walked arm in arm round the neighbourhood as we talked. On the way back we met a friend and stopped to have a word. 'Joshua,' said my companion, 'there was a chap i' London who was short of brass, an' 'e went to Rothschild for 'elp. Rothschild just took 'im by th' arm an' walked round th' Exchange with 'im. After that 'e could borrow anythin' fro' them as seed 'em.' Then he added, 'An', Joshua, I've bin round Weaste wi' t' parson.'

John H. Ritson, *The World is our Parish*, 1939, p. 41

As President of the British Conference, Ritson attended the Irish Conference in Belfast in June 1926.

There is something very attractive in the Irish Methodists. They are loyal to their Church and unswerving in their devotion to the Protestant position, but in all my visits to Ireland I have never heard the Methodists speak bitterly of the Roman Church. One of the ministers described the rebuilding of the Methodist Church in the town where he was stationed. Being friendly with the Roman Catholic priest, he asked him for a contribution to the new church. The priest replied, 'I cannot do that. My Church would not allow it. But it will surely allow me to give ten pounds towards pulling the old church down.'

John H. Ritson, *op. cit.*, pp. 313–14

John Mackintosh (1868–1920)

The world-wide success of 'Mackintosh's toffees' began in a family pastry shop in King Cross Lane, Halifax. Here the founder of the business tells his own story of those early days.

In those days there was very little in the way of toffee as we know it today. English toffee was mostly hard and brittle, a pure enough article, but lacking something; at least, so thought the originator of 'Mackintosh's Toffee'. It had been noticed that caramels were being imported into England from America. These were very soft to the teeth. Then came the great idea! Why not blend the English butterscotch and the American caramel? Experiments were made and an article was produced which was named 'Mackintosh's Celebrated Toffee'.

An advertisement was put out locally in Halifax, inviting the public to come and taste a free sample at our establishment. Hundreds came and before closing time we were 'Sold out'!

On the Monday morning following, another advertisement appeared, reading like this:

> ON SATURDAY LAST
> you were eating
> MACKINTOSH'S TOFFEE
> NEXT SATURDAY pay us
> another visit and eat it at
> your own expense.

And they did! When business opened on Saturday morning there was the largest display of toffee (or any other special sweetmeat) ever seen in Halifax. It began to look like a toffee shop. The pies and the cakes, the cheese tarts and the Eccles cakes, made a brave show, but the little mountain of deliciously inviting toffee made your mouth water.

It could only have one end. We kept the money separate for the toffee, and before long the takings for the latter outstripped the receipts for all the rest of the articles sold.

The window was painted in nice bold letters denoting that the establishment was intended to be a high-class pastry-cook's, but the public altered all that; they called it 'The Toffee Shop', and people came from all parts of Halifax for the popular commodity... That was the commencement of the wholesale business, which rapidly spread out first to the West Riding, then to the whole of Yorkshire, then to other parts of the North of England, and so on, until it was being sold North, South, East and West.

Nor did it stop there. The colonies quickly showed that they wanted this good old English toffee, and other countries, too, demanded it; so that today from China to Peru, and almost from Pole to Pole, there is scarcely a country that does not know 'Mackintosh's Toffee'. So from that little 'Toffee Shop' a huge factory employing over 1,000 people has grown and given to Halifax a new fame and a new name; for it is known today, the world over, as 'Toffee Town'.

Mackintosh developed an innovative flair for effective forms of advertising.

During the Premiership of the late Right Hon. Sir H. Campbell-Bannerman, when Parliament reassembled after the recess in February 1905, every member of the House of Commons received by post a presentation tin of 'Mackintosh's Toffee'. Six hundred and seventy tins were sent to the House, one for each member, accompanied by a carefully worded letter from Mr. Mackintosh, in which it was suggested that honourable members in the discharge of their duties would frequently be entertained at private houses, and that they might like to make some little return for the hospitality given to them. What could be better than to send the hostess a tin of 'Mackintosh's Toffee'? Members were politely informed that they might open an account with the firm. They need only send a card, when a tin would be forwarded to their recent hostess with the compliments of the honourable member. Many members took advantage of the suggestion, and several of them have kept up the practice to the present time.

The receipt of these parcels created considerable amusement among the members of the House, and everyone was talking toffee. The primary object was thus achieved, and a great volume of free advertisement secured for the firm.

G.W. Crutchley, *John Mackintosh, a biography*, 1921, pp. 33–4, 53–4

Mackintosh never lost his 'common touch', especially among those he had known through the fellowship of the Church.

Mr. Mackintosh never forgot Queen's Road [Methodist New Connexion] Church and Sunday School wherever he might be, and on Sundays his thoughts were always drawn to the place which had for him so many tender memories...

The overflowing good nature of the man was evident in the trouble he took, and the time he spent, looking up relations of friends at home who had removed to various parts of America. Nothing delighted him more than to visit them in their homes in the new world, no matter how humble they might be. He was always welcome, for the prosperous businessman was the unchanged friend whom they had known in former years. When he was in Philadelphia he visited the grandmother of one of the Queen's Road girls. When he arrived at the house the door was opened by the old lady herself. His greeting was:

'Are you Nellie's grandmother?'

Without asking the name of her visitor, she replied: 'Aye, lad, I am; come reight in.'

He followed her into her spotlessly clean and tidy kitchen. Then without speaking another word, she drew a big chair to the fire for him, placed the kettle on the hob, spread the white cloth on the table, got out the tea things, took off her apron, and sitting down in a chair by the hearth, said in the broad Doric of her native country: 'Well, lad, I dunnot knaw who tha' art, but if tha' comes fra' Halifax tha'rt reight welcome. Eh! but tha' knows I left mi heart i' Queensbury.'

Queensbury is a small township perched on the Yorkshire hills a short tram ride from Halifax. It was sweet to hear the familiar dialect and to receive such a hearty and homely welcome, and Mr. Mackintosh felt repaid for all the trouble he had taken to visit the old exile from home.

G.W. Crutchley, *op. cit.*, pp. 102–3

E. Aldom French (1868–1962)

The Dome Mission in Brighton was launched in 1907 during French's ministry there.

Mr. Aldom French tells a good story of the first mission services there. On the first Sunday night there were only 1,700 people and 2,400 seats. Mr. French walked home with his steward, who said, 'It's all right. Every seat will be full next week.' On the following Sunday it was so. On the way home Mr. French said to the steward, 'We have jumped up seven hundred.' 'No,' said the steward, 'it was the same congregation as last week.' 'How could it be?' cried the minister. 'Well, you see,' said the steward, 'I took seven hundred chairs out.' It should be added that before long they were put back again and were used.

Harold Murray, *Press, Pulpit and Pew*, 1934, pp. 62–3

C. Ensor Walters (1872–1938)

As a young man Ensor Walters' first appointment after leaving Richmond College was as assistant to Hugh Price Hughes at the West London Mission. Most of his ministry was spent in the West and East London Missions.

Let me tell you how the warm and lovable humanity of London was first revealed to me. It was in 1895, when I left college and was appointed to work in the West London Mission under the Rev. Hugh Price Hughes. Then London to me was just the mightiest City on earth. I knew nothing of its people and its real life. To be frank, I was in danger of becoming a snob. But I was saved by a little Cockney boy.

Picture me, complete with top-hat and umbrella, walking down a dingy street near the Middlesex Hospital. Suddenly I hear a voice: 'Tie my boot-lace, guv'nor.' I stop. Shall I ever forget? A white-faced London nipper, with his right arm missing, trying to tie a broken boot-lace with his left hand. Hurriedly I knelt on the pavement. My silk hat fell off and my umbrella went crash. But the boot-lace was tied.

I have been tying boot-laces ever since. There is only one way to help the reformation of humanity – the way of Him who washed his disciples' feet. Henceforth I looked at the poor people of the grey streets of London with new eyes, and they learnt to count me, I am proud to say, among their intimate friends.

I recall an incident outside King's Cross station in the days when we bought our newspapers from eager, quick-witted little Cockneys.

'Evenin' piper, sir?' cried one such lovable figure.

'Yes, thank you.'

And as I paid him, he said, 'You're Ensor Walters, ain't yer?'

'Yes,' I said.

'Yer belongs,' he resumed, with a friendly upward glance, 'to the West London Mission, don't yer?'

'Yes, that's right.'

'Well, so do I,' he said proudly. 'Shake 'ands.'

And we shook hands – fellow members of the same great Mission.

E.W. Walters, *Ensor Walters and the London He Loves*, 1937, pp. 29–31

Edgar C. Barton (1873–1953)

Barton was assistant to J. Alfred Sharp at the Book Room during the four years leading up to Methodist Union, and then became Book Steward in 1932.

I heard one good story in connection with Mr. Barton's appointment at the Book Room. At the time he was a circuit minister at Ilford. When he was suddenly called to join the late Dr. John Alfred Sharp, two ladies in that neighbourhood were heard talking of the news. One said, 'Have you heard about our minister?' 'No,' cried the other, keenly anticipating a bit of spicy gossip, 'what's he done?' 'Why,' said the first, 'he's going to leave the ministry and become a bookie!'

Harold Murray, *Press, Pulpit and Pew*, 1934, p. 56

Frank O. Salisbury (1874–1962)

Salisbury painted three different portraits of John Wesley, one of which was as a gift to Wesley's Chapel to mark the reopening of Wesley's House after its restoration in the 1930s.

Having collected my material and visualised my subject, it only remained for me to materialise it; but I needed a living personality who bore a likeness to Wesley and was of Wesley's age, about 75. It came suddenly to me that there was only one man who would do, and that was Charles Voysey, the famous architect, so going down to the Arts Club where I knew I should find him, I told him my idea. He looked at me in astonishment and said that nothing would give him greater pleasure, for he was a descendant of John Wesley.[42] This was a great surprise to me.

He came to the studio, put on the wig, the robes and the preaching-band, and might have been Wesley himself. I said I felt that all he lacked was the fullness of the lower lip of an orator, and begged him to push his lower lip forward, which he did, thoroughly enjoying doing it. After the first sitting in daylight from my model, I went on with the painting by artificial light well into midnight and went to bed very happy, feeling that I had got John Wesley. I painted also a portrait in profile and called it 'The Ecclesiastical Statesman'.

The portrait was completed in time for the Union of the Methodist and Wesleyan Churches, and the great meeting at the Albert Hall at which the deed of union was signed... The painting was exhibited at the Academy. At the completion of the restoration of Wesley's House, my wife opened the door with a golden key and the portrait was unveiled by Dr. Parkes Cadman.'

Frank O. Salisbury, *Portrait and Pageant*, 1944, pp. 99–100

Charles Hulbert (1878–1957)

Charles Hulbert was first and foremost an evangelist, who had an outstanding ministry in a succession of Central Halls. The outbreak of World War I found him beginning a seven-year

---

[42] Voysey was clearly mistaken here. According to the Oxford DNB he was, in fact, descended from one of John Wesley's sisters. John himself had no children.. Salisbury should have known this.

ministry at Thornton Hall, Hull, where experience of air raids foreshadowed what was to follow in 1939–1945.

The danger of panic was ever-present during crowded services because the air-raid alarm made an unpleasantly eerie sound readily heard in the hall. The possibility of two thousand people wildly alarmed by the siren and all struggling to get away was to be feared. As it happened, the employee who sounded the siren, a member of Thornhill Hall, arranged to give advance warning so that a steward at the back of the hall could flash a torch to the minister on the platform. Whenever that happened a hymn was sung to drown the noise, after which the people would be invited to go quietly home.

When a bomb fell one night on a row of small houses not far from the hall, two small boys were blown out of bed. They landed in the street wearing nothing except their shirt neckbands and wristbands. Taken to the hall, they were found to be as black as coal, and when the missioner saw them he turned to one of his workers – Charlie Russell, a converted coal trimmer – and said: 'Charlie, light a fire under that copper.' In that bath the minister of the hall bathed the two boys, afterwards allowing them to run about in front of the fire until they were dry. Next day Hull was talking about the practical parson, and Charles Hulbert was pointed out as 'the parson that bathed the kids'. The effect was remarkable. It broke down any barrier between him and the people – and more and more flocked to hear him preach.

Kenneth Hulbert, *Passion for Souls*, 1959, p. 31

In 1928 Hulbert succeeded John A. Broadbelt at the King's Hall, Southall.

One story will illustrate the kind of work that was being done among young people. A girl secretary in a manufacturing firm, had a spiritual experience at King's Hall. She asked other members of her class to pray for her especially because next day she was going to take down a letter at her boss's dictation which would contain a lie. She recalled a week later how, when she came to that part of the letter, she put down her pencil and refused to go further. The boss, of course, was angry. He told her he paid her to do as she was told. She replied that she had had a religious experience at the King's Hall which prevented her from recording a lie, and added that she could not go on. Her boss then altered the letter, but again his secretary refused to take it down, saying that although it now contained a white lie, it was *still* a lie. After a pause, her boss said that if *that* was the kind of religion they were teaching her at the King's Hall, he would trust her with everything in his office, and would never ask her to do a dishonourable thing again. This surely is the story of Christian Perfection in everyday life.

Kenneth Hulbert, *op. cit.*, p. 84

Evangelism was not just a matter of large congregations or house-to-house visiting, but also one of individual influences, where members would persuade friends to accompany them to a service.

Though Tommy Mayes, converted at Thornton Hall, was not gifted as a preacher or a speaker or a singer, he was used as a very wonderful instrument of evangelism. The minister told him to write in a notebook the names of men known to him whom he wished to see converted. Tommy was told to pray about them and to try to persuade them to attend the Sunday evening services. When they had become soundly converted, he was to tick their names off in his book. In after years, when the Methodist Conference was held at Thornton Hall, Charles Hulbert, tired of endless discussions on finance, procedure and reports of committees, left the Hall and took a stroll outside. One of the door stewards was none other than Tommy Mayes. 'Show me your notebook, Tommy,' said Charles. Gladly Tommy produced it, turning page after page of names, every one ticked off – every one entered in the Lamb's Book of Life. 'Tommy,' remarked Charles, 'there are not ten men in there who could show you a book like that.'

Kenneth Hulbert, *op. cit.*, p. 34

Wilbert F. Howard (1880–1952)

Drs Wilbert F Howard and A.W. Harrison had been close friends ever since they were together at Didsbury College, Harrison as Assistant Tutor and Howard as President's Assistant to Dr. John S. Simon during his Presidential year, 1907–8. Harrison died during his Presidential year, 1945–46, so the Conference of 1946 was presided over by Howard as his predecessor. Harrison's widow, G Elsie Harrison, recalled a moment during that Conference.

[Howard] was on the platform of the Hall, Mrs Harrison was on the floor below, and one of Charles Wesley's hymns was being sung, as only Conference can sing them. 'Howard turned, with a sprightly grace which seemed to spurn a little thing like a grave and to take death in its stride, and sought me out with a radiant smile, in just this verse:

Ready for all Thy perfect will,
   My acts of faith and love repeat,
Till death Thy endless mercies seal,
   And make the sacrifice complete.'

Edgar T. Selby, in *Wilbert F. Howard: Appreciations of the Man*, 1954, p. 24

Howard was on the staff of Handsworth College from 1919 until his retirement in 1951, becoming Principal in 1945.

He could concentrate on a game, as on anything else, particularly if it was cricket, and well on into his fifties he enjoyed the annual match against the College at the Garden Party, where his cutting and driving were always appreciated. He was, of course, much happier playing games than watching them; but besides being a regular supporter at College matches, he could often be tempted to watch the Villa or the Albion, preferably standing among the crowd, because the linguistic gymnastics of the spectators interested him as much as the finer points of the game. As an example of how he disliked being thwarted in any plan, particularly if a challenge to his physical powers was involved, I can remember how during the rail strike of 1919, rather than miss a preaching appointment at Birkenhead, he cycled the ninety miles there on the Saturday and returned on the Monday in time to take his 'private hours' with his students, an engagement which was sacrosanct and with which nothing must interfere.

Maurice F. Howard, in *Wilbert F. Howard, Appreciations of the Man*, 1954, p. 35

Isaac Foot (1880–1960)

Isaac Foot was the most prominent West Country Methodist of his day.

One of his favourite stories was about two Westcountry farmers who attended their Methodist service as usual one Sunday. The sermon consisted of a long discourse on the ten commandments and a harangue from the preacher to the congregation on the importance of obeying the commandments. When the service was over the farmers left the chapel and walked the few miles home in heavy silence and apparently deep in thought. On reaching their home they sat still, obviously taken up with contemplation of the subject of the fiery sermon. Finally the silence was broken by one saying thoughtfully: 'Well, in any case, we haven't worshipped any graven images lately.'

> Sarah Foot, *My Grandfather Isaac Foot*, 1980, p. 14

One day – as I have heard Isaac Foot himself relate – he found himself the sole passenger in an early morning bus. The conductor was humming a tune, as conductors will. 'What's that tune?' said Isaac. 'Isn't it "Dare to be a Daniel"?' 'Yes, sir, it's my favourite hymn.' 'Mine too,' cried Isaac. 'Let's sing it together!' And they sang it lustily from first verse to last, while the bus rolled on.

> Sir Carleton Allen, quoted in *Isaac Foot, a Westcountry Boy*, 2006, p. 344

Foot was an insatiable reader and an inveterate book collector. His library amounted to some 70,000 books and was said to have been the largest ever collected by one man in Britain. After his death it was sold to the University of California.

At fourteen he left school and went to London as a Boy Clerk at the Paymaster General's Department at the Admiralty and he recorded once: 'I learned to read while walking and also learned to measure distances by reading. That London walk took exactly one hour, and I found that if I began reading an essay on Macaulay as I entered the first gate in Kensington Gardens I could finish it comfortably as I turned from Green Park into Spring Gardens. I found a special route across Hyde Park and was rather proud of my discovery. Generally there was not a soul to be seen, Macaulay is all the better for being read aloud and one could freely declaim a rhetorical passage without being regarded as a lunatic.'...

Later in life when he had formed his own solicitor's practice of Foot and Bowden in Plymouth and he moved with his family from his home town to St Cleer on Bodmin Moor for a few years, each day he would walk the three miles or so to Liskeard Station declaiming poetry as he went. He had by this time memorised a hundred sonnets and 'I found I could do thirty of them in an hour,' he said.

In the 1930s during the 'National Government' when he was made Parliamentary Secretary for Mines he 'found that in my luncheon walk through St James's Park to and from the Reform Club, by dividing the poem into two, I could comfortably begin and complete the reading of fifty-five stanzas of Shelley's *Adonais*'.

> Sarah Foot, *My Grandfather Isaac Foot*, 1980, pp. 41–2

One day when walking in Callington, he met a gentleman who had just taken a book from the town library. 'What are you reading?' asked Isaac. The gentleman showed him his book and told my grandfather how much he enjoyed reading. 'You must come and see my library at Pencrebar one day soon,' he said.

Accordingly a date was set and the gentleman arrived at Pencrebar. As my grandfather led him from room to room his visitor was speechless, marvelling at the shelves upon shelves of priceless volumes. Eventually he got his voice back and remarked, 'I don't expect there is a finer library in all Callington.'

Sarah Foot, *op. cit.*, pp. 81–2

There was a strong bond between Isaac Foot and his sons, including Hugh Foot, who went into the British Colonial Service and found himself Governor of Cyprus at the time it achieved its independence.

We on our side would go to him for guidance and for encouragement. Once when I finally returned from Cyprus I was offered a commercial job at any salary I liked to state. I was not attracted by the prospect, but I went to him to tell him of the offer. He said he would think about it, and next day at breakfast he said: 'I have thought about that offer. If you accepted it your enemies would know what to say, but your friends wouldn't.'

And one day when the situation in Cyprus was at its worst and seemed to be in hopeless bloody deadlock, I received a telegram from my father which said: 'See Second Corinthians four verses eight and nine.' I turned from my anxieties to look it up and found this text to encourage me in my adversity: 'We are troubled on every side, yet not distressed; we are perplexed but not in despair; persecuted but not forsaken; cast down but not destroyed.' I sent back this telegram: 'See Romans five verses three and four.' 'And not only so, but we glory in tribulations also; knowing that tribulation worketh patience; and patience, experience; and experience, hope.' My father's opinion of my biblical knowledge was rightly low. The fact that I had been able to cap his text made him shake his head in wonder for long afterwards.

Hugh Foot, *A Start in Freedom*, 1964, p. 26

Jack Lawson (1881–1965)

Like Peter Lee, Jack Lawson began life as a coal miner and rose from humble beginnings to political prominence. He became an MP in 1919 and in 1924, in the first Labour government, was appointed Financial Secretary to the War Office.

It was worthwhile living to be one of the first of the new tribe to walk into those great buildings in Whitehall. My friend Clem Attlee (Under-Secretary of State to the War Office) said to me one day up in the officers' mess in Woolwich, after a meal there, 'That great chandelier must look fine when it is lit up.'

'Yes, it does,' I replied absently.

'Have you been here before?'

'Yes.'

'When?'

'The last time I was here I was serving these tables as officer's orderly on fatigue, after 'stables'.'

My fellow-member of the Army Council nearly needed a doctor to take the stitches out of his side.

From the first, I met courtesy and helpfulness departmentally and in all other matters. Let the superior smile in their wisdom... The social side did not attract me at all. The attraction of it is to me an increasing mystery, and I dodged it even when it was in the line of duty. But on one occasion, while in that Office, I could not. French military representatives had come over in respect of the evacuation of the Ruhr. A dinner was arranged for some half-dozen, Army, Air Service and visitors combined. The late Mr. Stephen Walsh, who was Secretary of State for War, was taken ill and could not attend, so the Financial Secretary had to take his place. It was a quiet, friendly, useful gathering. The late General Thompson, then Secretary of State for Air, kept the French General on my left fully occupied in that vivid way of his.

He had talked French some time when he suddenly leaned over towards me, saying, 'How old were you when you commenced working in the mine, Jack?'

'Twelve,' was my reply.

'How long did you work?'

'Nearly twenty years.'

This he conveyed to the General, who was plainly astonished.

'You – you – a miner, and now Finance Minister in the War Office?' he said in French, for he was limited to that language.

'Yes, I worked nearly twenty years in the pit, and I carry its marks on me,' I said in doubtful French, as I showed him my hands.

'You speak French?' he said.

'Yes, I replied, 'Durham French.'

But like all his ever-courteous countrymen, he swore I spoke it well – which was 'all my eye'. Still, we had a good 'crack'. But I think the fact of a real working miner in that Office shocked him more than my Durham French, for he kept looking at me and in varying terms expressing his astonishment. The Representative of a Republic, with its theory of equality, should have naturally expected such a thing; but it was the last thing looked for in fact, which only goes to show that there are different kinds of Republics, whatever you may call them.

Jack Lawson, *A Man's Life*, 1932, pp. 267–70

E. Benson Perkins (1881–1974)

With his high forehead and powerful jaw, Benson Perkins was always a formidable figure. In his later years the quip was that he was not born, but quarried. But he could tell a story against himself. His first appointment after leaving college was to Helston, where he had bachelor rooms in Coinagehall Street.

The outstanding event in my remembrance of the beginning of my work is the first drive out to a village service. The horse and conveyance would be brought to my door immediately after lunch and I would have to drive up through the town to collect my colleagues. Hitherto horses had no place in my life, but I disliked intensely the idea of looking the novice I knew myself to be. Fortunately, I found an article on horses in an encyclopedia, with illustrations of driving – the very thing I wanted. With a piece of string, I practised the correct way of holding the reins and handling the whip when driving. When we set off I felt sure I knew what to do and I could concentrate on preserving the correct style with the reins. My colleagues made no comment and the day passed uneventfully. The sequence came later. I was out for supper one evening and introduced to the wife of the Borough Surveyor, who belonged to one of the other Methodist churches. She said, 'Oh, I have seen you before,' and noting my surprise went on to explain. 'I was looking out for you on your first drive out, as you had to pass our house. I wanted to see what the new minister looked like.' 'Well,' I said, 'I hope the verdict was favourable.' 'Oh quite,' she said seriously, 'I said to my husband that you would be all right, as you knew how to drive.'

As the days passed I acquired a reputation as a furious driver, which was largely based on another incident. The man from whom we hired the outfit had bought another horse, which was a real high-stepper until tamed down by hard work. I was out with this fresh horse and supposed to pick up the Superintendent on my return from a village further away. He was not to be seen at the appointed place, and I went along the next morning to enquire about him. 'You want to know where I was last night?' he asked indignantly. 'When I heard you coming along like a fire-engine, I got into the hedge out of harm's way.' He wanted to make out that the horse was running away with me. Actually, I was enjoying myself driving an animal with some life. That horse could travel.

E. Benson Perkins, *So Appointed: an autobiography*, 1964, pp. 23–4

This is a reminder of what daily life was like in London at the height of the blitz.

During the daylight raid on Buckingham Palace I was in the basement of the shattered Stepney Central Hall, the headquarters of the East End Mission, where my brother-in-law, the Rev. Percy Ineson, Superintendent of the Mission, and my sister, had been living. Every shop and office in the area was closed down during the raid, but when we were badly needing some refreshment one of the deaconesses discovered that a fried-fish shop had a small chink open. She brought in the plebeian fish and chips, and could anything be more delicious! I referred to this in an article, and shortly afterwards I received a letter from the fried-fish proprietor with a donation for the Mission. He said it was the first time the fried-fish business had received honourable mention in the pages of the *Methodist Recorder*.

E. Benson Perkins, *op. cit.*, pp. 110–11

Robert F. Wearmouth (1882–1963)

The historian of Methodism's influence on trade unionism began his working life as a coal miner in County Durham.

The mine at Oxhill was notorious for mice; there were thousands of them. And very hungry they were, especially on a Monday morning. Whenever or wherever you sat down to eat a little food, out they came from their holes and corners and would almost beg for bread. It was easy to catch them...

In the South Moor Drift, where I laboured as a putter, there were numerous rats. They were fierce and furious when chased into a corner and would turn upon you to get away. Hungry and ferocious, they would not hesitate to tear or carry away your coat to satisfy their appetite. I never tried to catch them with my naked hands, but preferred to use a wooden drag when chasing them.

Happy the day when I laid aside the pick and shovel, the pit-clothes and shooting gear, to enter the Theological College of the Primitive Methodist Church. The last days of my pitman's career were unforgettable. In the period leading up to my final examinations for the ministry, I was labouring in an abnormal place. I had to hew and fill coal in a place two feet six inches high and six feet wide, with intensely cold water trickling ceaselessly from the roof and almost filling the place. Half-naked, I had to lie among the muddy water and at intervals ladle it out to prevent flooding. I worked in these conditions for more than three months.

The last place in which I laboured before going to college was dangerous to health and strength. The air was impure, almost non-existent. The candles would scarcely burn. One had to coax them by holding them upside down to allow the hot grease to warm the wick. To strike a match in such atmosphere was impossible. Every fifteen minutes it was necessary to leave the place to refresh the lungs with a purer air or to be rendered unconscious. At the end of each shift I was blown out almost like a football. I had to consult a doctor about my condition and he advised me to leave the mine immediately to prevent a breakdown. I did so through the permission of a kindly manager. I was under contract to work another week before going to college and he allowed me to break my contract.

R.F. Wearmouth, *Pages from a Padre's Diary*, 1958, pp. 9–11

Adolf Niemoller commanded a German Submarine in the first Great War, 1914–18, and after the war he became a minister of the German Protestant Church. One Sunday night in November, 1955, he preached to a large congregation in the Bainbridge Memorial Methodist Church at Heaton, Newcastle upon Tyne. I was a member of that congregation and after the service I had conversation with him in the minister's vestry. I told him of my experience the night Kitchener went down [in HMS Hampshire, off the Orkneys in 1916]. Along with over eight hundred soldiers returning from leave in England I sailed on a boat from Dover to Le Havre. After sailing a few miles out to sea we were chased back to Dover by German submarines. Seven hours elapsed before we reached the other side. I asked Pastor Niemoller where he was that night. I wondered if he was in charge of the submarines that tried to destroy us. He confessed that he was on duty that night, but it was impossible to tell exactly where without reference to his diary, which of course was among his papers at home.

Ibid., p. 138

Thomas Tiplady (1882–1967)

Later to be the Superintendent of the Lambeth Mission, Tiplady served in the Great War as an army chaplain on the Somme, witnessing both the carnage and the sacrificial courage of trench warfare. His descriptions of conditions in the battle zones, though marked by a degree of jingoism and (seen in retrospect) unfounded optimism about the post-war world, were remarkably vivid.

Last night I cycled into the neighbouring village to make enquiries about a lad who had perished in the fighting. As I drew near the church I heard sounds of music floating out through the shattered windows. If a seraph had stood in the streets of the village and sung heavenly songs to us, he could hardly have caused greater surprise to the occasional passers-by. The village lies forsaken. Every house is in ruins, or bears the marks of shells. There, at the crossroads, where the sentry stands, a shell burst a few weeks ago. The soldier on duty felt no pain and needed no burial. Now, on the same spot, stood another soldier wistfully listening to the music of the church. The civilians have fled and taken their belongings with them. A stranger race – an aforetime enemy – guards for them their land...

I placed my bicycle against the church wall and sought the back entrance. The right-hand corner of the priest's garden wall had been blown away. The damaged archway had been propped up with a pole and the path was blocked by a large shell-crater. The door of the vestry was off its hinges and the floor was littered with books, vestments and debris. Stepping over obstructions, I passed into the chancel. What a sight! A shell had been hurled through the centre of the wall immediately above the altar. The wall was two and a half feet thick, but it had broken before the invader like brown paper. A hole two yards wide gaped like a wound. The picture above the altar had been blown into a thousand fragments, and these were lying about the floor and window-sills. The altar, with its ornaments, lay crushed beneath a mass of masonry. The windows and the communion-rail were shattered to pieces and scattered far and wide. A lump of stone had been carried from above the altar into the pulpit. A still larger stone had been hurled to the other end of the church and lay in the central aisle. It seemed the work of some mad giant – some Samson insane with sorrow for the loss of his eyes... It was a scene of desolation – a holy place desecrated by the dance of devils. Yet, looking down from a picture on the wall was the sweet face of the Virgin. Straining to her breast her beautiful Babe, she seemed to be shielding Him from the horrible happenings about Him. But the figure of the suffering Saviour nailed against the wall on the opposite side showed how impotent even a mother's love may be...

Out from the soul of the organ came a chord sweet as the fragrance of violets at the unsealing of a maiden's letter and 'dear as remembered kisses after death'...

'It's enough to break a man's heart, isn't it, Sir?' said a soldier who had just entered the chancel and was looking at the ruins. From the soul of the organ came the answer:

Rock of ages, cleft for me,
Let me hide myself in Thee.

There was one sanctuary left unscarred; one Rock that towered above the surging floods of hate and lust; and the lad at the organ had found it... He was a simple soldier – a private in the Rangers – who a few days before had seen hundreds of his comrades fall at his side as he charged through a triple curtain of fire; and he was playing, from memory, the songs that soothed his spirit. He was holding companionship with the truths by which men live, and for which men die...

Last Tuesday I had my first Communion Service out here in France. We could not get a room of any kind, so we held the service in the corner of a field behind some billets. I spread my mackintosh on the grass and it served for a table; I used the Communion Service which was given me when I left the old country. Twelve men formed a semicircle round me, and the evening shadows were gathering over us when I began to read the words, 'Dearly beloved in the Lord'. Then in the twilight the twelve came one by one and knelt upon a corner of the mackintosh and received the broken bread and outpoured wine. As we knelt together in Holy Communion we could hear the voices of men returning from a game of football in a neighbouring field. As they passed through an opening in the hedge near us, they lowered their voices and passed quietly on to their billets in the village. When each of the twelve soldiers had partaken and returned to his place, I gave out, verse by verse, by the help of an electric torch, 'When I survey the wondrous cross'. In the utter stillness of the fields we sang, and, although between the verses we could hear the low booming of distant guns, we rejoiced in the love of God revealed in Jesus Christ.

Thomas Tiplady, *The Cross at the Front: Fragments from the Trenches*, 1917

Robert Newton Flew (1886–1962)

A leading Methodist scholar of the inter-war years, from 1910 to 1913 Flew was Assistant Tutor at Handsworth College, Birmingham.

At first Flew was disconcerted by Handsworth, so different from Oxford. He was heard to bemoan the lack of 'intellectual distinction'. This was hurtful to men several of whom had left school at the age of thirteen and who had no knowledge of the charmed world of Christ's Hospital, Merton, Marburg and Bonn. When this was pointed out to him by the students themselves, his contrition knew no bounds and the memory lingers still. Some thought his penitence excessive, but he would doubtless have applied to it his own rejoinder to one of his Handsworth students years later on the occasion famous in the oral tradition of Wesleyan Methodists, when F.L. Wiseman sought the forgiveness of Conference for some intemperate words the day before. The Handsworth man commented to Flew that Wiseman had gone far beyond what so venial an offence required, but Flew protested, his eyes shining, 'No! No! Never check a penitent as he makes confession. It is good for him to humble himself and lay bare his soul.'

Gordon S. Wakefield, *Robert Newton Flew 1886–1962*, 1971, pp. 22–23

For a short period following the 1918 Armistice Flew served as an army chaplain in the Middle East. His determination to visit a community of those known as Devil Worshippers at the time illustrates an aspect of the man very different from the dapper scholar and ecumenist, complete with pince-nez, of later years.

Flew had to surmount a good many obstacles on the part of the political and, especially, the military officers. 'It's all mountain country you know, Padre, and very difficult riding.' 'You may not be able to get horses, all the horses will be in the field ploughing.' 'It is rather dangerous out there, Padre. Who's going to punish the murderers if the Kurds swoop down and kill you as they did Scott last year?' 'You may be cut off by snow and kept up there a week.' 'You'll have to get official sanction for the cars from Brigade and the staff captain is a devil!'

There was real point in some of these objections, not least in the hint that Flew would have to overcome the devils of the plain before he met the worshippers in the mountains! And he nearly was marooned by snow! But he persisted and was given imposing credentials, notably a letter to the Amir or Mira of the Devil Worshippers, which stated that he was a priest of high degree and a truly great man...

Flew set off from Nineveh in a Ford van. Besides the driver and himself, the passengers were his servant and another Wesleyan chaplain, F.W. Beal, who was to remain with the party until the roads became impassable for motor transport and the van had to turn back. This happened just outside a Chaldaean Christian village called Tell Ushkof...

The Quri, the religious chief of Tell Ushkof, the Priest, Hormuzd, was waiting to do him honour. He treated him as a son, led him into the audience chamber, seated him on a settee or diva, while he himself sat on the floor in the corner and smoked his five-foot-long pipe, its bowl resting on a tray on the ground. Notables of the neighbourhood came in to see the stranger and other priests surrounded the Quri. 'There was no need to talk; the one necessity was to smoke and look profound.'...

After a meal, and provided with three ponies, one for himself, one for his servant and one for the baggage, Flew left the last vestiges of Christian civilisation and entered the country of the Devil. The servant, Mahmud, carried a rifle. Flew himself was unarmed, on the principle 'that a revolver is only a temptation to a Kurd to kill you for the sake of possessing it'. Mahmud knew the dialect of Kurdish which the Yezidis speak and had in fact lived among them for a few years. [Flew himself wrote:]

> On the road we had some conversation on the words to avoid. You must never say SHEITÄN (Satan) or even the first syllable of the dreaded name. You must not say keitan (thread); nor shatt (the common Arabic name for *river)*; nor must you use the words for malediction.

> Mahmud and I satisfied each other of our orthodoxy on this point. It is as well. For the old Yezidi rule is that if any of the faithful hears the word SHEITÄN spoken, he is bound either to kill the speaker or to kill himself. Neither Mahmud nor I wished to be in at the death!

> There was an amusing sequel to our conversation a couple of days later. We reached a spot amid the snows where the vast plain opened out before us, ringed with mountains, misty and immeasurable, and lo in the distance flashing in the morning sunlight was the River, the Tigris itself. Mahmud was nervous lest I be betrayed into an exclamation (Shuf, Esh Shatt –

see the River) and a Yezidi horseman was with us. So Mahmud himself cried: 'Shuf Sahib el mai kabir yem el Mosul!' (See, Sahib, the great water near Mosul!) I took him up at once and sagely answered, with an air of profound comprehension – 'Ah, it is the Dijla is it?' (i.e. the Tigris). And Mahmud grinned. He knew that we were safe.

The journey up the mountain track was perilous; a slip would have meant a fall into a ravine fifty feet or more beneath. But the ponies were well chosen and safe, and after five hours they discerned the tower of the Mira's castle at Ba'adri. They rode into a filthy courtyard, stabled their horses and Flew presented his letter, which was read while he waited in a dark, smoke-filled room in which his smarting eyes could discern the dim shapes of men. But before long the Mira's uncle appeared and besought him to enter the audience chamber. There he was hailed as a Bishop and put on the couch of honour. When Seyyid Beg, the Mira, entered, the letter was read once more and the Mira, in true Arab fashion, assured him that 'my house will be your house'. Flew reciprocated, wondering what his parents would think should the chief of the Devil Worshippers ever arrive in Ealing. Then came coffee, tea, and a meal served in a manner not calculated to aid the digestion of the squeamish. The Arab loaves, or chupatties, rather like pancakes, hung over the rim of the tray on which they were served, and touched the floor; the chicken was torn up by the fingers of the host and pieces passed round. To moisten the rice, chicken and plums, sour milk was drunk from a ladle shared by all the eaters.

The next day Flew rode to the shrine of Sheikh Adi, the Mecca of the Devil Worshippers – 160,000 of them – where there was a festival. The shrine is in a deep valley, surrounded by precipitous hills and mostly hidden from the sun... [He] made his way into the court of the temple and cringed a little before the sinister symbol of the snake carved in relief on the door of the shrine and blacked to heighten its effect... [He] was led through the shrine in his stockinged feet. Beyond the lamps and the tomb of the saint, he noticed a small door. When he asked what was on the other side of it, the Faqir hurriedly answered 'Nothing! Nothing!', but Flew had every reason to believe that it opened onto a steep stone staircase descending to the bowels of the rock. Wigram the author of *The Cradle of Mankind* had penetrated this in 1907, when the Yezidis were enduring Muslim persecution and the shrine was in charge of a Mullah, who himself believed that the abyss was the home of the foul fiend. But Wigram, though guided only by matches, saw enough to convince him that here was the source of the sacred spring which feeds the temple tanks. Devil-worship had derived from the yet more ancient cult of fountain-worship...

Back in Ba'adri, there occurred a remarkable episode:

It was after our evening meal. I had wielded the wooden spoon manfully, especially as there were almonds and other nuts hidden amid the rice and I had eaten wings of chicken and Hussein Beg had torn morsels off the breast for me with his own fingers (Allah reward him according to his works). After I had sighed the sigh of contentment and had tucked up my feet under me and was sitting solemn on the couch, the Kurdish minstrel sang. It was a passionate ditty, they told me, of the man serenading the woman, now half moaning, now rising furiously – and all in one monotonous cadence so unlike anything ever heard at the Queen's Hall. When it was over and I had congratulated the singer, I announced that I would sing an English love song! 'All were silent and fixed their gazing eyes.' One needs to quote Virgil to give the true effect. Then from my high couch I thus began: 'Drink to me only with thine eyes...' and so on to 'I would not change for thine.' The sensation was so profound and the effect so immediate that I could not proceed to the second verse. The Scribe, whose religion was Chaldean (Christian), decided to sing himself, so he wailed a Chaldaean hymn (applause). All looked to me to repeat my triumph. So as the atmosphere was now more religious I sang 'How sweet the name of Jesus sounds...' to the new tune of T. Tertius Noble, remembering where Rosalie and I first heard it and striving vainly to fit in the religion of Swanwick with my present company. No, even Swanwick revellers in their wildest revels never imagined that the hymn would be sung in the Palace of the Devil's Own.

Gordon S. Wakefield, *op. cit.*, pp. 55–60

Back in civilian life, Flew was appointed to Clapham and then to Muswell Hill in north London, where he showed his rapport with children and young people.

One Harvest Festival at Clapham, the children's gifts had been received and dedicated at a special service in the afternoon. They had been placed on a table which was discreetly removed before the evening worship. Flew noticed that it was gone and refused to begin the service until it had been replaced. On a Sunday morning at Muswell Hill, a little girl had mislaid her penny when the collection plate was brought round, but she found it just as the children were leaving in the hymn before the sermon. Without demur she broke from the line of departing boys and girls and walked straight up the pulpit steps to give it to her friend Mr. Flew.

Gordon S. Wakefield, *op. cit.*, pp. 69–70

When Raymond George became a student at Wesley House, Cambridge, Newton Flew was tutor there, with Maldwyn Hughes as Principal.

He was becoming prominent in ecumenical circles, both nationally and internationally. I was one Sunday, with others, being entertained to tea by him and Mrs. Flew, and he asked me: 'Who do you think called here after lunch today?' Somewhat mischievously I replied, 'William Temple,' pitching it high so that he would have to admit it was some lesser mortal. 'Yes,' he said, 'and how did you guess?' I naturally resolved that next time I would say, 'the Pope'.

A. Raymond George, *Memoirs Methodist & Ecumenical*, 2003, p. 22

Colin A. Roberts (1886–1975)

The Christian Commando Campaigns of the later war years, in which teams of ministers targeted particular towns and cities, gaining access to factories and other work places, were initiated and led by the Rev. Colin Roberts, Secretary of the Home Mission Department.

The Barrow[-in-Furness] campaign in March 1944 was expected to be tough going: the team had been warned, 'Barrow will break your heart in three days.' The warning proved incorrect, though there were some anxious moments especially when Colin Roberts, Bill [Gowland] and another member of the team met the night shift at Vickers Armstrong. The yard was working round the clock, building battleships, destroyers and submarines. They arrived at the main gates only to be confronted by two burly security officers, one of whom spotted their clerical collars and growled to the other, 'Three of the b---s!' In the canteen they found two thousand bleary-eyed workers peering at them through the smoke. Roberts was equal to the occasion. 'Good evening,' he said cheerfully. 'As we came in tonight, two of your security officers gave us a typical Barrow welcome;' and after relating the incident he announced, 'Now, b... number one is going to speak to you. Up you get, Gowland.' No doubt such an introduction would raise eyebrows in a church. But two thousand tired shipyard workers called for unusual techniques, and Roberts caught his audience in the first five seconds.

David Gowland and Stuart Roebuck, *Never Call Retreat*, 1990, pp. 62–63

J. Arthur Rank (1888–1972)

The son of Joseph Rank became involved in the film industry in his eagerness to use contemporary media as a means of evangelism.

Rank relied heavily on God's inspiration and he always consulted his Maker on every decision he ever made. And, when things went right, he counted it as a blessing from God. On one occasion at a Rank Films board meeting when new films for a series of documentaries were being considered, Rank stopped the discussion, looked around the room, and said:

'Do you know, gentlemen, what's the most wonderful monument in London? [Long pause] Cleopatra's needle. And do you know why, gentlemen? [A further long pause] Because it is the only monument in London upon which the eyes of our Lord Jesus Christ have gazed.'

Not necessarily historically accurate, perhaps, but a reminder to all, even in important meetings discussing film ideas and finance, that the Sunday School teacher was never far away. Rank was able to live in the two worlds and make them both work.

Michael Wakelin, *J. Arthur Rank, the Man behind the Gong*, 1996, pp. 118–19

His daughter Shelagh has one particular memory which indicates Rank's involvement in high places. She was home on leave when, the day before D-Day, her father stood all evening, looking out of the window. She and Nell [his wife, Laura Ellen] couldn't understand what he was doing. They asked him what was wrong, but he said he was only thinking. When morning came they heard on the wireless that the D-Day invasion had begun and Rank was able to say why he had been so anxious.

Apparently Eisenhower had been down to see him in secret. He had taken Rank out into a field where no one could hear, and had explained his mission. He told Rank of the plans for the top-secret D-Day operation. Adverse weather conditions had been indicated which might delay the troops' landing by another three weeks. What Eisenhower wanted was, in the event of bad weather, to borrow all Rank's cinemas on the south coast in order to entertain the troops, and keep them hidden and well briefed for the invasion. Rank had agreed to the proposal, but was sworn to secrecy, even from telling his family. So his relief when he heard that the invasion had gone ahead on schedule was understandable.

Michael Wakelin, *op. cit.*, pp. 148–9

Rank's critics often enjoyed quoting that his business genius had triumphed over his Methodist principles. They used, among other things, a commercial film, *The Wicked Lady*, to make their point. It was released in 1945, with James Mason, Margaret Lockwood and Pat Roc, [and] was a phenomenal success in the box office. It was held in great contempt by the critics for its racy content, and caused a storm of protest in the *Methodist Recorder*. It told the story of a highwaywoman who was also a prostitute. Queen Mary asked if she might be invited to the première. This caused slight consternation: apparently there was someone in the projection box throughout the showing, ready to turn down the sound so that any potentially offensive words would become inaudible to royal ears. However, at the end of the film, Queen Mary said to Arthur: 'A very good film, Mr. Rank, and a fine moral.' Rank was delighted with such royal approval:

'Queen Mary is the only person to see in the film what I see myself. I only agreed to it because there's a moral in it. You have two pretty girls, Margaret Lockwood and Pat Roc. One of them falls to temptation, and gets shot in the end; the other lives happily. That's the moral. Both girls are pretty, you see; it wouldn't have meant anything if one of them had been plain. Oh yes, I didn't like some of the dialogue... I didn't know about that.'

> Michael Wakelin, *op. cit.*, pp. 187–8

A member of staff at Methodist Publications Ltd., working under Walter Knights, was found stealing payments made for advertisements. Knights couldn't sack him, but he had the man suspended and informed Rank. Then it was also discovered that the man had other debts and was threatened with proceedings. Rank's response was, 'This fellow has fallen in the gutter, hasn't he? If Christ came along and saw a man in the gutter, what would he do?' Knights replied, 'Pick him up and give him another chance,' so Rank said, 'That is what you and I must do with this man. Find out how much he owes and I will send him a cheque.' Rank helped him get another job with the Eat More Bread campaign.

The man then stole again and ended up at Bow Street Magistrates Court. While in the dock, he claimed that Rank was a friend and Rank was summoned. In court, Rank admitted to having helped the man. When the man was sentenced to eight months in prison, Rank got Knights to find out where he was and arranged to visit him. The man had a wife and three sons and Rank paid for the children to be looked after while their father was inside so that the mother could work to earn money and keep them all more comfortably when her husband was released. That way the family stayed together.

> Michael Wakelin, *op. cit.*, pp. 202–3

R. John Tudor, later Superintendent of the Central Hall, Westminster, recalls an encounter with Rank in the 1950s.

I was a junior minister at East Ham mission and the Superintendent invited Lord Rank to come and chair the evening service... When he arrived he said, 'Take me to the gallery, young Tudor. Tell me, how many people do you get here on a Sunday night?' This was the time in the fifties when people were beginning to drift away. 'About three, four hundred, perhaps five.' He pointed out that it seated two thousand. 'When this place was built and my father gave money for it, it was packed.' I said, 'Yes, and there were no cinemas, no films on a Sunday, all the things there are that take people away from church today.' Then he turned on me and really took me to task, and for two minutes we argued, and then he put his arm round me and hugged me, saying, 'You'll do, you'll do.' He really was the kind of man that if you challenged him, he loved you.

> Michael Wakelin, *op cit.*, p. 217

G. Bramwell Evens ('Romany') (1890–1943)

Known to many outside Methodism through his writing and broadcasting on natural history, 'Romany' was a nephew of 'Gipsy Smith'. His first appointment after his marriage was to the Goole Circuit.

Sometimes on Sundays, if there was a seat to spare, he would take me with him in the antiquated high dogcart which took the various preachers to their village appointments. We had to make an early start, for we were always sure of being provided with the oldest worn-out mare the ostler had in his stables, and not even Bram's experienced handling of her would make her change her sabbatic walk to a trot. She knew every inch of the road and would stop at the various chapels of her own accord...

We loved these outings, in spite of the fact that at some of the smaller chapels his congregation often numbered less than a dozen people. On one occasion we cycled out ten miles to the tiny village of Adlingfleet to find a congregation of only one, but he preached with as much vigour and sincerity as though the chapel had been full. When the service was over, and he had shaken hands with the old man, he turned to me and said, 'I hope you were listening, for he's stone deaf.'

Eunice Evens, *Through the Years with Romany*, 1946, p. 43

He had a great gift for adapting himself to the various types of people he met. The humblest person was never embarrassed in his company, and I often envied him this trait. On one occasion, when preaching in a colliery village, he was taken home by a miner to dinner. The first thing he noticed was that the womenfolk did not join the men at table. They waited on them, and had their meal afterwards. He then saw that the men looked ill at ease. It suddenly occurred to him that they were not accustomed to wearing their Sunday jackets at meals. Getting up, he pulled off his own, saying, 'My word, it's warm.' He had broken the ice, off came theirs, and he at once became one of the family.

Eunice Evens, *op. cit.*, pp. 48–9

During the Great War the population of Carlisle was augmented by an influx of munition workers.

In spite of the increase in population, the various congregations of the city churches showed little increase, and so, with the backing of his officials, he rented one of the cinemas with the idea of holding a more popular type of service after the usual evening one. Only those who have lived in quiet cathedral cities can appreciate the reaction of many people to such an innovation and the many discouragements which he received.

We went through an agony of apprehension before the opening service. As we neared the cinema our hearts fell. It was a quarter to eight, the place was in darkness, and only a couple of hundred people were queued up outside. 'Why haven't they put on the lights?' he exclaimed impatiently. When we reached the entrance, we were met by excited perspiring stewards. The building was packed to the doors, and they had put the lights out to discourage new arrivals. Though the attendance varied according to the number of munition workers who came and went, there were rarely vacant seats during the six years that my husband conducted those services.

When he had applied for the cinema, the manager, a tall, good-looking man, was inclined to be somewhat cynical and critical of the venture. The first Sunday he walked in and out occasionally in his smart tail-coat, as cinema managers do, to see if the rules and regulations were being observed. The second Sunday he stayed longer, for the naturalness and simplicity of my husband's talk held him longer than he intended. After that he rarely missed a service, and many an evening he joined our late supper parties at the manse. He joined up the next year, and within a month was killed at Mons, much to our distress.

Eunice Evens, *op. cit.*, pp. 62–3

When he was younger he was inclined to be intolerant of those who knew little of his pet subject. If we met a party of hikers walking briskly along a main road, looking neither to right nor left, talking loudly as they went, he was irritated. 'Eyes have they, but they see not,' he would say. Some years later a friend took us over his engineering works. The marvellous ramifications of cranks, gears and shafts meant nothing to either of us. Teasingly, I whispered, 'Eyes have they, but they see not.' He saw at once what I meant, and in later years, if he lectured at a school where the children seemed unresponsive and ignorant of even the names of the commonest birds, instead of being impatient, his attitude was more one of pity that they lived in surroundings far from green fields and running streams.

Eunice Evens, *op. cit.*, pp. 158–9

A. Victor Murray (1890–1967)

While he was still a boy, Victor Murray's family moved to Berwick-on-Tweed, where they attended the Primitive Methodist chapel in College Place.

There were one or two odd things about the services. For example, the congregation always *sat* during the singing of the second hymn. No one knew the origin of the custom but no one ever questioned it. And it applied only to the second hymn. We discovered its existence at our first appearance, for we stood up and had to sit down again in some confusion. But no one had warned us. It was just taken for granted that we knew...

I think it must have been at Berwick that I solved to my own satisfaction something which had long been a problem. I noticed that when my elders came into chapel they spent the first minute or two with bowed heads and shut eyes. They appeared to be saying something but what it was I never could make out. Neither my father nor my mother were very religious people so I couldn't imagine that they were praying. Yet if they weren't praying what else could they be doing? This was a perpetual worry until one of my contemporaries, a bright lad of 12, hit on the solution. 'They are counting 21,' he whispered to me in confidence. On the scientific principle of experiment following hypothesis, I tried it out next Sunday in chapel. I counted 21, and sure enough the heads of my parents bobbed up at exactly the right time. Later I discovered that they were not always so well synchronised, but this I put down to the wrong tempo on my part. At any rate it was sufficiently accurate to satisfy me, although why they should count anything at all was a mystery that has never been solved.

A. Victor Murray, *A Northumbrian Methodist Childhood*, 1992, pp. 57–9

The 'penitent form' was a feature of the chapel which Murray found it puzzling to identify.

We had pews in our chapel, not forms, and so it was difficult to know what precisely the preacher was asking the sinners to do and where to go. It apparently was a metaphor and not a place, although it was expected that if you were really penitent you would be willing publicly to make the journey from the back pew to the front.

I once went up to the penitent form myself. I was nine years old at the time – which even our people considered to be a little early for any effective conviction of sin; but I was still very much missing my grandfather who had died the year before, and I felt a devastating sense of loneliness. The preacher was Matthew Lowry, a miner from Pegswood, – he was particularly appealing in the prayer-meeting. I think it was probably affection I needed more than anything else, and the idea that Jesus really loved me and cared for me just as my grandfather did was too much for me. I crept out of my pew when everybody else had their eyes shut and I was down on my knees at the penitent form before anybody but the preacher knew what was happening. He put one arm round me and whispered just the things I was wanting to know – how God was concerned about people who were bereaved and that we were never able to get away from His love. He said nothing about sin or salvation or any of the things which he had been talking about in his appeal to the grown-ups, and I believe I profited just then by his wisdom.

The effect did not last, however. By the time I was ten I was helping myself pretty freely to the chocolate and sweets that we sold in the shop and even on occasion to an odd penny or so from the till. I had no pocket money then, and to be left in charge of the shop from time to time with no supervision was too much for me.

A. Victor Murray, *op. cit.*, pp. 70–1

During his Vice-presidential year, Victor Murray visited Shebbear School in North Devon.

We were to meet him at the Rougemont Hotel, Exeter. 'You will know me at once – not a hair on my head.' My wife was in a nursing home for a few days. I took my daughter to the rendezvous as hostess. True enough, a tall man removed his hat at the entrance to the foyer and we recognised our man. We sat down and he consulted the menu: then he remarked, turning to my daughter, 'Horse doovers! I say, this *is* going to be a lunch!' We were well away.

He spoke to seniors after prep in the library – not the easiest time to win their attention. 'Which is better, service in Chapel or on the radio?' he queried. 'Radio, sir,' came a bright voice. 'And why?' 'No collection, sir.' We all joined in the laugh. (The V Former was later to become a Methodist minister.)

'Do you remember our Lord being asked whether Jews should pay tribute to Caesar, and his answering query – Whose superscription is this?' and the Professor slipped out a silver coin of the Emperor Tiberius and passed it round, handled again by English schoolboys after nearly two thousand years. They questioned him and listened to him until I had to take him away and send them to bed at ten o'clock. What an example of one who considered and knew how to hold and enthrall his audience!

J.B. Morris, *Two Decades of a Country Schoolmaster*, 1986, pp. 55–6

Harold V. Mackintosh (1891–1964)

The head of the confectionery firm founded by his parents, Harold Mackintosh was very active in public life, including the national savings movement. His involvement in the introduction of Premium Bonds was controversial among his fellow Methodists.

I was taken aback when... the Treasury came to me with the idea of the Premium Bond. This was something we had looked at rather wistfully from time to time. Till now the Treasury had darkly frowned on it, because of the 'cleavage of public opinion' which would follow if the State raised money by a lottery. But the new idea was to confine the lottery to the interest. The investor could not lose his stake... The Chancellor intended to launch this as a new government security. The question was, would I let it be called the Premium *Savings* Bond? Would I sponsor it with the National Savings Movement – and what about the Churches?

Mr. Macmillan [then Chancellor of the Exchequer] realised that there was likely to be some opposition from this quarter. I had for some years been a member of the Churches' Committee on Gambling, and my views were clear and well known. But, in all honesty, I could not see any harm in the scheme, as the point was that the money was not at stake, only the interest. Practising the virtue of hope, you could win, but you couldn't lose because your invested capital was never in jeopardy.

I must admit that I had suffered some qualms before introducing a security which had an element of luck, however small, attached to it. They were not qualms of conscience, because, after the most careful consideration, I had found personally nothing objectionable in the scheme. I thought, however, that it might upset some of our voluntary workers and that was the last thing I wanted to do. I told Mr. Macmillan that on no account would I risk doing anything that would damage the movement.

Mr. Macmillan announced the Premium Bond in his Budget speech in April 1956, but I would not approve it as a National Savings security till the Annual Savings Assembly had met in May.

I need not have worried. When the Assembly met, and I explained the scheme, it was received with unanimous approval. The Chancellor waited in an ante-room for the result. He was outwardly calm and indeed I have never in my life seen him otherwise, but I hoped he was feeling as relieved as I was when, as I led him in to address the Assembly, the audience burst into a spontaneous cheer. At the end of his speech he was given a standing ovation. In reply Mr. Macmillan said: 'We politicians get so few encores that I am going to give you one now.'

We had an extra five minutes' talk from him.

Shortly after this I was at a small dinner party at which the Archbishop of Canterbury, Dr. Fisher, was also a speaker and in the course of his observations he mildly criticised the introduction of Premium Bonds. When I followed him I retorted with equal mildness. 'I know it is the business of the Churches to save sinners, but I didn't know it was their duty to stop sinners saving.'

I then went on to remind him that these Bonds were not introduced for the saintly souls like His Lordship and myself, but were meant to attract people who were throwing their money away on football pools and other forms of gambling. If he could induce these people to invest their money in Premium Bonds, we should be doing more good than by a purely negative approach to the problem.

By Faith and Work. The Autobiography of The Rt. Hon. The First Viscount Mackintosh of Halifax, 1966, pp. 132–34

Leslie D. Weatherhead (1893–1976)

As a young man during the First World War, Weatherhead served with the British army in the Middle East.

Other aspects of the western way of life must also have seemed curious to the Arabs. Belasim [the Arab sheikh whose tribe he was visiting] treated his guest with great courtesy. He gave him a tame gazelle. He organised horse races, and when Les won he made him a present of the Arab pony he had ridden. One night as Les sat before the door of his tent, he saw a glimmer of white approaching, which proved to be the gauzy white robe of a young girl. An Arab held her lightly by the elbow, his other hand extended palm up, offering her. Her eyes were lowered and her hands hung by her sides. Les shook his head.

The Arab shrugged lightly and returned into the darkness. Shortly the glimmer returned; now Sheikh Belasim himself propelled the girl forward. Les saw difficulties arising as the oriental courtesies came up against the gritty resistance of British morality; after all, he was supposed to be fostering good relations up and down the river, so he sent for his interpreter. 'Thank the Arabian Lord profusely,' he instructed him, 'and explain that the British officer prefers to sleep alone.' Belasim uttered a voluble protest. 'He says, Sir, that she is a virgin.' Another protest followed: 'She would be honoured to sleep with you, he says.' 'Tell him,' said Les, recalling the images from an Arab love-song he had once heard, 'tell him that she has the soft eyes of a dove, her hair is of silken threads, and her skin is as soft as the skin of a pomegranate, and it is not on account of any failing in her beauty that the Arab Lord's lavish generosity is declined. Tell him all that,' he said,' and then explain that it's just part of our curious British way of life.'[43] To his relief he saw that the sheikh had got the message; as the interpreter concluded the piece, Belasim threw back his great head and rocked with laughter. There was clearly no resentment. He withdrew again into the dusk, the girl by his side; and then within a few minutes a servant appeared carrying on his shoulder what turned out to be a huge Arab carpet, woven in turkey reds and golds and greens and brown, a gift not less exotic but certainly more durable as a souvenir. It lay on my father's study floor for fifty years, 'Just to think how I came by that carpet,' he used to say.

Kingsley Weatherhead, *Leslie Weatherhead, a personal portrait*, 1975, pp. 46–7

Weatherhead's first English appointment after his return from India was to the Manchester (Oxford Road) Circuit.

---

[43] Telling me this story many years later, with the carpet in question spread out at our feet, Weatherhead added at this point that he was aware that in saying this he was being economical with the truth. [JAV]

61 Cecil Street, my parents' first English home, was unusually shabby: the linoleum was dark brown and cracked; there was dry rot in the passageway, a gas-pipe leaked in the cellar and fumes pervaded the whole house. The kitchen sink, a large stone piece, had settled at one end, and it was necessary to push the dirty dishwater uphill with a scrubbing brush to get it to go down the drain. But when my mother demonstrated this defect to the steward, he said, 'But you seem to manage expertly,' and the sink remained as it was. The letter Les published in the paper purported to have been written by a minister's mother-in-law to her husband and was signed Amelia Ray Tatwunce. It opened, 'Any girl who marries a Wesleyan minister is either a heroine or a fool.'...

The church was a large unsightly building, seating a thousand people. For some weeks that autumn the Sunday congregations were sparse, thirty perhaps in the morning and forty at night; Les's carefully written sermons echoed among empty pews. One aged church member told him pointedly, 'In my father's day, young man, the church was full, and the street was lined with carriages.' In an amazingly short time, however, things were like that again. With some university students he knew, Les visited three thousand houses in Manchester to attract people to the church; each week he held discussion groups for students at his house, and at the end of the Sunday evening service he organised a social hour. Gradually word about his preaching spread though the circles of church-goers or potential ones. Once again the church galleries were opened on Sundays, and the street was lined with motor cars. He was shortly able to say to the aged church member, 'This must remind you of your father's day', to which the old fellow replied, 'Young man, don't be carried away by numbers. They are no sign of success.'

Kingsley Weatherhead, *op. cit.*, p. 55

Les was apt to gesture quite a bit in his sermons... Once, when he was preaching the university sermon in St. Giles' Cathedral, Edinburgh, all the lights had been switched off except one which burned above his head. Suddenly, with one out-flung arm he contrived to switch this one off too, plunging the cathedral into darkness. For a moment the blackout produced a breathless silence in the old church, until he remarked casually, 'I seem to have extinguished my halo,' which brought a gust of laughter from the student audience, and later, in the vestry, brought from one of the elders the observation that no one had ever laughed before in St. Giles!

Kingsley Weatherhead, *op. cit.*, p. 68

During his ministry in Leeds, the Weatherheads had a stillborn son.

Les laid him in a box with some arum lilies and then carried him into the study and read the baptism service.

I know many would say it was useless [he wrote] but I believed he existed somewhere and that was all I had of him. I offered a little prayer, giving him back to God, and I put a card on his breast, 'David Leslie, Darling Son of Leslie D. and Evelyn Weatherhead. Safe in the arms of Jesus.' And there I truly believe he is or perhaps my dear parents are taking care of him for God. I am sure he is alive somewhere. He lived and was loved in a sacred cradle for months though we could not see him. The next day he was buried under a tree in the churchyard of Moor Allerton Parish Church.

The vicar had put on a cassock and read prayers over the grave. 'I have no resentments, least of all against God,' Les wrote. 'I feel as if I had had him for a long time. I know I shall see him in the Morning.'

Much later, in séances to which my father used to go, the medium would frequently say to him, 'There's a boy here who says he knows you' – a boy of eight, or ten, or twelve – whatever it might have been. And Les would count the years since 1932 and deduce that it was David Leslie in the other world, where he was regularly reported as being happy, as far as I recall.

[In his farewell sermon at Leeds he spoke of the 'amazing courage of ordinary people'.] 'I have seen men take the most crushing blows and be brave,' he said, 'and I have seen women go through hell and keep their courage.' And then, his own voice faltering, he added, 'And I too leave a tiny grave behind.'

Kingsley Weatherhead, *op. cit.*, pp. 103–4, 106

In 1947 the Rev. Herbert T. Lewis, a Presbyterian minister known as 'John', became assistant minister of the City Temple congregation.

He was a sportsman with a dry wit. Les and he got on fine. They played golf together and Les was a good loser. Once they were disrobing after service on a Sunday, and John was shaking his head solemnly. 'What's up?' Les asked.

'You said a terrible thing in your sermon,' said John. Les was not entirely unused to such protests; sometimes in letter, sometimes in head-shakings as now, and sometimes in my mother's comment, 'Oh, Les, you were *awful!*', he would be told he had said something offensive. 'What've I said, John?' he asked. 'Is it the Catholics, or the Plymouth Brethren, or the Christian Scientists?'

'All of them,' said John. 'You've just outraged hundreds of good honest-minded men and women.' He went on to explain that in his sermon illustration Les had had two teams playing each other - Leeds United and Sheffield Wednesday, they might have been.

'Well?'

'Man, *they're not even in the same Division*! They *couldn't* play each other!'

Kingsley Weatherhead, *op. cit.*, p. 167

Harold Roberts (1896–1982)

Methodist statesman and scholar, Dr. Roberts remained a confirmed bachelor until late in life.

In 1966 Southlands College in Wimbledon became co-educational. The Principal, Miss Myra Johnson, thought that her students should receive regular lectures on sex. She asked me to undertake this responsibility and thus there began a very happy association with the college... Miss Johnson was a gracious lady with a charming presence. I recall the day when Dr. Harold Roberts, a great friend and former Principal of Richmond College, came to my office to tell me rather shyly that he and Myra were to be married. It so happened that on the day after the conclusion of the honeymoon I met Harold Roberts at a function in Cambridge attended by the Queen Mother. He looked very fit and bronzed. I overheard a very elderly lady say to him, 'Oh, Dr. Roberts, you do look well.' 'Yes,' he replied, leaning back on his heels in a characteristic stance, 'I've had a little sun.' 'Oh, how wonderful,' replied the old lady, 'when did he arrive?' The Doctor seemed lost for words.

Kenneth G. Greet, *Fully Connected: A Volume of Memoirs*, 1997, p. 67

James ('Jimmy') Butterworth (1897–1977)

The Anglican-Methodist 'Conversations' were a preoccupation of the leaders of both Churches in the 1960s, but rather less so in the wider world.

The Rev. Jimmy Butterworth, the founder of Methodism's London Clubland, told me once that when there were some extensions to their premises, a *Church Times* reporter came up to him and, notebook at the ready, asked him, 'What do you think of the Conversations?'

'I haven't time to go into that now,' said Jimmy, 'ask him.'

He pointed to a certain rugged character who (though not a church member and something of a rough diamond) was one of his most regular helpers.

'Excuse me, sir,' said the man from the *Church Times* to this individual, 'could you tell me what you think of the Conversations?'

The man scratched his head, pondered the question for a few seconds, and said, 'Well, where I work, they're bloody spicy.'

Douglas J. Cock, *Every Other Inch a Methodist*, 1987, p. 74

H. Cecil Pawson (1897–1978)

The future Vice-President of the Conference was the son of the Rev. D. Ledger Pawson and grew up in the manse adjoining the Newcastle Mission where his father served and which saw dramatic conversions verified by an equally dramatic change of life. One such was that of a cabman called Tot.

Tot ... had the reputation of being one of the hardest-drinking men on Newcastle Central Station Cab Stand. He drank so heavily one night that the publican, wanting to be rid of him, promised two men free beer if they would land Tot home in the nearby street. When Tot awoke out of his drunken stupor, he found he had been robbed of several pounds and – to a cabman – his indispensable watch, for in those days public clocks were not so numerous as today. He realised what a fool he was and resolved to rid himself of this sinful habit. He found his way to the People's Hall, Rye Hill, and there found the new life which Christ offers to every man. My father once told me that for thirty years thereafter, Tot lived such a consistent, faithful Christian life that he never gave his minister five minutes' anxiety about his progress.

Soon after his conversion, Tot was seen running after a gentleman. When he arrived back at the stand, a fellow cabman said:

'Was he trying to *do* ye, Tot?'

'No, he gave me half a sovereign over and above the fare.'

'You don't mean to say you took the half quid back, do you?'

'Yes,' said Tot. 'I thought he only meant to give me sixpence for a tip.' Nothing more was said then, but the next day when some of the cabmen were chaffing Tot about becoming a Christian, the inquirer of the day before stepped forward.

'Shut up, you chaps. The next man that says owt more against Tot and his religion, I'll fell him. If religion will make Tot Reed give up half a quid for sixpence, there's something in it.'

After his conversion, Tot longed for his wife to share his wonderful experience of Christ's love. She had shared with him in many a drunken orgy. It was not to be, for though he sought for this crowning blessing for his home, he could not persuade her to become a Christian. Indeed, he had to endure such taunts and conduct with obscene language from her, and some of her associates, because of his Christian life, that my father said his home was often like hell... Three times he went to sign the papers making possible a separation, but each time he laid aside the pen, and said, 'I cannot do it. I encouraged her in my sinful days, and with all her persecution, I love her still.'

> H. Cecil Pawson, *Hand to the Plough*, 1973, pp. 29–30

Pawson lived through a time of great changes, not least in inter-Church relations.

When King George V was crowned in 1911, the [Bakewell] Town Council desired to hold a service on Sunday afternoon in the Market Square. The Vicar (then Suffragan Bishop of Derby) and the Free Church ministers, consisting of my father and the Congregational minister, were invited to take part. The Vicar absolutely refused to stand on the same platform as my father, whom he described as a dissenter in most discourteous, if not rude, fashion. He thereupon arranged a service in the Parish Church for the same hour.

Many years later I received a letter from the Headmaster of Lady Manners Grammar School, saying that he had discovered that I was an 'old boy' and inviting me to present the prizes and make the speech. He said it was the custom to have a service in the Parish Church at 11 a.m. – the prizegiving being in the afternoon – for parents, staff and scholars, and asking me to be the preacher, added that this invitation had the warmest support of the present Vicar. I was led to the pulpit in due course for the sermon, and as I mounted the pulpit steps, I thought I could hear the sound of my father's voice from heaven, saying 'Hallelujah'!

> H. Cecil Pawson, *op. cit.*, p. 41

One of the most remarkable answers to prayer in my preaching experience is worthy of record. One Sunday morning my wife felt constrained to look in our letter box – a quite unusual action, as we have no deliveries on Sundays. She discovered an unstamped envelope and, from the hand-writing, judged it to be a request for financial help of some kind and felt inclined not to pass it on to me until I had finished my preaching work for the day. Yet a sense of constraint led her to change her mind. I glanced at it and almost made the same decision to leave it unopened but, as with my wife, later felt that I must open it. It contained a letter from a woman I knew, whose husband often deserted her, pawning things taken from the home for money for his own purposes. Enclosed was a solicitor's demand for payment of a certain sum of money, amounting to some pounds, within two days, otherwise they would take steps to dispose of what she had left of personal possessions. She begged me for help to tide over their financial crisis.

Now it so happened that I had given more financial help during that week than I felt was justified as a married man with a growing family, and I honestly felt – much as I sympathised with the woman – that it would not be right for me to send her this sum in time for Tuesday morning. So in a brief prayer, I asked God to undertake for me in this dilemma. Thereupon *I forgot all about both the woman and the letter.*

After the service, several persons kindly came to shake my hand. The last one to approach was a man.

'I want you to know that I re-dedicated my life to God at the end of your sermon,' he said. Then, apparently quite casually, he added, 'And what you are holding in your hand, God told me to give you as we were singing the last hymn. I do not know for what purpose, but you will be guided.'

He left the church and I opened my hand and unrolled a number of pound notes. I rushed after him and told him that I never accepted a penny for my services. Then I asked him to read the letter and enclosure I had received that morning. He looked the astonishment we both felt that the sum he gave me was the exact figure of the solicitor's demand! I told him that I would take the money to the woman that same day and would leave an envelope with her addressed to him. He wanted to let the gift be anonymous, but I insisted otherwise. I always felt that this incident was an example of the truth that if we have done all we can in His guidance and power and still feel our duty has not been completed, we can rely on His providential completion.

H. Cecil Pawson, *op. cit.*, pp. 73–75

Richard Tyldesley (1897–1943)

Dick Tyldesley played cricket for Lancashire in the early years of the twentieth century, remembered here by Neville Cardus.

There is a story about fat Dick Tyldesley ... a Lancashire man, round, red-faced, bulky but very nimble. He was fielding in the leg-trap during a Lancashire and Yorkshire match. Towards the end of the day's play, a Yorkshireman made a stroke on the leg side. Dick bent down and made what appeared to be a marvellous catch. Just as the batsman was about to depart, Dick told the umpire that the ball had touched the ground. In my report in the *Manchester Guardian*, I congratulated Dick for his sportsmanship: he had made an honest gesture not at all common in a Lancashire and Yorkshire match of that period. And when I saw him on the Monday morning I went over to him and said, 'You showed wonderful sportsmanship in letting the umpire know that the ball touched the ground.' Dick replied, 'I thank you.' What I reported him as saying was, 'I thank you, Mr. Cardus. Westhoughton Sunday School, tha knows.'

R. Daniels, *Conversations with Cardus*, 1976, p. 63

Raymond Cook (1899–1972)

Raymond Cook was most widely known as the founder of a Christian travel firm which specialised in group tours in the Holy Land and elsewhere.

The move to Inglis Road [Southsea] brought us into closer contact with some of our friends. Among these were Mr. and Mrs. Hansell and their daughter Muriel. Mr. Hansell was my Sunday School superintendent. He seemed to be a very tall man beside my father who was only 5 ft. 4½ in. Although he was probably no taller than my present 5 ft. 9 in., it helped him to appear to me a very stern man, 'upright' in both senses of the word. He was a traveller for Peak Freans biscuits and a story my mother used to tell me was that he set out one day without saying his prayers. As a result he got caught in some heavy rain and contracted a chill that developed into pneumonia from which he nearly died.

> Raymond Cook, *Life in Many Parts*, 1972, p. 30

Cook was the nephew of a fervent Dover Wesleyan named George Clark.

Although I saw other sides to Uncle George, he was true gold and the greatest little man I ever knew. He often took me to work with him and then asked me back for a meal. I met several well-known evangelists there on these occasions, including Gipsy Smith and Josiah Nix... If the meal was lunch there were always B.A.s (baked apples) for the 'sweet' and I grew so tired of them that I have never liked them since.

During the meals Uncle George used to give me lectures on spelling, pronunciation and subjects of general knowledge. He himself was not grammatically faultless, it seemed to me, for he often used the old-fashioned 'ain't' and 'you was'. He also had a habit of qualifying a remark by adding, 'to a certain extent'. He was a local preacher for 39 years and one Sunday declared to his congregation that, 'We shall all go to hell – to a certain extent.' Maybe we shall find he was right!

> Raymond Cook, *op. cit.*, pp. 44–5

Cook's first Holy Land tour took place in 1935.

Just before we got married the Rev. E. Osborn Martin had come back to live in Dover, and Mrs. Martin became one of my wife's earliest friends in the town. In 1934 Mr. Martin went out to visit his son, Harold, in Egypt, where he was a Flying Officer. While there, Mr. Martin explored the Holy Land and returned with the idea that if a party of thirty people could be formed it should be possible to organise a tour there for no more than 30 guineas. He submitted his plans to one of the Christian travel bodies but they turned it down, as it failed to include sufficient walking for their kind of holidays. Mr. Martin showed me his scheme and wanted me to commiserate with him over his disappointment. Instead of this I told him that if he would be the guide, I would provide the people. I was confident I had enough advertising experience to ensure this, and in a short while we had more than forty applicants.

We went out to Port Said on the S.S. Orama (which was sunk in the Hitler War) and from there we visited Cairo and the Pyramids before catching the night train from El Kantara across the Sinai Desert to Jerusalem... By 1935 little had changed in Palestine since the days of the Turk. The Mount of Olives had only recently been replanted. The roads were still rough, and travel along the mountain-sides in the primitive motor vehicles with their reckless Arab drivers was often hair-raising. But we saw it all before it became spoiled by modernisation and prior to the outbreak of fresh political troubles. We went where we liked without let or hindrance. There were no boundaries to cross and there was no fear of border incidents. Although it was August the heat was not unbearable except down on the Dead Sea and this we were careful to visit in the cool of the evening...

The other incident concerns a member of our party who tried swimming in the buoyant salt waters of the Dead Sea. All of us would have liked to do the same, but most lacked the courage. This was not without reason, for the swimmer returned to shore covered from head to foot with sores and blisters resulting from opposition to his immersion on the part of the denizens of the Dead Sea. And the victim was no less a person than Leslie A. Newman who later, as the Rev. Dr. Leslie Newman, B.A., became one of Methodism's foremost evangelical preachers, as well as one of my greatest friends and a regular leader of our parties.

Raymond Cook, *op. cit.*, pp. 72–4

Cook attended the 1955 Conference in Manchester, but found himself travelling to and from Buxton, where he was billeted.

With me on these journeys was the Rev. Frederick Poad of the Lambeth Mission... and our driver was a well-known figure in Newcastle, Dr. George Miller. One evening, after we had taken the late Dr. W.E. Sangster to his billet, we drove on across the open country listening to our driver telling us some of his experiences. He was relating one incident after another to show us how God had never let him down. Suddenly his engine stopped. There wasn't a house in sight, let alone a garage. Mr. Poad and I winked at each other. Nothing daunted, however, after discovering the car had run out of petrol, Dr. Miller got out and sauntered along the road to a five-barred gate leading into a field where a tractor was at work. Within five minutes the driver had produced a can of petrol and we were on our way. God hadn't let us down!

But Dr. Miller had rarely finished his stories before we reached Buxton. Yet he didn't want to drive beyond. So one night he went to a roundabout and kept driving round and round it until he had finished all he wanted to say! He then let us get out.

Raymond Cook, *op. cit.,* p. 106

William E. Sangster (1900–1960)

Sangster's private life and outstanding ministry were both greatly enhanced by his marriage to a wife who learned to play a supporting role to his dynamic personality. In the days of their courtship they were united by their loyalty to the Radnor Street Mission in London.

On one extraordinary occasion the two loyalties appeared to clash. On a wretched foggy night in 1917 only two people attended the prayer meeting at Radnor Street, Will and Margaret. The purpose of such meetings, inaugurated by John Wesley, was a series of extempore prayers by all the members present. Most young men, perhaps, might have found a more suitable occupation for an evening alone with their betrothed. Will never hesitated. Margaret he placed alone in the audience. He prayed. Margaret did not take a turn, so Will prayed again, and he conducted the meeting through to its conclusion.

Paul Sangster, *Doctor Sangster*, 1962, pp. 36–7

Some of his duties a young probationer must have found very difficult. His own church at Littlehampton was divided on his arrival by a serious quarrel between two women. He talked to each alone, and then to them both together. He pleaded for a reconciliation and attempted to cement it in prayer, so the three knelt down in the chapel vestry. All went well until one of the two women added a line or two of prayer in a helpful way; her rival interpreted what she said as a deliberate violation of the treaty that had only just been ratified, and the minister had to jump to his feet to prevent murder. He was, fortunately, very agile in those days. One inhabitant of Littlehampton recalls seeing him leap over the back of an open moving car into a seat, in order not to miss it.

Paul Sangster*, op. cit.*, p. 61

He was always anxious to preserve the friendliest relations with the other churches of Conway, and though he could never understand a word of Welsh it seemed a friendly gesture to be a visitor at the Welsh Methodist Church when they had their special sermons. Merely to smile in acknowledgement of the greetings of the congregation would appear boorish, so he learned to say 'bore da', 'good day'. It was singularly unfortunate that only the day before this visit his wife came home from the shops and told him about a kind of currant loaf that was new to her and which was called 'bara brith'. The words got mixed up and he stood in the church porch after the service, solemnly shaking hands as the people went out, fixing each with a warm smile and saying with great distinctness in his best Welsh, 'Bara brith!' He noticed at the time that people seemed a little puzzled, but he didn't work it out until afterwards.

Paul Sangster, *op. cit.*, p. 78

In 1932 Sangster was appointed to Queen Street Central Hall in Scarborough. Its affairs were in the hands of a group of wealthy laymen.

One of the first shocks that a new minister of Queen Street received in those days was the information that he was not to preach in his own church for ten Sundays in the season. Visiting preachers of distinction had that honour and the minister was seconded to the missions and country places. Occasionally a minister struck back. One man, famed for his honesty and forthrightness, was told by Westborough Church that his services would not be required there for ten Sundays as the appointments were already filled. He answered, 'All right. I'll have the other three Sundays of the quarter for my holidays and I'll see you in the autumn.' He was as good as his word...

My father quietly accepted the arrangement, but there was a strange sequel. It was noted that the distinguished visitors drew smaller crowds than their own minister. Consternation. A top-level meeting of the 'Big Four'. Solution. Would Mr. Sangster consent to preach at his own church during the season for an additional £2 2s. a week? Satisfaction to all, especially my father, who enjoyed the joke of being paid for what he wanted to do.

Paul Sangster *op. cit.*, pp. 96–7

On 3 September 1939, the Sunday on which war was declared, Sangster began his ministry at the Westminster Central Hall, London. This was the climax of his reputation as a preacher.

Congregations at the Central Hall increased during the war years until at the evening service the Great Hall was regularly full. On special occasions the last to arrive would have to sit on the stone stairs or parapets of the galleries. The absolute capacity reached in this way was over 3,000. It was on such an occasion – Easter Day – that a self-important lady arrived only five minutes before the service began and asked a steward for a seat at the end of a row so that she could leave easily before the end. She was told that no seats were left anywhere, but that she might be squeezed in behind the choir, if she could manage to share a stone step with two others.

She was outraged. 'If that's the way you treat visitors,' she said, 'no wonder the churches are empty!'

> Paul Sangster, *op. cit.*, p. 140

Throughout the war the Sangsters lived and slept on the premises at Westminster and Sangster himself exercised a memorable ministry among those who took refuge in the local air-raid shelters. In 1944 his house at Wandsworth was hit by a flying bomb.

The next morning we travelled to see the remains of our house. Report had much exaggerated the truth. The roof was badly damaged, all the windows were blown in, the garage and car were a heap of wreckage and the garden was an immense crater, but the house still stood.

My father was looking in the crater at the remains of our only casualty – a pigeon – when our neighbour, the now aged Rev. Dr. Luke Wiseman[44], wandered in. The old man appeared with his Greek Testament under his arm, wearing the strange old shovel hat he often wore. The two men stood side by side and, without conferring, began immediately to sing the only appropriate hymn for the occasion.

> And are we yet alive,
>   And see each other's face?
> Glory and praise to Jesus give
>   For his redeeming grace.

> Paul Sangster, *op. cit.*, p. 198

Sangster was elected President of the 1950 Conference, 'the youngest President since Methodist Union, the first born in the 20th century, the 160th since John Wesley vacated the chair at his death'. The twelve months that followed, like every presidential year, were packed with engagements and continual travelling.

What he most enjoyed, perhaps, was recounting the happiest events of his Presidential year, especially the story of his prowess on Easter Monday. He told it with huge delight. 'At the

---

[44] i.e. Frederick Luke Wiseman, not his father Luke H. Wiseman. For what may well be a variation of this anecdote, see under the former.

Harrogate Branch of the [National] Children's Home which I visited the boys were having a football match. It was a poor day, already threatening the snow which afterwards fell. Standing on the touch-line, I was challenged by the boys to take a penalty kick. I walked over the squelching turf, saying to the Lord under my breath: 'You must help me now, Lord.' He did! The ball went smack! Right into the net. The goalkeeper never had a chance. And I came away feeling that the presidential dignity had been maintained again in a somewhat unusual way.!'

Another reminiscence – though in this case pure invention – concerned the hospitality he had received. At one home where he had been entertained, he said, a number of hens were present at his arrival, but gradually they 'entered the ministry'. 'As I went down the path on my way to the station,' he added, 'I think – though I am not sure on this point – that the two remaining birds burst triumphantly into the hymn, 'And are we yet alive?'.'

Paul Sangster, *op. cit.*, pp. 218–19

Sangster had a strong Puritanical streak in him. The Central Halls were part of the Forward Movement', dual-purpose buildings that were secular in design and intended to attract those who had no connection with the Church. But this carried risks with it.

Any humour which hinted of vulgarity he detested. On one terrible occasion at a concert in the Central Hall, Westminster, a famous comedian told a series of obscene stories. My father's face grew more and more angry. As the comedian finished, my father marched to the front and took his place on the platform. He began to tell stories himself. At first the audience was shocked into silence at the sight of a frock-coated parson interrupting the concert. Then, little by little, they began to enjoy his jokes. After a final story had provoked a gale of laughter, my father stopped and said, loudly and distinctly, 'You see? You can be funny *and* clean.' He left abruptly.

Paul Sangster, *op. cit.*, p. 326

In those days [the mid-20th century] most Methodist ministers used to wear clerical collars and often black suits, day in day out, no matter what secular errand they might be on. And once when my brother and I were walking in the country in the August heat and had taken some ears of wheat and stripped them to chew the grain, there came a great voice booming across the shimmering fields, 'Ah, my boys, emulating the disciples, I see,' and there in black amid the golden corn was Will Sangster, at the end of the lane in the depths of rustic England, wearing his dog-collar, on duty as always.

Kingsley Weatherhead, *Leslie Weatherhead, a personal portrait*, 1975, p. 123

He wore no mask, except the mask of his humanity, which we all wear, and on just two occasions I saw even that veil partially lifted. The first occasion was just after the war, when he heard that another son of a colleague had been killed. He received the news at breakfast and it numbed him so that he said nothing. After breakfast he announced that he was going for a short walk on the Common. Uninvited, I accompanied him. We had not walked more than a few paces when to my acute embarrassment he burst into tears. I had never seen that happen before. His exact words I cannot remember, but in his anguish he asked God what was the purpose of it all. Why bring sons into a world as mad as this one? The happier a man was in his family, the more unhappy he must become. He could, I think, have attempted some sort of an answer to the problems from the pulpit, but his grief for a little while overcame his reason and he cried to God for the answer.

Paul Sangster, *Doctor Sangster*, 1962, p. 335

Dr. W.E. Sangster was guest in our home for the Methodist Conference in Newcastle in 1958, and it was during that week he received confirmation from his London consultant that he had contracted the disease called muscular atrophy, for which there was no known cure; he knew that in consequence his days were definitely numbered. He had been feeling ill for some time, but gallantly discharged his responsibilities in the Conference. On the Sunday morning, however, his Conference-appointed service at Sunderland was taken by the Rev. Dr. Harold Roberts. After lunch that day he requested that he might have my summerhouse to himself the whole afternoon, that he might face the challenge, at 58 years of age, of his life being cut short. I was told to bring him a cup of tea at 4 p.m., and to see he was not disturbed till then. When I took him his tea there was a silence I shall never forget, and then I felt guided by God to speak.

'Will, you would like to preach tonight, wouldn't you?'

'I would give my right arm to do so, Cecil,' was his immediate response. 'But it rests with you. Bring the notes of a sermon in your pocket, take the service up to the hymn before the sermon, and I will tell you then, but not before, if I can preach.'

With prophetic insight, Dr. Arthur Hill of Ipswich (the unofficial honorary physician friend to the Methodist Conference) said,

'Let him attempt it. I'll be to hand in the service if anything happens. Who knows, it might be the last time he can preach.'

Half way through the all-important hymn, Dr. Sangster stepped forward.

'I'll preach,' he whispered. He spoke powerful words on the Perils of Procrastination (Felix to Paul – 'When I find it convenient I will send for you again,' Acts 24:25 NEB). After some 20 to 25 minutes his voice began to thicken (a symptom of his trouble) and he wisely brought his sermon to a close and gave out the last hymn. In the second verse he stepped back.

'Shall I make an appeal?' he whispered.

'I cannot decide that, Will,' was my immediate reaction. He resumed his place at the platform desk, then in the last verse turned back to me again and said just three words with great intensity.

'You *must* say.'

'Well, then,' I replied, 'I would if I were you.'

And two young men and a young lady in their twenties stood up in silent response to his invitation to give their lives to Christ.

Eleven years later I was at that church again. I ascertained that of the young men concerned, one was a fully accredited local preacher, while the other held several offices including Sunday

School Superintendent; the young lady was now in London and, it was believed, true to her vow made that Sunday evening in 1958. That was the last service at which my friend preached – he passed away in 1960.

H. Cecil Pawson, *Hand to the Plough*, 1973, pp. 161–3

Elsie Cooper (1902–1995)

Towards the end of her long life, the wife of a Methodist minister, Frank Cooper, published a book of reminiscences. One of their earliest circuit appointments, in the early 1930s, was in the Leeds area, where the effects of the depression were particularly felt.

The Great Depression still prevailed and, as he travelled around the area, Frank discovered a group of men who, through their anxiety and anger about unemployment, had become hardline Communists. They and their families were certainly in great distress and in need of help.

We talked the matter over and came to a decision. Frank would make himself known to them and invite them to tea at the manse on a certain Friday afternoon. I made real efforts to provide a really substantial 'tea' and the party duly took place. Once the initial shyness had worn off – these men were not used to manses – our visitors began to talk, and talk and talk. Their resentment, their sorrow, their anger poured out in floods of dialect speech. We listened, made mental notes, and began to understand. These people needed friends who understood and cared, and they needed a place where they could express their feelings and talk about their problems.

Thus began a long series of Friday afternoon meetings, where we provided lots of sandwiches, cakes etc. – and a platform for our Communists.

During this period, Frank discovered that a local drinking club was breaking the law about hours, etc. The drunkenness was becoming both a nuisance and a menace. With the co-operation of the doctor he reported the club to the local council. This caused enormous resentment among the club's clients.

One evening we had a visit from one of our Communist friends. He came to warn Frank that the angry members of the club were 'out to get him' unless he agreed to drop his complaint, and he felt he had to let him know, so that he would be on his guard. Frank took the news quite placidly and told our friend that he had a lightweight boxing medal from his army days – but we were both touched about the warning. We felt that we were beginning to be understood and to understand.

A few weeks later, a very old man, poor, ill and destitute, drowned himself in a local lake. Frank and the doctor were present when the body was brought ashore.

At our next Friday meeting a Communist friend said to me, 'What I say is – if he'd had somewhere like this to come and talk, he'd never 'ad done it!' That was the only expression of thanks we ever had, but it was enough.

Elsie Cooper, *Endless Song, a Celebration of Life*, 1986, p. 63

Maldwyn L. Edwards (1903–1974)

Maldwyn was a great historian and, like the best of scholars, a real enthusiast for his subject. In 1971 Bill [Gowland] was invited to give the Beckly Lecture at Conference, and Maldwyn was asked to chair the meeting. Conference met in Harrogate, but the lecture was due to take place one evening in Bingley, so Maldwyn suggested that they should travel together. It happened that on the way they passed the prayer cell of John Nelson, one of Wesley's early preachers. Not wanting to miss the opportunity of seeing it, Maldwyn asked if they could stop for a while. The prayer cell seemed very ordinary to Bill, not much more than a shed at the bottom of a garden.[45] But Maldwyn was enthralled by it and retreated into rhapsodic memories of early Methodism, so much so that he lost all sense of time. Though punctuality is not near the top of his list of virtues, Bill began to be anxious about getting to Bingley on time. Unable to contain himself any longer, he broke into Maldwyn's musings and urged him to leave the cell and hurry on in case they were late for the lecture. 'Oh!' came the surprised reply. 'Is it tonight?'

David Gowland and Stuart Roebuck, *Never Call Retreat*, 1990, pp. 224–5

Donald O. Soper (1903–1998)

Soper's unforgettable open-air ministry at Tower Hill and in Hyde Park called for many gifts, including a sense of humour, especially when the joke was against himself. He told the following story himself of an incident on Tower Hill.

There was one very eloquent man who came for many years. He was a Cockney, a sailor, who was talking one day about alcohol, concerning which he was an expert. I said that he ought to sign the pledge. Whereat he retorted, 'Didn't Paul say, 'Take a little wine for thy stomach's sake'?' I agreed that Paul did, but suggested that Paul meant 'Rub it in.' He wouldn't accept that as the answer. So I tried to approach him on another track. I told him how dangerous it was to quote Scripture, and I quoted with what I hoped to be devastating authority, the words from Proverbs, 'Wine is a mocker, strong drink is raging, for at the last it biteth like a serpent and stingeth like an adder.' And he said he'd been looking for that sort of stuff for the last ten years...

A crowd can educate the speaker, as Donald has said more than once. And then there are the tales of times when the batsman has been bowled. One such moment dates from as far back as the days of prohibition in America. To a heckler who was describing the evils of the Eighteenth Amendment Donald said: 'Have you been in America?' 'No.' 'Then don't talk of things you know nothing of.' Instantly, from another part of the crowd, a long-established atheist opponent asked: 'Have you ever been in heaven?'

William Purcell, *Portrait of Soper*, 1972, pp. 55, 147

Soper's need of quick thinking and courage was not confined to the open air.

---

[45] Nelson's study is in the burial ground adjoining the Methodist chapel at Birstall. It is difficult to see how they could be passing through Birstall on their way from Harrogate to Bingley, unless by a deliberate diversion.

One Monday afternoon in the September of 1926, a man in Rivet Street, off the Old Kent Road, announced to his cowering family that he was about to cut his throat. At the same hour, the new probationer to the South London Mission, Oakley Place, opposite Rivet Street, between the Dun Cow and the Duke of Wellington pubs, was about to preside at the Women's Meeting. The Deaconess, informed of the matter, hurried to fetch him. 'When I got there,' he remembered, 'he was standing in the middle of the room, drunk and brandishing his razor. There were one or two children in various corners of the room. I offered to shake hands with him and luckily he put the razor down to shake hands with me, and then one of the kids nipped off with the razor and was two streets away before he could say "Knife".'

William Purcell, *op. cit.,* p. 59

In 1932 when the Methodist Missionary Society arranged its annual May Meeting it was decided that an emphasis should be laid on Chinese affairs because the staff there had been through some difficult revolutionary times and it was felt that the Church should be told about them. The rally was booked to take place in Westminster Central Hall and the Hall would be full. A Mission House Secretary gathered together a team of missionaries on leave to brief them on their performance. There were three of them – all thoroughly 'blooded' in war, tumult and escapes during the last few years. The Secretary explained the drill – short, terse, pointed, evangelical, and on no account was any speech to take off into rhetoric because one of the 'well-known Home men' would be the last speaker. He would see to the rhetoric. One of the men on leave interjected, 'He picks up the bits?' A very sour 'Precisely' was the answer he got.

On the night the Hall was crowded and the subject seized the mind of the great congregation. The interjector was third to speak, and, fresh from central China, near the place where Mao Tse-tung was a young man growing up, he described the social work of the Church. Using the vocabulary of the Chinese times he called the Christian Movement 'The Fourth International'. Dr. Soper rose to speak – the Home man to supply the rhetoric. He picked up this phrase, which clearly excited him, and for twenty minutes wove it into a dazzling picture of a world movement outshining anything the World Council agencies have since accomplished. Later, in the Speakers' Room, he caught hold of the young missionary. 'Thanks,' he said. 'I hadn't an idea of what line to take when I came in.' The Acts of the Apostles tells us that the Athenian crowd called Paul 'a seedpicker' – he too picked up the bits. It is not given to many departmental secretaries to have this skill.

Douglas Thompson, *Donald Soper: a biography*, 1971, pp. 49–50

Sir Ronald Gould (1904–1982)

Gould was both a teacher, trained at Westminster College, and a local preacher, and later became General Secretary of the National Union of Teachers.

Within two or three years of leaving college ... politics and local preaching produced a conflict. The General Strike, and the miners' strike which continued after the General Strike had collapsed, had caused great bitterness in our district. Slowly, the miners, driven by poverty, returned to work... In the end all the miners went back to work with the power of their organisations greatly diminished – so much so that a deputy manager, who was also a local preacher, ejected from his office a checkweighman, a friend of mine, who was not even employed by the management but by the men. (This post had been established by law so that the management could not fiddle the weight of coal produced by each team of miners.) The miners, dispirited and disorganised, did nothing to support him. I was young and impetuous and came to his aid in the only way I could. I told the local Methodist minister that as long as the deputy manager occupied pulpits in the area, I would not.

The poor minister had never before faced such a problem, but it was clear from his attitude that he regarded me as a nuisance. He cherished peace, even though it were peace at any price. However, he called a local preachers' meeting ostensibly to discuss the matter, but in reality to persuade me to forsake my foolish ways. I vigorously defended my action, and to my surprise (and the minister's disappointment) a quieter and much older man said that he agreed with me and would follow my example. My father had indicated that he would do the same, though he could not be present.

The minister was in a dilemma. His inclination urged him to support the deputy manager; wisdom advised caution, for a strike of three active local preachers, perhaps more, would have meant abandoning a considerable number of services. So he brought the meeting to a close with nothing decided. Soon after, he told me that the deputy manager had voluntarily decided to do no preaching for the time being. I doubt whether this was entirely a voluntary decision; I suspect that the minister had worked on him. However, I continued preaching; but the incident was discussed at street corners, in homes, pubs and clubs throughout the district. It made me a few enemies, but it brought me some support. For the first time in my life I discovered that victories are not won without wounds.

Chalk up the Memory: The autobiography of Sir Ronald Gould, 1976, pp. 62–3

Edward Rogers (1909–1997)

Ted Rogers and Kenneth Greet were colleagues in the Department of Christian Citizenship. In 1956 they crossed the Atlantic together in a liner called 'The Empress of Scotland'.

The food on the ship was more luxurious than anything I have experienced elsewhere. Alas, in mid-Atlantic we ran into a terrible storm. The numbers in the dining room dwindled to about six, one of them being Ted, who continued to eat his way through the menu. I lay on my bunk not caring whether I lived or died. The storm subsided and when we woke in the morning the ship was as steady as a rock. I called out to my travel companion in the lower bunk, 'Seems the storm is over, Ted.' 'Either that or we're on the bottom,' came the lugubrious reply from one who was always able to see both sides of an argument.

Kenneth G. Greet, *Fully Connected: A Volume of Memoirs*, 1997, p. 168

George Thomas, Viscount Tonypandy (1909–1997)

Thomas became Labour MP for Cardiff West in 1945 and describes the occasion of his taking his seat for the first time.

The chamber was absolutely packed. Members were standing below the Bar, around the Speaker's Chair, and sitting in the aisles. I sat next to Jim Callaghan and a man with a streaming cold, which I was afraid I would catch. He turned out to be Michael Foot. I was a great admirer of his radical father, Isaac, and remarked, 'Your father is a great Methodist – and a teetotaller.' Michael smiled and replied, 'My father is a good man; but I don't share all his views.'

George Thomas, *Mr Speaker: the memoirs of Viscount Tonypandy*, 1985, p. 54

As Vice-President of the Conference, Thomas attended the World Methodist Conference at Lake Junaluska, North Carolina, in 1956.

From there I went on a wide preaching tour. In Georgia I met with a difficulty.

My host had taken me on Saturday night to see the church in which I was due to preach the next day. It was an attractive white building, with colonial-style pillars and I said innocently, 'What a beautiful white church.' To my horror he replied, 'Of course it's white, you don't understand our problems.' My hackles rose and I asked as coldly as I could, 'Are you telling me that black people are not allowed to worship here?' He was equally disturbed: 'I told you, you do not understand our problems. Of course no Negroes worship there. They have their own church.' With some trepidation I said, 'I do not pretend to understand your problems; I am only a visitor. My trouble is that you do not understand my problem. I cannot preach in a church where blacks are refused admission. I believe in the Brotherhood of Man.'

I could not have caused greater offence. Soon the Bishop of Georgia was speaking to me on the telephone. His name was Moore[46], and I knew that he had Irish blood. He did not mince his words. He said he found it offensive that I should come to Georgia and create trouble. He wished he had never invited me. I listened to a lot more abusive references to people from the United Kingdom before I could get in a word by way of reply.

I finally managed to ask him if he could arrange for another preacher to take my place. He could not, but went on to ask that if he could make arrangements for me to preach in the 'Nigra' church in the evening, would I preach in his church in the morning. I jumped at the lifeline for it would mean everyone in the community would know I did not support segregation.

Next morning I faced a crowded congregation in the white Methodist church. Not feeling that I had the right to use their own pulpit to attack them, I avoided any reference to segregation. Even so, a man said, 'So you're another one-worlder!' I replied with a smile, 'That's right, Sir. How many worlds do you believe in?' I received no reply.

In the evening it was a totally different experience. I was the only white person in the church, and I felt that the congregation was rather embarrassed. But the welcome was warm and sincere. The minister said to everyone, 'We are greatly honoured tonight to welcome Mr George Thomas, a British Member of Parliament, who is also a Methodist like us. His face is white, but his heart is as black as ours.'

George Thomas, *op. cit.*, pp. 80–81

---

[46] Arthur James Moore, Bishop of the Atlanta area since 1940.

William Gowland (1911–1991)

Following his student days at Victoria Park College in Manchester, Bill Gowland's first circuit appointment was to the Isle of Man, where he faced what would now be called a 'steep learning curve'.

There were bitter family quarrels within individual chapels that tested Bill's diplomatic skills to the limit and, when all else failed, demonstrated his sledge-hammer tactics. At one of the earliest trustees' meetings over which he presided, he stared in disbelief as an argument raged over the tremulant stop on the organ. This item had been gifted by one of the trustees in memory of his wife, but it was regarded by another trustee as ruinous to the singing. The incident was part of a long-standing feud between the two families. Bill made several attempts to end the argument but, having failed, he pronounced the benediction, closed the meeting and bade farewell. Some days later in a cloak and dagger operation with the assistance of the organist, he removed the tremulant stop from the organ. At the next trustees' meeting, following a Sunday service, he innocently enquired if the tremulant stop was still adversely affecting the singing. He was told in no uncertain terms that the tremulant stop was as good or as bad as ever, whereupon Bill announced what he had done. He reported the matter to the Superintendent, expecting a reprimand. Instead he received a commendation for his sense of humour.

Such petty conflicts and rancorous divisions left a lasting impression on Bill and helped to shape his view of the mission of the Church… There were other people who ministered to Bill far more than he could ever do to them. A favourite port of call was the home of Willie and Eliza Keig, a couple in their nineties. Whenever he visited them they used to read the Bible and pray with him. On one occasion Eliza commented on how happy their married life had been: 'In more than seventy years together, we've never had a wrong word, have we, Willie?' Then Willie dropped the teapot, and Eliza made up in five seconds flat for everything she had not said during the past seventy years. Bill made a rapid exit without waiting for the benediction.

David Gowland and Stuart Roebuck, *Never Call Retreat*, 1990, pp. 30,33

Following his successful suburban ministry at Tilehurst, Reading, Bill Gowland was sent into the thick of urban mission in Manchester.

Soon after his arrival in Manchester, Bill attended his first Mission staff meeting, a large gathering of ministers, deaconesses and a lay pastor. Seating arrangements around a big table were strictly determined by seniority and status in an atmosphere that reeked of late Victorian attitudes. The Superintendent sat at the head of the table with the Albert Hall minister immediately to his right. The other ministers were positioned in accordance with the ranking order of their hall. The deaconesses sat on the opposite side of the table in order of seniority, while the lay pastor was almost out of sight at the bottom of the table. Bill took a seat next to the lay pastor, whereupon the Superintendent immediately beckoned him to his allotted position. Bill remained in his seat, indicating that his chair was perfectly safe and comfortable and knowing full well that he had to win the first battle or lose a long struggle against outdated attitudes.

David Gowland and Stuart Roebuck, *op. cit.*, pp. 77–78

Building on his involvement in the Christian Commando Campaigns, Gowland quickly decided that Methodism needed to be represented among the motley assortment of open-air speakers at Manchester's Deansgate equivalent of Hyde Park Corner.

At an early stage in his Manchester ministry, Bill was working in his dingy office in the Albert Hall when there was a knock on the door. Two young men stood there, one of whom wore gold-rimmed spectacles and a Cambridge scarf, carried an umbrella and introduced himself as Harry Morton. The other, less formally attired and seemingly less sophisticated than his suave companion, answered to the name of Colin Morris. They had no sooner entered Bill's office and sat down than they declared: 'We've been here two weeks. There's nothing going on in the city. There's no open-air witness. The Hartley Victoria college staff know nothing about life. What's to be done?' Morton and Morris belonged to an immediate post-war generation of mature students, many of whom whether in the armed forces or elsewhere had had some tough experiences quite beyond the comprehension of some of their college tutors: Morris himself had just emerged from the Marines. They chafed at the stultifying genteel atmosphere of college life, regarded their tutors as lesser mortals running a girls' school, and had taken one look at the ministry at large to conclude that it consisted of faded flowers. Bill listened carefully to their stories, momentarily wondering whether or not this was a case of student bellyaching. Eventually he decided to test their mettle by inviting them to the first open-air meeting.

The following Thursday lunchtime he went down to Deansgate carrying the stand on his shoulder. Morton and Morris were waiting for him. The site was packed with people, so Colin took the stand and began to erect it near the pavement. But this position did not suit Bill. He had long since learnt not to waste breath on passing traffic, but to take up a position in the middle of a site and to steal someone else's crowd. Eventually the stand was in a satisfactory position. The two young men stood back and waited for Bill to begin so that they might cast a critical student eye on a man who, they understood, was a rising star in Methodism, reportedly talking the language of men, riding the crest of the wave and heading for the top.

Such thoughts were sharply interrupted by Bill's voice. 'Up you get Morris. You wanted an open-air meeting, and now you've got one.' Morris expressed alarm. 'What, me? What shall I say?' to which Bill retorted: 'I don't know what I'm going to say myself. How can I know what you're going to say?' Morris reluctantly mounted the stand and began with the oldest mistake in the book. 'Now why are we here?' Before he could utter another word one Mancunian wit shouted: 'Because you're not all there!' For a moment Colin slipped back into the language of the Marines, and etched on Bill's memory is the astonishment of on the heckler's face as his eyes went back and forth from Colin to the words on the stand, 'Albert Hall – Manchester and Salford Methodist Mission'. Morris came off the stand and declared he would never attempt such a job again. Sensing that the man was made of sterner stuff, Bill scathingly responded: 'Don't be gutless. Are you a coward?' The glare of Morris' eyes clearly showed that he would not be beaten. Morton made no mistakes, since he had been involved in some open-air work with Donald Soper in London. Following the meeting they headed for the local Kardomah café which long remained their favourite retreat...

Bill has always retained a specially fond regard for the two young men who invaded his office in his early Manchester days. In Colin Morris's view, neither Morton nor himself would have remained in the ministry had they not met Bill and experienced at first-hand his informed and robust combination of evangelism and social concern.

David Gowland and Stuart Roebuck, *op. cit.*, pp. 79–80, 85

During much of his Manchester ministry Gowland conducted a mission among the prostitutes that plied their trade on the large city centre square called Piccadilly. This was potentially dangerous, and – unknown to him at the time – the local police were instructed to keep an eye on him to ensure his safety, but not to get in his way.

What is beyond doubt is that many lives were helped, reconstructed or transformed as a result of this ministry. For example, one night Bill was chatting with two policemen in the square when one of them pointed to a woman and challenged him: 'You want to go and have a word with her, Padre.' He went over and introduced himself. She saw his clerical collar and replied: 'You wouldn't want to know a person like me.' The comment hit him hard and he never forgot it. He explained why he was on the square, to minister to men and women irrespective of class, colour and creed and in the belief that every person is a child of God. Eventually she told her story. Her wealthy husband had died leaving a pile of debts while her son was still studying at Cambridge. She had no job skills, so she had gone onto the streets to earn money in order to support herself and her son until he completed his studies. At the end of a long conversation Bill sensed that this was a story of extraordinary self-sacrifice. He passed on her name and address to one of the deaconesses, with the slim hope that some contact could be maintained with the woman.

Some time later, however, Bill was conducting a Communion service in the Albert Hall. By now there were so many communicants that the bread and wine were distributed to people in their seats. When he came to the back row he found the woman sitting there. She took the bread after he had almost pushed it into her hands, but she refused the wine. He did not know what to do, but then he recalled the words of an old Scottish minister who had said to a girl refusing communion: 'Take it, lassie. It's for sinners like thee and me.' Bill tilted the woman's face towards him – something he had never done before or since – and said the same: 'Take it. It's for sinners. That's why I've taken it.' She took it, and for the only time in his life Bill saw a person's character change before his eyes. At that moment she began her struggle to lead a Christian life. She found a room in the slums of Ancoats, took in some children from the streets every Sunday afternoon, washed their faces, gave them tea, and told them a simple story about Jesus which Bill supplied to her each week. Years later, Bill returned to Manchester to conduct her funeral. Meanwhile, her son graduated with a double first from Cambridge, and eventually became a leading barrister without ever knowing what his mother had done for him.

David Gowland and Stuart Roebuck, *op. cit.*, pp. 90–91

Gowland's move to Luton in 1954 brought him face to face with the challenge of a once flourishing down-town church that seemed to be in terminal decline. At first he was at a loss to know what direction his ministry there might take. The vision of what became the Luton Industrial College, bridging the gap between the Church and the modern world, had still to be glimpsed.

Late one chilly November night, two months after his arrival in Luton, Bill was leaving the church for home when he noticed a middle-aged man standing beside the old church noticeboard and trying to read the board with the aid of a match. He went over to him – his clerical collar hidden by a muffler – and asked if he could be of any assistance. 'What's that got to do with you?' the man growled. There was something about the look of the man that prompted Bill to ask if he had been in prison. Back came the same response: 'What's that got to do with you?' Eventually the man explained that he had just spent fourteen years in Dartmoor. 'We're in the same boat,' commented Bill. 'You've got nowhere to go, and I've inherited all this lot, and I don't know where to go either. Let's go and have something to eat.'

Over the next few weeks a friendship began to develop between Bill and this man, whose name was Jimmy. Bill found him a labouring job and borrowed some money to pay for his lodgings. Shortly afterwards Jimmy attended a Sunday service and continued to do so regularly, always sitting on his own in the gallery and out of the congregation's eyeshot. At the end of the Easter Sunday evening service in 1955 Bill made an appeal for commitment to Christ. Many responded and filled the Communion rail to overflowing. Some had to kneel in the aisle, and Jimmy was one of them. Colin Roberts' words echoed in Bill's ears at this sight: 'If you get the worst, you'll also get the best.' Six months later Jimmy died of pneumonia. Bill paid for and conducted his funeral service with only the undertakers in attendance. At the end of the service he stood alone beside the grave, full of indescribable emotion and yet with an overpowering sense of spiritual certainty as he bade farewell to his friend: 'Jimmy, if He can save you, He can save me. I now know what to do in this job.' This moment was a turning point in his Luton ministry. Christ had at last spoken through the life of Jimmy. Yet again Bill had discovered that the best lessons about Christ are learnt through listening to the unexpected person in the ordinary course of daily life. He had played his hunches in coming to Luton. Now he felt driven by an impelling inner vision to reach out to the non-churchgoer. The first part of the sealed orders had been opened.

David Gowland and Stuart Roebuck, *op. cit.*, pp. 124–25

A. Raymond George (1912–1998)

Raymond George was a leading scholar, liturgiologist and ecumenist in the second half of the 20th century, and a notably humble man.

When he was President of the Conference [in 1975] Raymond was invited to lunch at Buckingham Palace. With that simplicity that was ingrained in him, he walked from Westminster Central Hall, where he had attended the morning service, down Birdcage Walk, and up to the railings of the Palace. To the policeman on duty, he said mildly, 'The Queen has asked me to lunch with her.' 'And who might you be?' asked the sceptical constable. Raymond showed him his invitation. 'Oh yes, Mr. George, come this way, please,' and he was ushered into the royal presence.

John A. Newton, memorial service in A. Raymond George, *Memoirs Methodist & Ecumenical*, 2003, pp. 273–4

Oliver A. Beckerlegge (1913–2003)

Chapel trusts were invariably short of funds, if not actually in debt, and the difficult war years exacerbated their problems. Early in the post-war years, Beckerlegge found himself stationed in the Alston Circuit.

[One problem] was the renovation of the Alston chapel which, though not dirty as you perhaps find in an industrial area, was in a deplorable state; it was a typical square galleried chapel, but the trustees had clearly – on their own admission, in fact – been scared of the job. The plaster was missing from places on the walls and the ceiling; the linoleum in the aisles was so old that it was paper-thin, and the organ was in a parlous state; quite literally the organist played with a screwdriver on the keyboard, as the pedals were so loose. I got quotations for both the chapel and the organ renovation, and then called a trustees' meeting. I have rarely known a church meeting last so long – three and a half hours. We dealt with the two matters, the chapel and the organ; the estimate for each was in the region of four or five hundred pounds – considerable sums in those days. Happily I had had the good sense to have a word with the organist beforehand. So when someone suggested that we do only the chapel, I turned to Mr. Carr and asked, 'What will happen then?' 'The organ will break down at the re-opening service.' So it was suggested that the organ be done first. 'What will happen then?' 'We shall get dust in the organ and have to do it again.' So we decided to do the whole job at one go.

Oliver A. Beckerlegge, *A Methodist Life*, 2000, pp. 118–19

With his extensive knowledge of the Wesley hymns, Beckerlegge was closely involved in the preparation of Hymns and Psalms as the successor to the Methodist Hymn Book of 1933.

The greatest tussle of all concerned 'O for a thousand tongues to sing'. We have, of course, always used a selection of the original eighteen verses, the selection varying from book to book. The *MHB* version had as its last verse,

> See all your sins on Jesus laid:
>   The Lamb of God was slain;
> His soul was once an offering made
>   For every soul of man.

Now there were those on the committee who felt that was not the right note on which to end the hymn, and they proposed to end it with the verse beginning, 'My gracious Master and my God', finishing on what they no doubt considered a more positive note. But they had failed to realise that the verse 'My gracious Master' follows on from the last line of the previous verse, 'The triumphs of his grace'. Charles Wesley often has such verbal connections between verses, and to have wantonly destroyed one would be to have shewn ourselves guilty of the most disgraceful illiteracy. After long argument, we finally kept the verse in its right place and came up with a fresh last verse:

> In Christ, our Head, you then shall know,
>   Shall feel, your sins forgiven,
> Anticipate your heaven below,
>   And own that love is heaven

to the improvement of the hymn.

Oliver A. Beckerlegge, *op. cit.*, pp. 192–3

Norman Nicholson (1914–1987)

Cumbrian poet and playwright, Nicholson spent all his adult life in his native Millom and was brought up by his stepmother in the local Methodist Church.

Marmaduke Fawcett was the third of the old Methodists who towered over my boyhood. His odd surname singled him out, though at times it gave rise to confusion – one Dutch bulb firm regularly addressed its catalogue to:

'His Grace, the Marmaduke Fawcett'.

I am not sure exactly what office he held in the chapel, but I remember that he taught in the Sunday School, for I was in his class, and now and then he would offer sixpence to any boy who could learn a set psalm by the next Sunday...

There was, indeed, an extraordinary matter-of-factness about these old Methodists. To call them 'fundamentalists' is to underestimate them. They did not just take the Bible literally; they took God literally. One can imagine them arguing back with God.

'But Thou said'st so-and-so,' they would point out, quoting chapter and verse of the Bible.

I remember that once Henry Foss and I met Marmaduke Fawcett in the street. He was beginning to be rather bent by that time, his legs bowed by sciatica, but he still had the leanness of a dalesman, and his sharp, little, gingery beard jabbed up and down as he walked. He was wearing a black coat and hat, so maybe he was on his way to some mid-week service. We talked for a minute and said goodbye.

'I'll see you again,' he said, and began walking away.

Suddenly, he stopped and turned and stared, his hoary, leathery face slowly taking on a new brightness, as when the sun strikes a lichened stone.

'I'll see you again up there,' he said, raising his stick towards the chimney pots.

It was as if, for a moment, the whole street stopped dead-still, listening.

'Both of you,' he went on. 'I'll be going there before you, but I'll be waiting for you. Think on't. I'll be expecting you.'

It was not just a promise: it was a pact between him and us and God. I felt that, if I failed to keep it, I should have let Mr. Fawcett down.

Norman Nicholson, *Wednesday Early Closing*, 1975, pp. 90–1

Kenneth G. Greet (1918–2014)

As a native of Bristol, Kenneth Greet knew Wesley's 'New Room' in the Horsefair well.

In later years I have preached on a number of occasions in this old Chapel. Particularly memorable was the great service to mark the 250th anniversary of the Wesleys' conversions.

The warden, the Rev. A. Raymond George, had asked me to finish preaching two minutes before 'a quarter before nine', the hour which Wesley records in his Journal as being the time when he 'felt (his) heart strangely warmed'. The arrangement was that immediately after my sermon this famous page from the diary would be read. Suddenly, however, as I finished preaching, a bearded fellow appeared from nowhere, entered the pulpit and began to read a diatribe against black immigrants. As soon as his purpose became clear the great congregation with one voice shouted 'Shame!' Mr. George signalled the organist and we rose to sing the last hymn. The intruder disappeared as quickly as he had come. I leaned across to Lord Tonypandy who had been presiding and said, 'When you give the closing prayer, will you invoke the Lord's blessing on black and white alike?' This he did in his mellifluous Welsh voice. The response of the congregation was a thunderous 'Amen'. So an ugly interruption was transformed into an act of witness of which, I think, John Wesley would have heartily approved.

Kenneth G. Greet, *Fully Connected: A Volume of Memoirs*, 1997, pp. 14–15

For many years, candidates for the Methodist ministry were not allowed to marry until the end of their seven years' probation. This rule was not swept away until the mid-1950s.

During the sixth year of probation, by which time I was in college, John Stacey, George Lockett and I got up a petition asking for permission to marry a year early. We obtained the signatures of about two hundred ministers and spent a few pounds that we could ill afford on a trip to London. We arrived at 1, Central Buildings, the Westminster Headquarters of the Methodist Church, with the modest petition in our pocket. We were received by the head of the Ministerial Training Department, Dr. Sydney Diamond, a saintly soul with an aristocratic stoop and silver hair. He welcomed us warmly and rang for a cup of tea. Then, to our dismay, he suggested that we should pray about our problem. We knelt around his desk and Dr. Diamond informed the Lord that he had great sympathy with these young men but that, of course, rules were rules and there was no hope of their being changed. We came away with the petition still in our pocket. If ever an army was defeated without a shot being fired, this was surely a case in point.

Kenneth G. Greet, *op. cit.*, pp. 27–8

As President of the Conference in 1980, Dr. Greet presided over the Irish Methodist Conference the following summer.

At one of the sessions there was a lively debate on 'the Irish situation'. The Methodist Church in Ireland is one church, north and south, but the discussion became rather tense. One minister rose to say, 'Mr. President, I note that the resolution we are debating says nothing about the victims of violence.' I invited him to propose an amendment to remedy this omission. This he did. Then another member with a mischievous twinkle in his eye rose to say, 'Sir, I have to point out that, alas, many victims of violence are dead, so our brother is inviting the Conference to pray for the dead.' The mover of the amendment turned red, leapt to his feet, and said, 'I beg leave to withdraw my amendment.' This the Conference declined to allow him to do. It was an interesting sidelight on certain strangely conservative theological concepts.

Kenneth G. Greet, *op. cit.*, pp. 104–5

Having come to the end of my anecdotes, I will follow the advice of the King of Hearts and just stop.